STATUS IN CLASSICAL ATHENS

STATUS IN CLASSICAL ATHENS

DEBORAH KAMEN

PRINCETON UNIVERSITY PRESS
Princeton and Oxford

Copyright © 2013 by Princeton University Press

Published by Princeton University Press, 41 William Street, Princeton, New Jersey 08540

In the United Kingdom: Princeton University Press, 6 Oxford Street,

Woodstock, Oxfordshire OX20 1TR

press.princeton.edu

Cover design by Jason Alejandro

First paperback printing, 2019

Paperback ISBN 978-0-691-19597-1

The Library of Congress has cataloged the cloth edition as follows:

Kamen, Deborah.

    Status in classical Athens / Deborah Kamen.

      pages cm

    Includes bibliographical references and index.

    ISBN 978-0-691-13813-8 (hardcover : alk. paper) 1. Athens (Greece)—Social conditions. 2. Greece—Social conditions—To 146 B.C. 3. Social status—Greece—Athens—History. I. Title.

    DF275.K28 2013

    305.0938'5—dc23   2012040983

British Library Cataloging-in-Publication Data is available

This book has been composed in Baskerville and John Sans

For HBK

CONTENTS

PREFACE

THE IMPETUS FOR THIS BOOK COMES FROM TWO SOURCES. THE FIRST IS MY Ph.D. dissertation on manumission in ancient Greece (Berkeley 2005). One relatively small part of this project involved assessing the legal and social status of freed slaves in classical Athens, which led me to try to map out the full range of Athenian status groups. That map, in all of its complexity, proved so compelling to me that it took on a life of its own, eventually expanding and developing into this book. The second is my interest in contemporary issues of status. As is well known, some residents of the United States, despite their participation in the country's social and economic spheres, are not granted access to full citizen rights (e.g., green card–holders, people on student and work visas, undocumented immigrants), nor are all U.S. citizens able to exercise the totality of their civic rights: prisoners, ex-cons, gay people, homeless people, people with disabilities, and racial minorities (to name just a few groups) face both legal restrictions and social stigmatization. The gap between the ideology of equality (inscribed, for example, in the Constitution) and the reality of inequality (dramatically voiced, while I was writing this book, by the Occupy Wall Street movement) is of course not directly parallel to what we find in classical Athens, but I hope that by critically reflecting upon similar tensions in the ancient world we might view with new eyes the range of statuses—and status inequalities—in our own societies.

I have many people and institutions to thank for their assistance in writing this book. First, my teachers. My interest in the ancient world was kindled in high school, thanks in no small part to my Latin teacher Michael Fiveash. For continuing to shape my intellectual interests, I will always be grateful to the terrific professors I had at Bryn Mawr (especially Richard Hamilton and Corey Brennan), Oxford (in particular Robert Parker), and Berkeley (especially the members of my dissertation reading committee: Ron Stroud, David Cohen, and Marianne Constable). Greatest thanks are owed to my dissertation advisor, Leslie Kurke, whose encouragement and mentorship over the years have been invaluable.

Writing this book would have been impossible without the support of my fabulous colleagues at the University of Washington, especially Ruby Blondell, Alain Gowing, Sandra Joshel, and Kate Topper. The impressive Classics graduate students in my Athenian citizenship seminar at the University of Washington (fall 2009) helped me think through the ideas of this book while they were still in the development stage. The Mellon Fellowship I held at Stanford facilitated the beginning of this project, and the Royalty Research Fund Grant I received from UW was key to its timely completion.

For offering very useful comments and/or bibliographic suggestions while this book was in manuscript form, I am grateful to Ruby Blondell, Sarah Levin-Richardson, Peter Liddel, David Mirhady, Lauri Reitzammer, Daniel Tompkins, and Princeton's two anonymous reviewers. Radika Bhaskar and the members of Lunch Circle provided tremendous support throughout the book-writing process. I also thank Rob Tempio for his generosity and skill in guiding me through the process of publishing my first book; Natalie Baan for shepherding the book through production; and Emma Young for her careful copyediting.

Finally, I am thankful for the love and encouragement I receive from my family and friends. Most of all, I am indebted to my partner Sarah Levin-Richardson, who makes my work better and my life much more enjoyable.

CONVENTIONS AND ABBREVIATIONS

IN THIS BOOK, I TRANSLITERATE GREEK WORDS FOLLOWING THE CONVENTIONS of the *Chicago Manual of Style,* 16th edition, Table 11.4. For Greek proper names and place names, I use the same system of transliteration, except when Latinized versions of these names are more familiar. Inevitably, this leads to some inconsistency: for instance, I use the spellings Aeschines, Chaeronea, and Pericles, but also Apollodoros, Aigospotamoi, and Thrasyboulos. All translations of Greek texts are my own unless I specify otherwise.

Throughout this book I refer to prices and wages using units of Greek currency: six obols = one drachma; one hundred drachmas = one mna; and sixty mnas = one talent. For reference, a loaf of bread in classical Athens cost about one obol, and a day's pay for a skilled workman ranged from one to two drachmas.

With some exceptions, the abbreviations of ancient works are used in accordance with Simon Hornblower and Anthony Spawforth, eds., *The Oxford Classical Dictionary,* 3rd edition (1996); those of modern works for the most part follow the *American Journal of Archaeology* 95 (1991): 1–16.

ANCIENT WORKS

Ael.	Aelian
VH	*Varia Historia*
Aesch.	Aeschines
Ammon.	Ammonius grammaticus
Andoc.	Andocides
Ant.	Antiphon
Aristoph.	Aristophanes
Ach.	*Acharnians*
Lys.	*Lysistrata*
Thesm.	*Thesmophoriazousai*
Arist.	Aristotle
Pol.	*Politics*
Prob.	*Problems*
Rhet.	*Rhetoric*
[Arist.]	ps.-Aristotle
Ath. Pol.	*Athēnaiōn Politeia*

Oik.	*Oikonomika*
Athen.	Athenaeus
Dem.	Demosthenes
Ep.	*Epistles*
[Dem.]	ps.-Demosthenes
Din.	Dinarchus
Dio Chrys.	Dio Chrysostomus
Diogenian.	Diogenianus Paroemiographus
D. L.	Diogenes Laertius
Harp.	Harpocration
Herod.	Herodas
Hesych.	Hesychius
Hyp.	Hyperides
Is.	Isaeus
Isoc.	Isocrates
Lycurg.	Lycurgus
Lys.	Lysias
Macrob.	Macrobius
Sat.	*Saturnalia*
Men.	Menander
Dys.	*Dyskolos*
Her.	*Hērōs*
Phot.	Photius
Pl.	Plato
Grg.	*Gorgias*
Rep.	*Republic*
Plut.	Plutarch
Mor.	*Moralia*
Per.	*Life of Pericles*
Sol.	*Life of Solon*
Them.	*Life of Themistocles*
Poll.	Pollux
Rutil.	Rutilius Lupus
Schol.	Scholiast
Theocr.	Theocritus
Thuc.	Thucydides
Xen.	Xenophon
Ages.	*Agesilaus*
Hell.	*Hellenica*
Oik.	*Oikonomikos*
[Xen.]	Ps.-Xenophon
Ath. Pol.	*Athēnaiōn Politeia*

MODERN WORKS

AAntHung	*Acta Antiqua Academiae Scientiarum Hungaricae*
ABSA	*Annual of the British School at Athens*
Ag. Inv.	Agora Inventory Number
AHR	*American Historical Review*
AJA	*American Journal of Archaeology*
AJAH	*American Journal of Ancient History*
AJP	*American Journal of Philology*
AncW	*Ancient World*
AntCl	*L'Antiquité classique*
Bekk. *Anec.*	I. Bekker, *Anecdota Graeca*, 3 vols. (Berlin 1814–21)
C&M	*Classica et Mediaevalia*
CA	*Classical Antiquity*
CJ	*Classical Journal*
CP	*Classical Philology*
CQ	*Classical Quarterly*
CR	*Classical Review*
CSSH	*Comparative Studies in Society and History*
CW	*Classical World*
DAGR	C. V. Daremberg and E. Saglio, *Dictionnaire des antiquités grecques et romaines* (Paris 1877–1919)
ECM/CV	*Échos du monde classique / Classical Views*
ERH/REH	*European Review of History: Revue européenne d'histoire*
FD	*Fouilles de Delphes* (Paris 1902–)
G&R	*Greece & Rome*
GDI	H. Collitz and others, *Sammlung der griechischen Dialektinschriften* (Göttingen 1884–1915)
GRBS	*Greek, Roman and Byzantine Studies*
HSCP	*Harvard Studies in Classical Philology*
HThR	*Harvard Theological Review*
IG	*Inscriptiones Graecae* (Berlin 1873–)
Jensen	C.C. Jensen, *Hyperides: Orationes sex cum ceterarum fragmentis* (Leipzig 1917)
JFH	*Journal of Family History*
JHS	*Journal of Hellenic Studies*
JJP	*Journal of Juristic Papyrology*
JNES	*Journal of Near Eastern Studies*
JRS	*Journal of Roman Studies*
LSCG	F. Sokolowski, *Lois sacrées des cités grecques* (Paris 1962–69)
LSJ	H. G. Liddell, R. Scott, and H. S. Jones, *Greek–English Lexicon*, 9th ed., with Supplement (Oxford 1968)
MAAR	*Memoirs of the American Academy at Rome*

NDI	M. d'Amelio and A. Azara, *Nuovo Digesto Italiano* (Turin 1937–40)
Osborne	M. J. Osborne, *Naturalization in Athens*, 4 vols. (Brussels 1981–83)
P. Oxy.	*The Oxyrhynchus Papyri* (London 1898–)
P&P	*Past & Present*
PCPS	*Proceedings of the Cambridge Philological Society*
QUCC	*Quaderni Urbinati di Cultura Classica*
RE	Pauly-Wissowa, *Realencylopädie der classischen Altertumwissenschaft*
REA	*Revue des études anciennes*
REG	*Revue des études grecques*
RIDA	*Revue internationale des droits de l'Antiquité*
RO	P. J. Rhodes and R. Osborne, *Greek Historical Inscriptions, 404-323 BC* (Oxford 2003)
SCI	*Scripta Classica Israelica*
SEG	*Supplementum Epigraphicum Graecum* (Leiden 1923–)
TAPA	*Transactions of the American Philological Association*
ZPE	*Zeitschrift für Papyrologie und Epigraphik*

STATUS IN CLASSICAL ATHENS

INTRODUCTION
Spectrum of Statuses

MOSES FINLEY FAMOUSLY ARGUED THAT WE OUGHT TO RECOGNIZE A SPECTRUM of statuses in ancient Greece, with the chattel slave at one extreme, the full-fledged citizen at the other, and a range of statuses in between.[1] Taking up his challenge, this book maps the range of social and legal statuses in classical Athens (451/0–323 BCE). My aim is to provide a thick description of Athenian status, ultimately broaching larger questions about the relationship between Athenian citizenship and civic ideology. By "civic ideology" I refer to the conception that all Athenian citizens—and only Athenian citizens—were autochthonous (that is, descended from ancestors "born from the earth" of Attica) and engaged in the political and military life of the city.[2] This survey of statuses will demonstrate, among other things, that Athenian democracy was both more closed and more open than civic ideology might lead us to think: on the one hand, only some citizen males exercised full citizen rights;[3] on the other, even non-citizens and naturalized citizens were, to varying degrees, partial shareholders in the Athenian polis.[4]

But first, my choice of "status" as a heuristic term requires some explanation, since a debate on the definitional terms "class," "status," and "order" dates back to Marx and Weber.[5] Within the field of ancient history, the Marxist pole is best represented by G.E.M. de Ste. Croix, who holds that *class*—"the collective social expression of the fact of exploitation, the way in which exploitation is embodied in a social structure"[6]—underlies the

---

[1] See Finley 1981 [1959], 1981 [1960], 1981 [1964], 1973. For a recent reiteration of the need to recognize intermediate categories, see Bearzot 2005, 91–92.

[2] On Athenian civic ideology, see, e.g., Loraux 1993; Boegehold and Scafuro 1994; Lape 2010.

[3] See, e.g., Mossé 1979 on "active" vs. "passive" citizens.

[4] See, e.g., Ober 2005 [2000], who argues that the ideology of Athenian democratic inclusiveness led to the development of "quasi rights" (granted to rich and poor citizens alike), one unintended result of which was the extension of negative liberties even to noncitizens.

[5] For a concise analysis of this debate, see Ober 1991, 113–16. Hunter and Edmundson's edited volume *Law and Social Status in Classical Athens* explicitly avoids entering into this debate: see Hunter 2000a, 1. As we shall see, de Ste. Croix explicitly aligns himself with Marx, whereas Finley's analysis is heavily indebted to Weber. For Weber's influence on Finley, see, e.g., Finley 1981 [1977], ch. 1; Finley 1985, ch. 6; Shaw and Saller 1981, xvii–xviii, discussing Weberian influences on Finley in the spheres of social analysis ("order" and "status") and methodology ("ideal type"); and Tompkins 2006, on Finley's personal and intellectual influences in general, focusing on his early days.

[6] de Ste. Croix 1981, 43. A particular class, on the other hand, is "a group of persons in a community identified by their position in the whole system of social production, defined above all according to their

differentiation of ancient Greek society.[7] Finley exemplifies the Weberian pole, arguing that class is less salient than *status*, which he terms "an admirably vague word with a considerable psychological element."[8] Finley's main objections to class are, first, that there is no consensus on how to define it; and, second, that a Marxist definition does not actually hold for ancient society—if it did, the slave and free wage laborer, because neither owns the means of production, would belong to the same class, which they clearly do not.[9] De Ste. Croix in turn contends that Finley misunderstands and misrepresents Marx,[10] and that while status can indeed *describe* ancient society, it cannot be used to *analyze* it.[11]

While de Ste. Croix and Finley each argue for a preferred definitional term, both acknowledge the usefulness of the term "order," referring, in Finley's words, to "a juridically defined group within a population, possessing formalized privileges and disabilities in one or more fields of activity, governmental, military, legal, economic, religious, marital, and *standing in a hierarchical relation to other orders*."[12] The orders in classical Athens were, in Mogens Hansen's words, "three clearly differentiated groups": the privileged (citizens), the underprivileged (metics), and the unprivileged (slaves).[13] Most scholars accept this division of Athens into three juridically based categories, even if not all of them refer to these categories as "orders."[14]

---

relationship (primarily in terms of the degree of ownership or control) to the conditions of production (that is to say, the means and labour of production) and to other classes" (43).

[7] On "class" as his category of choice: de Ste. Croix 1981, 42–69. De Ste. Croix admits that "class" is not the only category we need for analyzing the ancient world, but he asserts that it is nonetheless the "fundamental one" (1981, 45).

[8] Finley 1973, 51. "Class" is also rejected by Austin and Vidal-Naquet (1977 [1972]); for a focus on slaves in particular not being a "class," see Vidal-Naquet 1986 [1981], ch. 7.

[9] On his objections to the use of the term "class," see Finley 1973, 48–51. Hansen 1991, 86–87 has a similar criticism of "class." For a critical analysis of Finley's rejection of class in favor of status, see Nafissi 2004. Although Finley retained his Weberian orientation throughout his career, he later used the term "class" "in the sense intended in ordinary discourse, not in a technical sense, Marxist or other" to analyze ancient politics (Finley 1983, 10n29). Ober 1991 uses the term "class" in the same way in his discussion of Aristotle's *Politics*.

[10] See de Ste. Croix 1981, 58–59 for a critique of Finley's understanding and representation of Marx.

[11] De Ste. Croix 1981, 92–93; on the problems with "status" more generally, see 81–98.

[12] Finley 1973, 45 (emphasis in original); on orders more broadly, see 45–48. See also de Ste. Croix 1981, 42 for a definition of "orders" as "status-groups (*Stände*) which are *legally recognised* as such and have different sets of juridical characteristics (privileges and disadvantages)" (emphasis in original); and 94–95 on the Greek orders. See further Ober 1991 (esp. 128), who argues that Aristotle was using something like "orders" (i.e., juridically defined groups with legal privileges and disabilities) as his organizing principle.

[13] Hansen 1991, 86. Hansen argues that the difference between citizens, metics, and slaves does not correspond to a division "according to social status (with all its psychological implications)," since, e.g., metics, citizens, and slaves work side by side. The differentiation, he says, is found primarily in the political sphere (87).

[14] Todd 1995, ch. 10, and Hunter 2000a refer to these three groups as "status groups." (Hunter 2000a does acknowledge, however, that more groups than three existed, including *nothoi* and *atimoi*, but says that such groups "have not been included here because the collection as a whole concentrates on the three major status groups" [2n4].) Austin and Vidal-Naquet use the term "legal category," as in "three legal categories," to refer to slave, metic, and citizen (Austin and Vidal-Naquet 1977 [1972], *passim*); they make a point, however,

In determining the usefulness of any of these terms—status, class, and order—we should remember that none of them has an equivalent in Greek. This is not to say that these *concepts* were unimportant to the Greeks, simply that there is a certain arbitrariness, and inevitable imprecision, in ancient historians' use of such terms. In fact, we sometimes see a blurring of these terms in the scholarship. For instance, de Ste. Croix says that the term "status" is useful when it "partakes of some legal recognition and can therefore be considered as constituting an 'order' in the technical sense."[15] Virginia Hunter, in turn, explains that the term "status groups" is used in her coedited volume *Law and Social Status in Classical Athens* to refer to the three "juridically defined orders" of society, "status" to the "standing of each group within the resultant social hierarchy, together with its attendant privileges and disabilities, honour or lack thereof."[16] By Hunter's definition, the term "status" seems to encompass legal status *along with* honor (*timē*).[17]

Indeed, to the extent that there is any consensus among scholars, it is that a category encompassing both social standing and legal rights is a useful one. The question then becomes what to call this category. "Order," to my mind, is too redolent of Rome (with its Struggle of the Orders), and "class" inevitably carries with it the baggage of exploitation.[18] "Status" too has its flaws—potentially connoting social estimation of honor and prestige in a strict Weberian sense—but I think it is also the least loaded of the three terms, perhaps because of its "vagueness." In this book, then, I take "status" to refer to *both* legal rights *and* social standing, in keeping with the double way in which modern sociologists use the term.[19] Wherever I want to emphasize one aspect of status, I will specify "legal status" or "social status,"[20] but I see both as subsets of a larger overarching category, "status."[21]

---

of saying that the legal categories do not correspond to "social categories" (see esp. 103–6), since within each legal category there is a lot of social variation.

[15] De Ste. Croix 1981, 94.

[16] Hunter 2000a, 1–2. This definition is adopted by C. Patterson 2009, 354.

[17] This is more or less the definition of status I will be using. However, although I will touch briefly on the level of honor (*timē*) possessed by each status group, I will not be engaging in the scholarly debates about whether Athens was an agonistic society in which the courts provided a setting for competing over honor (a view espoused by, e.g., D. Cohen 1995, esp. chs. 4 and 5, and challenged by Herman 2006, esp. ch. 6).

[18] Cf., however, Wright 2005, for a brief summary of the different ways in which sociologists use the term "class."

[19] In fact, sociologists use both "status" and "social status" in this double way: "In a narrow sense, the term refers to one's legal or professional standing within a group; in a broader sense, it means one's value and importance in the eyes of the world" (Middleton 2008, 621); see also Kantzara 2007. In this book, I reserve the term "social status" for standing or esteem in the eyes of the community (cf. Weberian "status").

[20] See also Todd 1995, who says that "social status is different from (and often more complex than) legal status" (173).

[21] In so doing, I subscribe to the following words of Finley: "It may be objected that I am now confusing political and social categories with proper juristic ones. To that I would reply that such 'confusion' is inherent in Greek thinking and in Greek institutions. To separate them might be more elegant, more Roman, but it

What, then, were the status groups of classical Athens? As mentioned above, the majority of scholars adopt the tripartite classification found in most of Greek literature: slave, metic, and citizen. These are in fact the three *major* status groups, but, as I argue in this book, they are not the *only* status categories: instead, they are three nodes on a much broader spectrum. One of the earliest discussions of a range of statuses in antiquity can be found in a 1945 article ("Between Slavery and Freedom") by Finley's teacher William Westermann, who takes as his starting point the second-century CE lexicographer Pollux's discussion of those "between free and slave" (*metaxu ... eleutherōn kai doulōn*; 3.83), including indigenous enslaved populations (like the Spartan Helots) and manumitted slaves. From this, Finley developed the idea of a spectrum of statuses in ancient Greece: "If we think of ancient society as made up of a spectrum of statuses, with the free citizen at one end and the slave at the other, and with a considerable number of shades of dependence in between, we shall quickly discover different 'lines' on the spectrum."[22] He elaborated on this idea in "The Servile Statuses of Ancient Greece" (1960)[23] as well as in "Between Slavery and Freedom" (1964). In *The Ancient Economy* (1973), among other works,[24] Finley further clarified the *nature* of his spectrum, stating that it "is not meant to be understood as a mathematical continuum, but as a more metaphorical, discontinuous spectrum, with gaps here, heavier concentrations there."[25]

But Finley's concept of a spectrum of statuses—even his nuanced version thereof—has not won universal acceptance. Just as de Ste. Croix objects to "status" as an insufficiently analytical category (since, he says, there is "no organic relationship" between statuses), so too does he find the idea of a *spectrum* of statuses problematic (since a spectrum has no explanatory force).[26] Yvon Garlan, in turn, takes issue specifically with Finley's (implicit) notion of one spectrum encapsulating all of the intermediate statuses in all periods and areas of ancient Greece.[27] Yet another objection to Finley's spectrum has been voiced by Charles Hedrick. He agues that because the various noncitizens in Athens were defined (all together) in relation to the citizen, rather than against one another, viewing Athenian society as a spectrum—giving equal weight, in a sense, to the various noncitizen groups as separate identities—does

---

would no longer be Greek" (1981 [1960], 147). Cf. Mennen 2011 for a recent exploration of "status" in the Roman Empire in the sense of "*social* status" (6; emphasis in original).

[22] Finley 1981 [1959], 98.

[23] Finley 1981 [1960], esp. 147–48.

[24] See especially Finley 1981 [1964].

[25] Finley 1973, 68. He also called the spectrum "metaphorical" and "too smooth" in 1981 [1964], 132.

[26] De Ste. Croix 1981, 92–93.

[27] Garlan 1988 [1982], 85–118, esp. 87.

not accurately represent the prevailing classical Athenian ideology.[28] In fact, even Finley admits that the metaphor of a spectrum "breaks down" in classical Athens. That is, while the full spectrum was "visible" before the rise of the polis, with a diversity of statuses recognized and spoken of, it became ideologically obscured in the classical period and only re-emerged as visible in the Hellenistic period.[29]

However, even while classical Athenian society was thought of, and written about, as being defined by a tripartite division of slave/metic/citizen—or sometimes by a simple antimony of slave vs. free, or citizen vs. noncitizen—there simultaneously existed an (often unacknowledged) range of statuses between these nodes.[30] That is to say, Athenian ideology "masked" the reality of a spectrum.[31] I do think, then, that it is productive to speak of a spectrum of statuses in classical Athens. First of all, the (relatively) limited temporal and geographic scope of my study (Athens of the period 451/0–323 BCE) avoids the potential difficulties pointed out by Garlan: unlike Finley, I am speaking of status not in "ancient Greece" (broadly construed) but in a specific polis at a specific time. Secondly, there clearly was a level on which the Athenians *did* recognize a multiplicity of statuses between slave and citizen, each of which (as we shall see) had its own set of defined legal and political rights.[32] Moreover, each of these intervening status categories served an ideological purpose of its own. As Stephen Todd puts it, since these categories "occur always on the rising side of the main status groups"—e.g., *privileged* slaves, *privileged* metics—their function may in part be "to highlight the depth of the gulf between the main statuses."[33] Therefore, rather than *countering* Athenian ideology, a study of the intervening status categories gives us a richer sense for the full spectrum of Athenian status, while simultaneously illuminating the primary significance of the "big three" categories. In pursuing this study, I hope not only to describe but also to *analyze* Athenian society and ideology.[34]

---

[28] Hedrick 1994, 307.

[29] Finley 1981 [1964], 132. Cf. Cartledge 2002, 144, who argues that the concept of a spectrum of statuses "could not have been entertained widely, let alone normatively" before the Hellenistic period.

[30] See also Vlassapoulos 2009, who argues that "while there was a categorical and simple division between slave and free in Athenian law, in social practice the situation was very complicated" (348).

[31] For the notion of ideology as a mask, see Geertz 1973, 201–3. I am inspired, in part, by Hunt 1998, who demonstrates that the ideology of a rigid slave/free binary masks the reality of slave participation in the Greek military.

[32] In the words of Finley 1981 [1964], 116, the ancients "could hardly have been unaware of certain gradations."

[33] Todd 1995, 173–74.

[34] Cf. Ober 2005 [2000], 101: "Focusing exclusively on the binary opposition between 'citizen' and 'other' elides too much of the ideological complexity central to Athenian politics and society." I would argue that this holds as well for focusing on the tripartite division of Athenian society.

In mapping out this spectrum of statuses, I am again following the lead of Finley, who proposes an effective way of analyzing status in ancient Greece.[35] His methodology, rooted in contemporary (i.e., twentieth-century) jurisprudence,[36]

> involves first breaking up the traditional notion of rights into a number of concepts, including claims, privileges, immunities, powers, and their opposites (duties and so on). Second it involves envisaging status (or freedom) as a bundle of privileges, powers, and so on, and therefore the definition of any particular status, or of any individual's status, in terms of the possession and location of the individual's elements of the bundle.[37]

Finley then provides a list of categories by which status may be analyzed:

> (1) claims to property, or power over things—a complex of elements requiring further differentiation both in its range (from *peculium* to full ownership) and in its application to different categories of things (e.g. cattle or land or agricultural produce or money); (2) power over a man's labour and movements; (3) power to punish; (4) privileges and liabilities in legal action, such as immunity from arbitrary seizure or the capacity to sue and be sued; (5) privileges in the area of the family: marriage, succession, and so on; (6) privileges of social mobility, such as manumission or enfranchisement (and their inverse); and (7) privileges and duties in the sacral, political, and military spheres.[38]

To my mind, the greatest advantage of this kind of approach is that it entails investigation into *all* areas of life, encompassing privileges and liabilities not only in the juridical sphere but also in the spheres of politics, religion, and the economy, among others. In this way, it allows for a unique and (I believe) unprecedented view of the complexity of status in classical Athens.

One goal of this book, then, is to fulfill for Athens the agenda proposed (but never accomplished) by Finley. Thus, adopting his suggested method of analysis, and following the order of his schema, I lay out in each of the following chapters a distinct status group (or set of status groups), although I show that the lines between groups were not entirely clear-cut. These groups include chattel slaves (chapter 1); privileged chattel slaves (chapter 2); conditionally freed slaves (chapter 3); metics (chapter 4); privileged metics (chapter 5); bastards (chapter 6); disenfranchised citizens (chapter 7); naturalized citizens (chapter 8);

---

[35] The approach I am taking is also suggested by Hunter 2000a, 3, according to whom "a thorough analysis of status and its concomitants" would entail adopting an approach like Finley's.

[36] See, e.g., Hohfeld 1919 for a systematic categorization of legal relations, mapping "jural opposites" like right/no-right and privilege/duty, and "jural correlatives" like right/duty and privilege/no-right. Finley 1981 [1976] does cite Hohfeld 1919.

[37] Finley 1981 [1960], 148. See also Finley 1981 [1976], 77.

[38] Finley 1981 [1960], 149. Essentially the same catalogue is found also in Finley 1981 [1964], 131.

female citizens (chapter 9); and male citizens (chapter 10). Ordering the chapters in this way—starting with the chattel slave and slowly building up to citizen status—has, to my mind, two heuristic advantages: 1) it brings (still-needed) attention to the least enfranchised status groups in Athens; and 2) it helps citizens be viewed, in the end, in a new light: namely, less as the default status group in Athens and more as possessors of an exceptional bundle of rights and privileges. In the conclusion, I summarize the book's findings and propose an explanation for why ancient Greek literature maintains the fiction of three status groups despite the reality of a full spectrum of legal and social statuses. Most important, it seems, was the fact that freeborn Athenian citizens defined themselves (ideologically) in opposition to noncitizens and slaves. As a result, the very fact of a spectrum of statuses, not to mention movement between status groups, was likely a source of anxiety for them.[39]

A few points about my methodology should be made at the outset. First, in order to capture the most accurate picture of a particular group's status (both legal and social), I expand on Finley's model by looking *beyond* legal provisions: that is, I tease out what rights each group had de facto, in addition to the rights they were granted de jure. Second, the status groups I outline are not exactly parallel to each other—some are more precisely defined by law than others, some include large numbers of people whereas others are more exceptional—but each possesses a sufficiently unique "bundle" of privileges and liabilities to render it a distinct category. Finally, although I have chosen to divide Athenian society into ten status groups, there is, naturally, variation within each group, and so I could have parceled up the spectrum into even narrower categories. My taxonomy, therefore, is neither exhaustive nor the only possible one, but is meant to demonstrate the *complexity* of the spectrum, or at least to get closer to its complexity than a tripartite model of status does. Indeed, as Finley himself has said, "No classification or taxonomy, no matter how detailed, is a sufficient account of the nature of a given society and its transformations. It can only be deemed to be more or less useful than competing classifications as an analytical tool in a particular inquiry."[40] I hope only that my classificatory scheme is more, rather than less, useful in fleshing out our picture of classical Athenian society. Ultimately, my aim is to reveal a social and legal reality otherwise masked by Athenian civic ideology.

---

[39] On anxieties about status boundary-crossing in Athens, see, e.g., Davies 1977/78; Jameson 2004 [1997].

[40] Finley 1998 [1980], 140.

CHAPTER 1

CHATTEL SLAVES

ALTHOUGH WAR AMONG THE VARIOUS GREEK POLEIS WAS COMMON, THE Greeks were nonetheless (in principle) averse to the enslavement of their fellow Greeks (see, e.g., Pl. *Rep.* 469b–c; Xen. *Hell.* 1.6.14, *Ages.* 7.6).[1] Most chattel slaves, therefore, were of "barbarian"—that is, non-Greek—origin, acquired mainly through Mediterranean trading networks.[2] In the archaic period (ca. 630–480 BCE), slaves were primarily Scythians and Thracians, coming from areas northeast of Greece. After the Persian Wars, traders began to acquire more slaves from the east, particularly from those areas (like Caria) near the Greek cities of Asia Minor. And in the fourth century and into the Hellenistic period (323–330 BCE), slaves came from all over Asia Minor, with the number of slaves from Africa also increasing.[3] Augmenting these regular supplies of slaves were those captured in war or, less frequently, by pirates or bandits.[4]

For classical Athens, some of our best evidence for the sources of slaves is epigraphic. So, for example, gravestones attest to the various ethnic origins of foreigners living (and dying) in Attica, many of whom were slaves.[5] The Attic Stelai, records of property confiscated from Athenians convicted in the sacrilegious Defamation of the Mysteries and Mutilation of the Herms incidents of 415 BCE, preserve the names of thirteen Thracian slaves and ten Anatolian slaves; and in the funerary and dedicatory inscriptions from the silver mines at Laureion, many of which date to the fourth century, the names of twenty Anatolian slaves and two Thracian slaves are recorded.[6] The picture we get from inscriptions is complemented by Aristophanic comedy, which presents slaves of a wide range of ethnicities.[7]

---

[1] For this aversion, see Garlan 1987, 17–19, and 1988 [1982], 47–53; and Rosivach 1999, who credits Philip of Macedon with the "innovation" of enslaving Greek men, in addition to women and children. For "antidotes to the enslavement of Greeks," see Garlan 1987, 19–23; see also Ducrey 1999 [1968], 235–46; Pritchett 1991, 245–97.

[2] On the slave supply, e.g., Finley 1981 [1962]; Garlan 1987; Klees 1998, 52–56; Braund 2011.

[3] For concise summaries of sources of slaves in Greece, see Garlan 1988 [1982] 46–47; Bäbler 1998, 14–17; Fisher 2001 [1993], 36–37.

[4] On the acquisition of slaves in warfare, see Ducrey 1999 [1968], 74–92, 131–40; Garlan 1988 [1982], 47–48; Garlan 1987; Pritchett 1991, 223–45; Klees 1998, 20–50. For the relationship between piracy/banditry and slavery, see Ducrey 1999 [1968], 171–93; Garlan 1987 and 1988 [1982], 48–49, with further bibliography in n37; and Klees 1998, 50–52.

[5] See, e.g., Bäbler 1998, 69–198.

[6] For all of these numbers, see Morris 2011, 184. For a discussion of the slaves in the Attic Stelai, see Pritchett 1956, 276–81. For the origins of the slaves at Laureion, see Lauffer 1979, 129–39.

[7] On slaves in Aristophanes, see Ehrenberg 1943, 123–41, esp., on their ethnic origins, 127–28.

Although the population of chattel slaves was evidently at times quite high in Greece, exact numbers are nearly impossible to ascertain. Even for classical Athens there is no direct evidence for slave numbers; the closest we come is Athenaeus's (third-century CE) account of the census taken at the end of the fourth century BCE:

> Ktesikles, in the third book of the *Chronicles*, says that in the 117th Olympiad [312–308 BCE], there was a census taken by Demetrius of Phaleron of those residing in Athens, and 21,000 Athenians, 10,000 metics, and 400,000 slaves (*oiketōn*) were found. (Athen. 272c–d)

This passage is quoted nearly every time scholars hazard a guess as to the number of slaves in classical Athens, but both its meaning and validity are contested.[8] Also often cited by scholars are two other passages: Thucydides's report that after the Spartan occupation of Dekeleia in 413 BCE, 20,000 slaves (*andrapodōn*) deserted from Attica (Thuc. 7.27.5), and a fragment of Hyperides suggesting that more than 150,000 slaves "from the mines and the countryside" be enlisted to fight (fr. 29, Jensen). Drawing cautiously from these ancient accounts of slave numbers, coupled with modern estimates both of the total population of Athens[9] and of rates of slave ownership, scholars have proposed a range of estimates for classical Athens, varying from a low of 20,000 slaves to a high of more than 150,000; the most likely number falls somewhere in the middle, representing 15–35 percent of the total population. Moreover, these numbers do not remain constant throughout the classical period, but fluctuate: slave numbers were at their highest immediately before the Peloponnesian War, fell dramatically during the war, and began to increase again afterward.[10]

Orlando Patterson has famously argued that slaves experience a process of desocialization and depersonalization, which he refers to as "social death."[11] In this chapter, I demonstrate some of the ways in which chattel slaves in Athens were socially dead (their "social status"), in addition to being deprived of nearly all legal and political rights (their "legal status"). There is no question that slaves were desocialized: in most cases torn from their natal communities, they were deprived of all family and community ties.[12] Chattel slaves were also depersonalized, in a process Igor Kopytoff describes as "commoditization." Once enslaved, an individual "is stripped of his social identity"—that is, desocialized—"and becomes a non-person, indeed an object and an actual or potential

---

[8] See Garlan 1988 [1982], 56n51 for bibliography on the reliability of Athenaeus's numbers.

[9] For a summary of the scholarly debates (up to 1998) about the population of Attica, see Scheidel's addendum in Garnsey 1998, 197–98.

[10] For concise summaries of the debate on slave numbers in Athens, see Garlan 1988 [1982], 55–60; Fisher 2001 [1993], 34–36.

[11] O. Patterson 1982 borrows this term from Meillassoux 1975, 21–22; see also Meillassoux 1986, 106.

[12] On the desocialized nature of the slave, see Finley 1968; Garlan 1988 [1982], 41; Garnsey 1999 [1996], 1.

commodity."[13] In fact, Aristotle calls the chattel slave "animate property" (*ktēma ti empsukhon*) (*Pol.* 1253b32), and scholars have defined the chattel slave either exclusively or at least in part by his or her status as a piece of property.[14] In this capacity, a slave could be bought and sold, hired out (Xen. *Poroi* 4.14–16), or bequeathed in a will (e.g., Dem. 27.9). In addition to being conceived of as a possession, however, the slave was also recognized as a person (of sorts) with limited legal rights, as we shall see.

Finally, chattel slaves in classical Athens, as in many other slave societies, were almost entirely stripped of honor (*timē*),[15] rendering them the very lowest social *and* legal status group on the spectrum of statuses.[16] But even within the legal category of "chattel slave," there existed a large range of sub-statuses,[17] generally dependent on the type of labor the slave performed (and related to this, their economic status).[18] This labor, in turn, was sometimes correlated with the slave's ethnicity: so, for example, Thracians and Anatolians generally performed manual labor, Scythians served as policemen-archers, and Phoenicians were at least sometimes bankers and traders (see chapter 2).[19] This correlation did not always hold, however: a striking example is the Thracian slave-overseer Sosias, who was wealthy enough to lease 1000 mining slaves from the general Nicias (Xen. *Poroi* 4.14).

In this chapter, I will focus on the legal and social status of the "basest" chattel slaves—that is, those performing the basest forms of labor, like working in the mines or mills.[20] I will reserve for chapter 2 discussion of what have (rightly or wrongly) been called "privileged" slaves, who exercised greater independence despite their legal status as chattel.

Chattel slaves in Greece had no legal claims to property, either moveable or unmoveable. They also, in theory, had no power over their labor or movement: they performed the tasks that were assigned to them and

[13] Kopytoff 1986, 65.

[14] Finley defines the chattel slave in two (coexistent) ways: as property, from a legal point of view, and as an outsider, from a sociological point of view (1968). See also Garnsey 1999 [1996], 1: "A slave was property. The slaveowner's rights over his slave-property were total, covering the person as well as the labour of the slave. The slave was kinless, stripped of his or her old social identity in the process of capture, sale and deracination, and denied the capacity to forge new bonds of kinship through marriage alliance." Cf. Vlassopoulos 2011, who stresses the understanding of slavery as a relationship of domination.

[15] See Fisher 1995.

[16] For overviews of the status of the slave, see Morrow 1939, esp. 73–89 (with a focus on Plato's *Laws*); Harrison 1968, 163–80; MacDowell 1978, 79–83; Hansen 1991, 120–23; Todd 1995, 184–94; Hunter 2000a, 5–15.

[17] "It is apparent that, though household servants, slaves with a *peculium* and slaves working in chains on a large farm all fell within a single juridical category, the legal status masked the economic and social differentiations among them" (Finley 1973, 64).

[18] "We distinguish several kinds [*doulou . . . eidē*] of slave, as their employments are different" (Arist. *Pol.* 1277a37–38). For slave professions, see Finley 1981 [1959].

[19] On Phoenicians as bankers and traders in Athens, see Bäbler 1998, 119–22.

[20] On mining slaves, see Lauffer 1979; see also Rihll 2010, who stresses the skilled nature of some mining work.

engaged in no movement that was not mandated by their master or mistress. In practice, this ideal behavior was not necessarily realized: although specific tasks were assigned to slaves, the ways in which they conducted these tasks were within their control, and many slaves (particularly in households with few slaves) were "multitaskers" who presumably had some degree of control over which tasks they did when, and how. That said, to the extent that they did not choose their occupations, and did not own the means or fruits of their production, slaves, at least ideologically, had no control over their labor. Slaves' movement, too, was notionally circumscribed by their masters, and there were certain public places from which they were barred, including citizens' *gymnasia* and *palaistrai* (Aesch. 1.138; Plut. *Sol.* 1.3).[21] However, the realities of slave labor necessitated that slaves exercise some autonomy over their own movements. Take, for example, the labor of domestic servants, which encompassed, among other things, "child-minding, caring for the sick, answering and guarding the door, cooking, woolworking, carrying messages, fetching water, [and] shopping."[22] For slaves sent out to the marketplace to buy food, their task was set but their path probably was not.[23] Stephanie Camp's work on geographies of resistance in the American South has illuminated the ways in which slaves can carve out their own spaces and movements even while appearing to follow the rigid guidelines set out by their masters.[24] Moreover, some slaves (as discussed further in the next chapter) were leased out by their masters to work in the mines or to do other dangerous labor; while this often involved extremely unpleasant tasks, it also represents a case where the slaves' movements were, by necessity, not overseen by their immediate master.

Chattel slaves were defined at least in part by the fact that, unlike free people, they had to answer for their wrongdoings with their bodies (*sōmata*) (see Dem. 22.55, 24.167).[25] One way in which this manifested itself was through corporal punishment by their masters, who were permitted to inflict nearly any form of violence on their slaves. Physical abuse could take a number of different forms: whipping, flogging, hitting with sticks, fettering, rape, tattooing, and branding.[26] A vivid description of such violence, apparently written by a young male slave, can be found in a fourth-century lead tablet from the Athenian Agora: "I

---

[21] There were, however, exceptions in practice: see Golden 2008, ch. 2. On the limited participation of slaves in Greek athletics more broadly, see Crowther 1992; Golden 2008, ch. 2.

[22] This catalogue of tasks performed by slaves in the Athenian household comes from Golden 2011, 140.

[23] See also Todd 1995, 187–88, "The moment you send your slave out to do the shopping, you are expecting him or her to take decisions on your behalf."

[24] Camp 2004. See also Joshel and Petersen forthcoming on slave movement in ancient Rome.

[25] See, e.g., Hunter 1992; duBois 2003.

[26] On the punishment of slaves in Athens, see, e.g., Hunter 1994, 162–73; Klees 1998, ch. 6.

am perishing from being whipped; I am tied up; I am treated like dirt—more and more!" (Ag. Inv. IL 1702, line 4).[27]

Slaves had some, albeit few, protections against extreme violence directed against them. They could run away to a slave asylum, like the Theseion or the altar of the Eumenides in Athens (Aristoph. *Knights* 1311–12); here they were protected, but rather than being given their freedom, they were sold to a new master.[28] There were also some legal measures in place to protect the slave. Technically, a master was not supposed to kill his slave (Ant. 5.47), but if he did, it was unlikely that anyone would press charges.[29] Nonetheless, a master who killed his own slave would still want to purify himself, since all bloodshed was thought to be a source of pollution (Ant. 6.4; cf. Pl. *Laws* 868a).[30] If slaves were harmed by someone who was not their master, their master could bring a *dikē* (private suit) for *blabē* (damages), under which the slave was viewed, legally, as a piece of property that had been damaged. This is the same suit used if someone hurt your donkey or broke your furniture.[31] If, however, slaves were *killed* by someone who was not their master, the master could file a private suit for murder (the *dikē phonou*) (Isoc. 18.52, [Dem.] 59.9).[32] The case was brought, via the Basileus (the "king" archon, one of the city's chief magistrates), to a special court called the Palladion and was heard along with cases of unintentional homicide of citizens, as well as the murder of metics ([Arist.] *Ath. Pol.* 57.3; Dem. 23.71; see also Dem. 47.68–73). If a man was convicted of murder at the Palladion, he faced exile (Dem. 23.72; [Dem.] 59.10).[33] Finally, the master, or any other citizen in Athens, could in theory bring a public suit, called a *graphē hubreōs*, against someone who committed an act of *hubris* against a slave—that is, an assault against the slave's honor.[34] Many scholars have struggled to account for the fact that slaves were included in the law against *hubris* despite their lowly status.[35] Was it that slaves were protected *qua* vehicles

---

[27] This lead tablet was first published (and translated) by Jordan 2000. Jordan, however, believes that the letter writer is either a metic or a citizen, arguing that the word *despotai* ("masters") in line 2 "evidently has a looser sense" than literal masters (98). See also Harris 2004, who argues convincingly that the writer is in fact a slave.

[28] On the Theseion as a slave sanctuary, see Christensen 1984.

[29] Since only relatives or the owner of the deceased could bring a murder charge (*dikē phonou*) (Dem. 47.70), and since slaves could not initiate suits and a master was extremely unlikely to incriminate himself, such cases were likely never brought to court.

[30] On the pollution caused by bloodshed, see Parker 1983, 104–43.

[31] On the *dikē blabēs*, see Todd 1995, 279–82.

[32] On the murder of slaves in Athens, see Morrow 1937 and MacDowell 1963, 20–22, 69, 94–96, 104, 126–27.

[33] But cf. Lycurg. 1.65, which implies that a fine was the penalty.

[34] "*Hybris* [*hubris*] is essentially the serious assault on the honour of another, which is likely to cause shame, and lead to anger and attempts at revenge" (Fisher 1992, 1). For this and other interpretations of *hubris*, see Fisher 1992, esp. 1–5 with bibliography.

[35] For an excellent discussion (and resolution) of this "apparent paradox," see Fisher 1995. For a brief summary of the issue, see Todd 1995, 189–90.

of their masters' honor?[36] Was it that they themselves possessed some small degree of honor, *qua* human beings?[37] Was it that the protections offered by the *hubris* law were simply a byproduct of the burgeoning ideology of Athenian democratic inclusiveness?[38] The Greeks themselves suggested (Dem. 21.47–49; Aesch. 1.16–17) that the protection of slaves was (at least in part) a means of demonstrating how serious the Athenians were about prosecuting any and all acts of *hubris*.[39] Since we have very little evidence for *graphai hybreōs* actually being brought to court on behalf of slaves,[40] the question is perhaps more interesting on an ideological than on a practical level. That is, the fact that slaves *could* be protected by this suit implies that, at least by the period under consideration here, they were conceived of as having some honor—even if it was only a small amount, or only by proxy—worth protecting.

In terms of legal personality, the chattel slave had very few rights. Plato's Kallikles describes slaves as those who, when treated unjustly, cannot defend themselves or anyone else they care for (*Grg.* 483b). They could be neither a plaintiff nor a defendant in court, though a case could be brought on their behalf (see above). Legally (as well as conceptually), they were the equivalent of a minor,[41] represented by their master just as a father or other guardian represented his children's legal interests. If slaves incurred a debt, their master was liable, as we see most clearly in the case of a slave who ran up huge debts running a perfume business for his master (Hyp. 3). If slaves committed a private offense, their master was generally held responsible (Hyp. 3.22; [Dem.] 53.20), though the master could in turn punish the slave. It may be the case that slaves could be directly sued, but our only evidence for this practice cites it in the context of saying that it is inappropriate to do so, since (the logic goes) slaves act only on the orders of their masters (Dem. 37.51, 55.31). For public offenses, on the other hand, slaves had to assume liability for their own actions, and most often the punishment entailed being whipped by a representative of the state. Thus, for example, a slave who became the lover of a freeborn boy was punished with fifty lashes (Aesch. 1.139).[42]

While slaves could not serve as witnesses (*martures*), their statements could be elicited by judicial torture (*basanos*) and used as evidence (see Is. 8.12 for an explanation). However, although litigants are attested

---

[36] E.g., Mactoux 1988, 336–38; Ostwald 1990, 145.

[37] This is the main argument of Fisher 1995.

[38] See Ober 2005 [2000], who classifies such protections as "negative liberties."

[39] See again Fisher 1995.

[40] Cf. Christensen 1984 (esp. 25), who suggests that slaves may have been resold following a master's conviction in a *graphē hubreōs*, and that these trials may have been held at the Theseion itself.

[41] See Golden 1985 on the use of *"pais"* to describe both children and slaves, who occupied a similar status in the Greeks' minds.

[42] On the public whip more generally, see Hunter 1994, 155–62.

challenging their opponents to produce slaves for torture, in almost all cases the challenge is rejected, and there is little evidence of *basanos* being carried out (but see Dem. 37.20–22; Aristoph. *Frogs* 618–22). As a result, scholars have debated whether *basanos* ever actually took place.[43] For our purposes, however, the "reality" of this practice is less important than its ideological ramifications; that is, whether or not it was performed, the presuppositions underlying *basanos*—namely, that slaves were lesser beings capable of "speaking" only through their bodies—served to reinforce the slave's already base status.[44] In certain exceptional cases, slaves were called upon to offer information (*mēnusis*) before a magistrate, presumably without torture, in return for which they were given their freedom.[45] After the Mutilation of the Herms and Defamation of the Mysteries in 415 BCE, slaves were encouraged to give information in exchange for their freedom (Thuc. 6.27.2; Andoc. 1.12–18, 27–28); slaves were assured manumission for informing against their masters in cases of sacrilege or damage to sacred olive trees (*hierosulia*) (see Lys. 5 and 7); and in Plato's ideal city in the *Laws*, slaves are to be freed for informing on those who steal treasures or neglect their parents (914a, 932d).

In the course of the fourth century BCE, practical considerations led to a gradual improvement in the legal capacities of at least some slaves. Probably due to their increased involvement in mercantile affairs, it appears that starting around 350 BCE slaves could bring lawsuits and be prosecuted in certain kinds of commercial suits dealing with imports and exports (*dikai emporikaí*) (see chapter 2). Most likely, the slaves participating in these *dikai* were "privileged slaves," to be discussed in the next chapter. Legally speaking, however, this right was open to all chattel slaves, even if they were not in a position to exercise it.

Slaves had virtually no rights in the areas of sex and marriage.[46] Female slaves in particular were at the sexual disposal of their masters (e.g., Xen. *Oik.* 10.12).[47] Slave-prostitutes of lower status (*pornai*) were whored out by brothel-keepers,[48] themselves often freedwomen ([Dem.] 59.18;

---

[43] For opposing views, see, e.g., Mirhady 1996 and Gagarin 1996. The former (following Headlam 1893) argues that *basanos* likely did take place and functioned as a dispute-ending procedure, an alternative to the *dikastērion*. The latter (following Thür 1977) argues that *basanos* was essentially a legal fiction, a way of making one's opponent look bad by issuing a challenge he would have to reject. For slave torture in the context of institutionalized "dares," see Johnstone 1999, ch. 3.

[44] See duBois 1991, who argues that slave torture was a way of drawing the line between slave and free, marking the slave as "other"; cf. Hunter 1992, who makes a similar argument about the ideological role played by the whip. See also Mirhady 2000 for Athenian justifications for slave torture.

[45] According to R. Osborne 2000, these exceptional cases, at least in Athens, always pertained to religion; cf. the suggestions that *mēnusis* was used in "certain cases with serious religious and/or political consequences" (Todd 1995, 187) and "cases of treason, sacrilege, or theft of public money" (Harrison 1968, 171).

[46] See Klees 1998, ch. 5.

[47] On sexual relations with slaves, see Klees 1998, 161–75; Golden 2011, 146–51.

[48] Cf. Glazebrook 2011, who contends that Athenian brothels were multipurpose spaces, which (like *pornai*) were not necessarily low-class or marginalized.

Is. 6.19). Male slaves, unlike male citizens, were banned from pederastic relationships with citizen boys (Aesch. 1.139; Plut. *Sol*.1.3). Slaves were not allowed to marry, but cohabitation with their slave-partners was occasionally granted as a reward (Xen. *Oik*. 9.5; [Arist.] *Oik*. 1344b17–18).[49] It was, however, most likely only "higher-up" slaves (managers and overseers) who were offered this sort of perk for good service. Children born to female slaves belonged to the master, who could either keep them in his household as slaves or sell them. However, despite the fact that slave "marriages" and "families" were not legally protected, later epigraphic evidence indicates that slaves themselves may have recognized relationships with their slave-partners and children. So, for example, some inscriptions attest to slaves and former slaves paying for the manumission of their slave-children, or to "husband"-"wife" pairs being freed together.[50]

Social mobility depended greatly on the type of chattel slave. A slave working in the silver mines of Laureion, for example, not only was unlikely to be freed, but also had little chance of attaining a higher-status profession as a slave. Domestic servants, on the other hand, were closer to the category of "privileged slave"—we might call them "semi-privileged"—and accordingly had more opportunities for advancement. If their work was respected, they might be elevated in the household status hierarchy, perhaps rising to the rank of overseer. Moreover, if they had a particularly intimate relationship with their owner or their owner's children, as was especially the case with wetnurses and male *paidagōgoi* (tutors),[51] they might even be granted their freedom (see chapter 3). This was generally done either upon the master's death or when the slave was too old to be of much use in the household. In the case of a nurse, this might be when she could no longer provide wetnurse services or when the children of the family had grown up (see, e.g., Dem. 47). Other frequently freed slaves are high-class prostitutes (e.g. [Dem.] 59) and attractive slave-boys (e.g. Hyp. 3), both of which groups I would characterize as at least semiprivileged. Citizenship, unlike manumission, was a near impossibility for slaves, particularly for the types of slaves who occupied the lowest rung of the slave hierarchy. We will turn to slaves who became citizens in chapters to come; these individuals invariably started at a "high" level of servitude, often as serving as bankers or performing other duties of a "privileged" nature.

Slaves had limited rights in the sacral sphere, but they were not entirely excluded. Sometimes they took part in their masters' household

---

[49] On slave "families," see Golden 2011, 143–46.

[50] On family relationships among slaves as attested in Hellenistic manumissions from Delphi, see Tucker 1982, 227–29.

[51] On wetnurses and *paidagōgoi*, see Golden 2011, 141–43; Wrenhaven 2012, ch. 3.

cult practices, as for example in the worship of the household guardian Zeus Ktesios ("Zeus of Household Property") (Ant. 1.17–19; cf. Is. 8.16). Masters often shared a portion of the sacrificial meat with their slaves, whether out of generosity or in the belief that it was a good way to maintain their slaves' loyalty ([Arist.] *Oik.* 1344b19–21; Men. *Dys.* 560–69). Some of the household festivals allowing the presence of slaves entailed a (temporary) leveling of status: these included the Anthesteria, a wine-drinking festival at which slaves were allowed to drink (*IG* II² 1672.204–5), and the Kronia, a harvest festival at which slaves shared a banquet with their masters (Macrob. *Sat.* 1.10.22; cf. 1.7.37).[52] Although slaves played no official role in most civic festivals and were explicitly banned from some (like the all-female Thesmophoria: Is. 6.49; Aristoph. *Thesm.* 294), they were allowed to participate in the Rural Dionysia (Aristoph. *Ach.* 247–50; Plut. *Mor.* 1098b). Finally, at least some slaves were initiated into the Eleusinian Mysteries (e.g., [Dem.] 59.21; *IG* II² 1672.207, 1673.24), though it is unclear whether this represented genuine religious devotion on the slaves' part or (more likely) was simply a prerequisite for them to perform the labor associated with these rites.[53]

It is sometimes said that slaves had little or no autonomous religious life apart from their masters.[54] But religious practices initiated by slaves themselves, rather than by their masters, are in fact attested. Our best evidence comes from fourth-century BCE Laureion: namely, a handful of inscribed dedications by both collectives (*eranistai*) of slaves and individual slaves. Within this small sample set, the most popular gods are Heracles and Artemis, with one dedication made to "a hero."[55] There is, moreover, some evidence for slaves consulting the oracle at Dodona. The nature of their queries (about, for example, whether to run away) strongly implies that these slaves were consulting Zeus for their own sake, rather than their masters'.[56] In addition, it is possible that the gods commonly involved in manumission were particularly attractive to slaves, but unfortunately most of our evidence for manumission, especially of a sacral variety, comes from the Hellenistic period.[57]

[52] On slave participation in the Kronia, see Bömer 1960, 174–75. See also Zelnick-Abramovitz 2012 on so-called cults of reversal, which she argues were more about equalizing status than status reversal.

[53] On slave participation in the Eleusinian Mysteries, see Bömer 1960, 109–118. For the possibility of a practical motivation in initiating slaves into the mysteries (acknowledged even by Bömer), see Parker 2005, 169–70, and 2011, 237.

[54] See, e.g., Bömer 1960, still the definitive work on Greek and Roman slave religion; see also Mikalson 2010, 143–44, and Parker 2011, 237–38. But cf. Geary and Hodkinson 2012.

[55] Inscriptions by *eranistai*: see, e.g., *IG* II² 2937–38, 2940; by individuals: see, e.g., *IG* II² 4598, 4633. On dedications by slaves (both communal and individual) in Laureion: Lauffer 1979, 128–31, 176–85. On *eranistai* of mine slaves: Lauffer 1979, 185–92.

[56] See Eidinow 2012.

[57] See Zelnick-Abramovitz 2005; Kamen 2012.

Of particular interest is the fact that there clearly existed collectives of slave worshippers, even if these groupings sometimes included non-slaves as well. In addition to the *eranistai* at Laureion, some evidence exists for *thiasoi* (cult groups) of slaves. By far the majority of this evidence comes from the Hellenistic period, but an Eleusinian inscription from the late fourth century records a dedication to a god (whose name is not preserved) by a *thiasos* made up at least in large part of slaves (*SEG* 24.223).[58] In addition, an association of slave (or at least foreign) fullers, albeit not a formal religious group per se, makes a dedication to the nymphs in a mid–fourth century inscription from Attica (*IG* II² 2934).[59] Through these kinds of group religious activity, it is possible that slaves may have found some sense of community, thus resisting the "social death" imposed on them by their masters. Even if they were for the most part worshipping the same gods as their masters, the fact that these practices were initiated by the slaves themselves indicates that they possessed at least some degree of (religious) agency.

It is easier to make broad statements about the political lives of slaves, or their lack thereof. Chattel slaves of the lowest rung had no role in the political life of Athens, since they lacked both the public rights and the public duties of citizens. They could not hold office, nor could they participate in the Assembly (Ekklesia) (Aristoph. *Thesm.* 294) or the Council (Boule). This complete lack of participation in the political sphere is one of the features that most clearly separates slaves from citizens.

Finally, slaves' role in the military sphere is a hotly contested issue. It used to be thought that slaves played no role in the military, an idea substantiated by the near silence on the part of the Greek historians about slave involvement in military affairs. But Peter Hunt has convincingly argued that the historians' reticence on this topic was ideologically motivated: since Athenian ideology held that it was the citizen-soldier who fought on behalf of his city, any insinuation that the military did not embody the citizenry was to be avoided.[60] However, we know for a fact that slaves served as personal attendants to their masters in war (Thuc. 3.17.3), and the instances of large-scale manumission of slaves at the Battle of Arginousai and other battles (see chapter 3) indicate that slaves were at least occasionally armed for battle. In fact, Hunt argues that this use of slaves in war was not quite as extraordinary as our sources would have us believe.

---

[58] As Parker 2011, 237 points out, however, most attested *thiasoi* including slaves also include free people, and therefore do not represent "slave cults" per se. On noncitizen (including slave) religious associations of various sorts in Athens, see Parker 1996, 337–39.

[59] For another dedication to the nymphs by a group of slaves, see *IG* II² 4650.

[60] Hunt 1998; see also Todd 1995, 186.

As we have seen, "socially dead" chattel slaves were denied nearly all rights and privileges, and stripped almost entirely of honor. Moreover, as both foreigners and slaves, they were doubly stigmatized, representing the polar opposite of the freeborn Athenian citizen. Socially and legally, then, the chattel slave represented the lowest rung on the Athenian status ladder. At the same time, however, despite all of the figurative stigmata they bore, many chattel slaves were at least superficially indistinguishable from free people.[61] Aristotle says that while nature aims to make the bodies of free men and slaves different, sometimes slaves have the bodies of free men and vice versa (*Pol.* 1254b27–33). Moreover, lacking any significant somatic or sartorial markers, many of them were not immediately recognizable as slaves, as the Old Oligarch, author of a treatise purportedly by Xenophon, crankily points out ([Xen.] *Ath. Pol.* 1.10). Nor was slaves' labor an immediate clue as to their status, since many slaves worked alongside metics and citizens on city building projects, as well as alongside their masters in the fields.[62] As a result, their baseness, since it was not immediately apparent, had to be reinforced ideologically.

[61] For the *literal* stigmata borne by slaves (including marks from corporal punishment as well as tattoos and brands), see Kamen 2010.

[62] For slaves, metics, and citizens working alongside one another on the Erekhtheion, see Randall 1953. For slaves and owners performing agricultural work together, see, e.g., Jameson 1977/78; R. Osborne 1995. On interactions and interrelationships between slaves, metics, and foreigners in Athens, see also Fisher 2006.

CHAPTER 2

PRIVILEGED CHATTEL SLAVES

A SUBCATEGORY OF CHATTEL SLAVE, BUT ONE SUFFICIENTLY DISTINCT (TO MY mind) to constitute a unique status group, is "privileged" slaves.[1] The term "privileged," as I am using it here, is not absolute but relative. To define this group, we first have to set up some parameters, especially since scholars have often lumped together two very different kinds of slaves—*andrapoda misthophorounta* and *apophora*-bearing slaves—into the category of privileged slaves. As Emily Kazakévich has demonstrated, the only similarity between these two types of slaves is that they both worked outside the confines of the household.[2] The first of these, *andrapoda misthophorounta*, belong squarely in the (basest) chattel slave category: they were leased-out slaves—conceived of as two-footed beasts of burden—who handed over their earnings to their masters. The type of work they did was generally lowly and often dangerous, like mining (see chapter 1).[3] *Apophora*-bearing slaves, on the other hand, have a better claim to being called privileged slaves. These are slaves who worked, and sometimes lived, apart from their masters, conducted their own businesses, and handed over some fraction of their earnings, called the *apophora*, to their masters.[4] Despite the fact that chattel slaves notionally could not earn or dispense money, in practice these slaves held on to the rest of their earnings, presumably to spend at their own discretion.[5] Rather than waiting until their master was benevolent enough (or

---

[1] "In both economic and social terms there was a gulf between the thousands of slaves who worked in the mines of Laureion under the worst imaginable conditions, sometimes in chains, and the minority of privileged slaves . . ." (Hansen 1991, 122). See also Fisher 1995, 69: "A reasonable number of slaves in Athens, and the most prominent of slaves at that, were fulfilling roles that entitled them, they must have felt, to be given more 'honour' and legal protection than the rest; and some of these groups also had more advanced legal status, that put them in some respects on a social level closer to that attained by metics (who included freed ex-slaves)." On privileged slaves, see further Todd 1995, 192–94; E. E. Cohen 1998 and 2003 [2000], ch. 5; and Fisher 2008 (he calls them "independent slaves"). Cf. Hunter 2000a, 11: "Whatever independence and responsibility such slaves enjoyed and however much wealth they accumulated, their status was not one acknowledged by the law"; see also Perotti 1974, 55.

[2] See Kazakévich 2008 [1960] for a discussion of these two types of slaves, as well as a critique of scholars' conflation of the two.

[3] On mining slaves, see further Lauffer 1979. On *andrapoda misthophorounta*, see also Perotti 1976.

[4] On the primarily financial but also ideological advantages for owners in allowing their slaves to work independently, see Fisher 2006, 338.

[5] For the gap between theory and practice in this instance, see Todd 1995, 187–88. Cf. Rädle 1969, 65–66, who suggests that the only restriction placed on slaves was on conducting financial transactions with their own masters.

otherwise motivated) to manumit them, slaves could, in some circum-stances, save up this money to buy their freedom, sometimes relying on legal fictions like "purchase" by a third party (see chapter 3).

It is generally *apophora*-bearing slaves that scholars have in mind when they speak of a category of privileged slaves called *khōris oikountes* ("those living apart").[6] But we must exercise caution in using this term. As Kazaké-vich points out, the phrase appears only once in Greek literature, in Dem. 4.36–37. Moreover, by surveying collocations of *khōris* ("apart") and finite forms of the verb *oikein* ("to dwell")—used to describe both freed slaves (Dem. 47.72) and free citizens (Dem. 43.19, 47.34–35)—Kazakévich con-cludes that *khōris oikeō* refers not specifically to slaves, but to any individu-als separating themselves from the "family compound" (*oikos*). It is often used, she says, in the context of division of property. In Dem. 4.36–37, she suggests, the phrase *khōris oikountes* might refer to some group of non-Athenians who were not registered as metics. I have argued elsewhere that this phrase most likely refers to freedmen, especially since Demosthenes's pairing of *khōris oikountes* with *metoikoi* indicates that the two groups were in some way parallel, without being identical.[7] However, given the difficulty of interpreting this phrase, I will refrain from using it to refer to slaves who worked independently, calling them instead "privileged slaves."

Light is shed on the labor of privileged slaves by the so-called *phialai exeleutherikai* ("freedman bowls"), dated to ca. 330–320 BCE. These inscrip-tions are generally thought to record freedmen's dedications of silver *phia-lai* to Athena, after winning (possibly fictive) *dikai apostasiou* (private law-suits for desertion) against their former masters and thus earning their complete freedom (see further chapters 3 and 4).[8] Because the freedmen's listed trades are likely the same as those they practiced as slaves, and many of these professions required working "independently," these inscriptions may yield valuable information about privileged slaves' occupations. Clearly, even before they were freed, and certainly afterward, these privi-leged slaves made up a large part of the Athenian labor force: we find work-ers in industry (crafters of metal, stone and earthenware, wool and fab-rics); agriculture (farmhands and vine-dressers); trade (general retailers, ironmongers, bakers, greengrocers, hot-food vendors and cooks, sellers of

---

[6] So, e.g., Perotti 1974; E. E. Cohen 2003 [2000], 130–54. For various interpretations of this phrase, see Kazakévich 2008 [1960], with bibliography listed in 347–49nn11–13.

[7] See Kamen forthcoming; see also chapter 4.

[8] For these inscriptions, see *IG* II² 1553–78; Ag. Inv. I 3183 (Lewis 1959); Ag. Inv. I 4763 (*SEG* XXV.178); Ag. Inv. I 5656 (Lewis 1968, #49 and 50; *SEG* XXV.180); Ag. Inv. I 5774 (*SEG* XXI.561); Ag. Inv. I 1580 (*SEG* XLIV.68) (possibly; see Meyer 2010, 141–42); Ag. Inv. I 4665 (*SEG* XLVI.180). A new edition of all of these inscriptions, with commentary, can be found in Meyer 2010. That these inscriptions represent dedications of *phialai exeleutherikai* after *dikai apostasiou* is the conventional wisdom (for a recent discussion, including whether or not the trials are "fictive," see Zelnick-Abramovitz 2005, 282–90 and *passim*). But cf. Meyer 2010, who radically argues that they represent instead prosecutions of metics in *graphai aprostasiou*.

particular goods such as dried fish, sesame, frankincense, hemp, wool, perfume, etc.); entertainment (kitharodists); transport (muleteers, donkey-drivers, porters, jar-carriers, skin-carriers); finance (moneylenders); clerical positions (secretaries, undersecretaries); and the domestic sphere[9] (house servants, nurses).[10] A surprisingly high percentage of women (over 80 percent) are labelled as *talasiourgoi*, literally "woolworkers," though the exact nature of their work has been debated; in fact, it has recently been suggested that term may have been a euphemism for prostitutes (who also worked wool on the side).[11] Although the professions listed in these records are not equally privileged—a secretary, for example, is considerably higher on both the status and the class ladder than the average vine-dresser[12]—most of them involve slaves working on their own terms. It was this relative independence that would have allowed at least some of them to afford a 100-drachma *phialē*. If they could not afford it, they (or more likely their former masters) had the option of seeking the assistance of *koina eranistōn*, collectives of men who make ad-hoc loans (*eranoi*).[13]

The occupations of some privileged slaves, moreover, allowed for the acquisition of vast sums of money. This fact, coupled with the perceived implication that free men may themselves be "enslaved" to such wealthy slaves, greatly disturbed the Old Oligarch:

> If anyone is also startled by the fact that they let the slaves live luxuriously there [i.e., in Athens], and some of them sumptuously, it would be clear that even this they do for a reason. For where there is a naval power, it is necessary from financial considerations to be slaves to the slaves in order to take *apophorai* from them, and it is then necessary to let them go free [*eleutherous aphienai*]. And where there are rich slaves [*plousioi douloi*], it is no longer profitable in such a place for my slave to fear you. ([Xen.]*Ath. Pol.* 1.11; translated by G. W. Bowersock, with slight modification)

Our sources speak of a number of privileged slaves, some of whom are in fact very rich. One difficulty in drawing conclusions from these

---

[9] As mentioned in chapter 1, I consider domestic servants "semi-privileged" in that, thanks to intimate relationships (sexual or otherwise) with their owners, they had a better chance than their baser counterparts of being freed. Unlike more economically privileged slaves, however, they likely did not have the money to pay for their own manumission.

[10] On slave professions as attested in these inscriptions, see Tod 1950.

[11] That the *talasiourgoi* were housewives, see Rosivach 1989; that they were woolworkers, see Labarre 1998; Meyer 2010, 70n202; that they were prostitutes, see E. E. Cohen 2003, 226, and 2006, 105–8; Wrenhaven 2009. On the relationship between gender and occupation in the *phialai exeleutherikai* inscriptions, see Todd 1997, 120–24.

[12] I would imagine, however, that the agricultural slaves listed in these inscriptions must be those of higher status (e.g., overseers), rather than the masses of slaves who performed the most laborious work in the fields. The extent of slave participation in Greek agriculture is much contested: for a summary of the debate, see Fisher 2001 [1993], 37–47, with bibliography.

[13] On *eranos* loans, see Millett 1991, 153–59; cf. E. E. Cohen 1992, 207–15, who argues, against Millett, that an *eranos* loan was not necessarily interest-free. For examples of *koina eranistōn* in the *phialai* inscriptions, see Meyer 2010, 16–17n23.

examples, however, is that it is not always entirely clear whether, at the time of the narrative, they are still slaves or have already been freed. It is therefore hard to know in many of these cases whether what we gather about their legal rights and social standing better describes privileged slaves or freed slaves.[14]

Among the privileged slaves most likely to become *plousioi douloi* were slave-bankers,[15] whose work constituted an important part of the Greek economy.[16] The most famous of these slave-bankers were two men named Pasion and Phormion (see further chapter 8).[17] Pasion began his career as the slave of the bankers Antisthenes and Arkhestratos (Isoc. 17.43; Dem. 36.43, 48; [Dem.] 59.2). At some point before 394 BCE, he was manumitted by his owners (Dem. 36.48) and was later granted citizenship for his financial services to the state (by 386 or after 377 BCE). Before he died (in 370/69 BCE; Dem. 46.13), he leased his bank and shield factory to Phormion, the slave-manager of his bank, who by that point had already been freed (if this is how we interpret *kath' heauton onti*, "being separate," Dem. 36.4; cf. 36.48) (in 373/2? BCE), but who was not yet a citizen (Dem. 36.6). In his will, Pasion made Phormion the guardian of his underage son Pasikles, and gave the ex-slave his wife Arkhippe to marry (Dem. 36.8). This latter arrangement vexed Apollodoros, Pasion's elder son, but the nature of the marriage was hardly exceptional.[18] Sometime between 364 and 362 BCE, Phormion's lease on the bank expired, and Apollodoros and Pasikles (the latter now of age) leased out the bank to their slave-assistants Xenon, Euphron, Euphraios, and Kallistratos (Dem. 36.13). At some point later, these slaves seem to have been freed by their masters (Dem. 36.14).[19] Meanwhile, in 361/0 BCE, Phormion was naturalized for his monetary contributions to the state (Dem. 46.13).

As slave-bankers, and afterwards as freedmen, Pasion and Phormion acquired enormous fortunes. Pasion is said to have possessed twenty

---

[14] Edward Cohen has argued that the denial of these individuals' slave status stems from a refusal to see the extent to which slaves could attain wealth and privilege in Athens (see E. E. Cohen 2003 [2000], ch. 5; and more recently on the "power" of wealthy slaves, E. E. Cohen 2007).

[15] On slave bankers, see especially E. E. Cohen 1992, ch. 4, and 2003 [2000], ch. 5.

[16] There is a debate among scholars about how important private banking was in classical Athens. For the view that it was only marginal, see Finley 1973; Millett 1991; that it was central and important is argued by E. E. Cohen 1992; Shipton 1997.

[17] For orations involving Pasion and Phormion (in small or major roles): Isoc. 17, Dem. 36, Dem. 45, Dem. 46, [Dem.] 49, [Dem.] 50, [Dem.] 52, [Dem.] 53, [Dem.] 59. On Pasion and Phormion, see E. E. Cohen 1992, ch. 4, and 2003 [2000], ch. 5; Trevett 1992.

[18] See, e.g., Dem. 36.28–29 for other examples of widows married off to bank managers. See also E. E. Cohen 1992, ch. 4.

[19] The Greek says *eleutherous apheisan* ("released as free"). Since this phrase is consistently used in Greek literature and epigraphy to refer to manumission, I believe that manumission is meant here (see also the translation in Gernet 1954 [the French *affranchis*]; E. E. Cohen 2003 [2000], 134n21). Another interpretation is that the phrase refers to the brothers simply releasing them from their duties: Davies 1971, 433; Trevett 1992, 38.

talents in real property, with an additional fifty talents of his own money loaned out at interest (Dem. 36.5); he also gave the state one thousand shields and, once he became a citizen, served five times as trierarch (Dem. 45.85), financing triremes (warships). Phormion also acquired great sums of money (Dem. 45.54, 73, 80). It was this wealth, combined with political savvy, that allowed these slave-bankers to earn their freedom, and later their citizenship. We have no way of knowing how exceptional Pasion and Phormion were,[20] but it is safe to assert that their social mobility, facilitated by access to and use of wealth, is characterisic of their status as privileged slaves.

Another group of privileged slaves includes those involved in mercantile affairs.[21] In Dem. 34 we learn of Lampis, the servant (*oiketēs*) of a man named Dion (34.5). The speaker claims that a certain Phormion (not the slave-banker, but a man of the same name) commissioned a ship from this Lampis, evidently not merely the manager but the owner (*nauklēros*, 34.6), to convey goods to the Bosporos; Lampis, in turn, made Phormion a loan of 1,000 drachmas (34.7). Lampis then put to sea from Athens, only to be shipwrecked, making his escape with "the rest of Dion's slaves (*allōn paidōn*)" (34.10). Modern scholars debate Lampis's status, but the label *oiketēs*, as well as Lampis's connection with Dion's (other?) slaves, suggest that he too was a slave.[22] And not just that: he was a *plousios doulos*, rich enough to own a ship and to make loans on a large scale.[23] In addition, he is said to have served as a witness (*emarturei*) before a private arbitrator (34.18), suggesting to some scholars the possibility that slaves in the fourth century could participate in certain kinds of lawsuits, including *dikai emporikai*, commercial maritime cases introduced around 350 BCE.[24]

Midas, of whom we learn in Hyperides's *Against Athenogenes* (Hyp. 3), was yet another slave dealing in large sums of money. Along with his sons, he was manager of one of a certain Athenogenes's perfume businesses. And he was definitely a slave: because the case centers on the fact

[20] Another slave involved in the banking industry (albeit on a lower level than Pasion and Phormion) was a certain Kittos (Isoc. 17.11–23, 49–55). It is unclear, however, at what point (if ever) he was manumitted.

[21] One such figure, Zenothemis, the *hypēretēs*, "servant/assistant" (32.4) of Hegestratos in Demosthenes's speech *Against Zenothemis*, may or may not have been a slave. For the view that he was a slave, see Paoli 1974 [1930], 106; E. E. Cohen 2003 [2000], 135; cf. Pearson 1972 on Dem. 32.4.

[22] On Lampis as a slave, see Gernet 1955, 163; Paoli 1974 [1930], 106–8; E. E. Cohen 2003 [2000], 135, 139–40. On the modern scholarly debate about his status (whether slave, metic, or freedman), see E. E. Cohen 2003 [2000], 140n4. Todd 1994, 135–36, and 1995, 193, says we cannot be sure of Lampis's status. Fisher 2006, 337, and 2008 suggests that Lampis was registered as a metic in Athens.

[23] Might this be the same man as the wealthy Lampis of Dem. 23.211?

[24] That slaves could also participate in other *dikai emmēnoi* (monthly cases), e.g., *dikai trapezitikai* (banking cases), is argued by E. E. Cohen 1992, 96–98; for a complete study of maritime cases, see E. E. Cohen 1973, as well as Lanni 2006, 149–74. David Mirhady (personal communication) has suggested, by contrast, that Lampis may have been allowed to testify because this is an instance of private arbitration, *not* a court case.

that a certain Epikrates buys Midas's and his sons' freedom, we know that they were slaves while managing the perfumery. During their tenure as slave-managers, they racked up a huge debt (five talents!), which Epikrates then became responsible for paying off. Perhaps it is misleading to call Midas and his sons "wealthy slaves," given the hefty debts they incurred, but they did traffic in large sums of money, indicating the *potential* for moneymaking in their line of work. And potential for acquisition is as much a part of status as is actual acquisition.[25] It is significant to note, however, that despite these slaves' privileges in the financial realm, it was still their master's responsibility to handle their debts.

A final example of a privileged mercantile slave is offered by Milyas, the slave (and then freedman) of Demosthenes's family. In Demosthenes's speech *Against Aphobos I*, we learn that Milyas was once foreman (*epitropos*) of the family's shield factory. Aphobos, who had charge of (*epimelētheis*) the factory, claimed that he (Aphobos) was sometimes not himself manager (*epimelēthē*), but that Milyas was instead in charge of (*diōikēsen*) financial matters—and that Demosthenes should therefore look to Milyas for an accounting of finances (27.19). Despite the fact that Demosthenes refers to Milyas in this speech as "our freedman" (*ho apeleutheros ho hēmeteros*; 27.19), one can argue that the designation *apeleutheros* indicates only that Milyas was a freedman at the time of the trial (years later), not that he was already free when he was in charge of the factory.[26] If Milyas *was* a slave during the events described in the speech—something we cannot definitively ascertain—he certainly had a remarkable degree of control over Demosthenes's family's tremendous finances, indicating a certain measure of de facto privilege.

Female slaves too "worked apart" and earned money. The ones about whom we hear most frequently, and who presumably earned the most money, were courtesans (*hetairai*). *Hetairai* could accumulate wealth in either (or both) of two ways. Money could be earned over time through their "work for hire"—if we assume that most *hetairai*, unlike whores in brothels (*pornai*), were (relatively) independent contractors and kept at least a portion of their earnings.[27] *Hetairai* might also stage one-time "fundraising campaigns" for their manumission, gathering money from

---

[25] Finley 1981 [1964], 131: "A man's status is defined by the total of these elements [claims, privileges, immunities, liabilities, obligations] which he possesses or which he has (or has not) the potential of acquiring. Actual and potential must both be considered."

[26] So E. E. Cohen 1992, 93n155 (verbatim in 2003 [2000], 140n51): "There is no indication that Milyas was not still a slave when he was operating the workshops." For the view that Milyas must have been free, see the bibliography listed in E. E. Cohen 2003 [2000], 140n51.

[27] On the distinction between *hetaira* (courtesan) and *pornē* (whore), see Davidson 1997, chs. 3 and 4; Kurke 1997. For a challenge to the polarization of these terms, see the articles in Glazebrook and Henry 2011. For a discussion of prostitution as a "liberal profession," including the relative freedom of prostitutes in Athens, see E. E. Cohen 2003 (along with E. E. Cohen 2006).

previous lovers. The *hetaira* Neaira provides an illustrative example. In a fourth-century lawsuit charging Neaira with posing as an Athenian citizen ([Dem.] 59), we learn that two young men purchased Neaira from her owner Nikarete, a freedwoman madam. They kept her as their (love-)slave, making use of her as they pleased. When they tired of her, they offered to let her buy her freedom. Graciously subtracting 1,000 drachmas from the price at which they bought her, they said that if she could find the means to pay them the remaining twenty mnas (i.e., 2,000 drachmas), she would be free. Neaira then collected an ad-hoc *eranos* loan from a number of her ex-lovers to contribute to the price of her freedom ([Dem.] 59.29–31).[28]

Yet another group of privileged slaves in Athens were the public slaves (*dēmosioi*),[29] who may have numbered as many as a thousand in the fourth century.[30] I should note, first of all, that *dēmosioi*, like privately owned slaves, encompassed a very large range of occupations. Public slaves included, for example, magistrates' assistants (*hypēretai*),[31] who performed such tasks as removing corpses from roads for burial ([Arist.] *Ath. Pol.* 50.2), aiding in the jury-selection process ([Arist.] *Ath. Pol.* 65.4), and keeping records.[32] They also included Scythian archers, who served as a police force,[33] and *ergatai* (literally "laborers"),[34] who did work such as road repair ([Arist.] *Ath. Pol.* 54.1). Not all of these public slaves were equally privileged, but those who were were closer to metic status than to that of the (basest) chattel slave.[35] At the same time, however, they remained de jure chattel slaves.

One particularly privileged public slave may have been a man named Pittalakos, who appears in Aeschines's speech *Against Timarchus*. But although Pittalakos is explicitly called "a public slave [*dēmosios*] who is the property of the city" (Aesch. 1.54; also 1.62), it is nonetheless not entirely clear whether, at the time of the events narrated in the speech, Pittalakos was a slave or a freedman. Edward Cohen, for instance, has no doubts that Pittalakos remains a slave throughout the narrative.[36]

---

[28] See Kapparis 1999 *ad loc.*

[29] On public slaves in Athens, see Jacob 1928. On the legal status of public slaves: Jacob 1928, 146–67; Harrison 1968, 177–78; MacDowell 1978, 83; Hansen 1991, 123–24.

[30] Robinson 1924, 120–21.

[31] On *hypēretai*, see Jacob 1928, 79–145.

[32] One such record-keeper was the public slave Eukles, attested in *IG* II² 120, 1440, 1673; on Eukles, see Hunter 2006, 8–12.

[33] On the Scythian archers, see Jacob 1928, 53–78.

[34] On the *ergatai*, see Jacob 1928, 13–52.

[35] Scholars tend to agree on this point. The "legal status [of *dēmosioi*] approximated closely to that of metics" (Harrison 1968, 177); "The legal position of a public slave was quite different from that of a slave belonging to an individual owner; it could even be called 'freedom'. It may have been something like the status of a metic" (MacDowell 1978, 83); "If any slaves came close to crossing the bounds that separated free and slave, it was the *dēmosioi*" (Hunter 2000a, 12).

[36] In fact, he considers any other interpretation a refusal to see the extent to which slaves could attain wealth and privilege in Athens; see E. E. Cohen 2003 [2000], 131. See similarly Hunter 2006, 2–8.

But as Stephen Todd points out, status distinctions are often murky in the orators, since those who had at one point been slaves were often still referred to as slaves in court.[37] It is therefore also conceivable that Pittalakos was a *freed* slave:[38] in fact, when a certain Hegesandros tries to claim Pittalakos as his own slave,[39] a man named Glaukon asserts (in a procedure called an *aphairesis eis eleutherian*, "release into freedom") that Pittalakos is in fact free (1.62). Another interpretation of this passage, however, is that this "freedom" was only freedom *from Hegesandros* and that he would still have been a *dēmosios*.[40] In any event, this Pittalakos, we learn, lives in his own house (*tēn oikian hou ōikei*, 1.59; see also 1.54, 55, 68), which he likely rented. We also learn that he "had plenty of money" (*euporōn arguriou*, 1.54), presumably earned in part by his service to the state and multiplied manifold by his side business, gambling. He used this money to seduce the citizen Timarchus, whom he spotted one day gambling; he then kept Timarchus in his house, continuing to expend money on him (1.54).

Other public slaves, who may not have been wealthy but earned an income nonetheless, include those *dēmosioi* working as guardians of official weights and measures.[41] The city's *dokimastēs* ("[currency] tester"), for example, was a public slave entrusted with the task of verifying that coins paid to the state were of pure silver and struck from the official die. His was not an ad-hoc job but an official position. Like his counterpart in the Peiraieus (who was also a *dēmosios*), the *dokimastēs* was paid by public officials called *apodektai*.[42] *Dokimastai* seem to have been in some sense "privileged": living and working apart from a master (since the state was their master), they were entrusted with work that was considered of great importance to the city. As privileged as they were, however, their standing was still very much servile: they were kept in their place, reminded of their bodiliness, by the punishment inflicted for poor service (i.e., not showing up at their post or testing the coins correctly):[43] namely, fifty lashes, apparently a standard legal penalty for slaves (Ag. Inv. I 7180, lines 13–16).[44]

[37] Todd 1995, 193–94; see also Kamen 2009. Fisher (2004 and 2008) argues, convincingly to my mind, that Aeschines is deliberately ambiguous about Pittalakos's status, presenting him as a slave only when it is rhetorically useful for him.

[38] Pittalakos as freed slave: Jacob 1928, 158–62; Fisher 2004, 66–67, and 2008; Vlassopoulos 2009, 352.

[39] It is possible that Hegesandros was the owner, and that Pittalakos was a public slave: Fisher (2001 [1993], 362, and 2004, 76) suggests the possibility that Pittalakos was owned at one point by the *genos* of the Salaminioi, to which Hegesadros may have belonged.

[40] Beauchet 1976 [1897], 466, says that the *aphairesis* was to prove that Pittalakos was a public slave and not a private one. Hunter 2006, 3n9, similarly says this freedom was only "relative."

[41] See Jacob 1928, 110–21.

[42] For a discussion of *dokimastai* in the context of the Athenian law on silver coinage (Ag. Inv. I 7180), see Stroud 1974.

[43] For this point, see also Todd 1994, 130; Hunter 2000a, 12. On the whip as a symbolic means of asserting status distinctions between slave and free, see duBois 1991; Hunter 1992, esp. 280–84, and 2000a, 13–15.

[44] See Stroud 1974, 178. Cf. *IG* II² 380, 1013, 1362; Aesch. 1.139.

Another possible *dēmosios* about whom we know a great deal is Niko-makhos, perhaps the most famous of the *anagrapheis* ("recorders") involved in the writing-up of the "Athenian Law Code" in the late fifth/early fourth century BCE (Lys. 30).[45] Most significantly for our purposes, Nikomakhos's relationship to the recording of law sheds light on the remarkable status of at least some *dēmosioi*. Both the specific tasks and the level of authority of the *anagrapheis* are debated: Some scholars believe that they not only "wrote up" the laws, but also had some role in deciding what the laws would be[46]—or at any rate, which laws to include. Other scholars, however, have argued that the *anagrapheis'* work was merely cler-ical, speculating that after the laws were compiled, they were passed on to the Boule or Ekklesia for careful study.[47] The nature and extent of the *anagrapheis'* authority may be unclear (to us), but we should not dismiss the possibility that certain privileged slaves may have had the right to vet laws in some fashion.

Having now surveyed a range of "privileged" slaves, we can at this point lay out the features that define this particular status group. First of all, unlike the average chattel slave, these slaves seem to have had some claims to property: they could not own land, of course, but the fact that they could hold on to the balance of their earnings after handing over an *apophora* indicates that they at least had some control over money, even if in a legal sense they probably did not "own" it.[48] Some slaves do seem to have owned (in some sense) their moveable property, perhaps especially if it was related to their work: so, for example, in the Attic Stelai inscrip-tions, the cobbler Aristomarkhos, slave of Adeimantos, is listed as owner of various items: two types of shoe, squared timber, two couches, and a table.[49] "Independent" slaves lived in houses or apartments owned pre-sumably by their masters, or in the case of public slaves like Pittalakos, by the state. It is hard to say whether these slaves "owned" the moveable property in their homes: legally they likely did not, but in practice they essentially did.

Privileged slaves' labor was mandated by a master, as was the labor of baser chattel slaves, but unlike the latter, privileged slaves had some

---

[45] According to Stroud 1968, 24–25, the impetus for this writing-up was a need for legal documents to be gathered and centralized, in order to form a more coherent body of law (if not quite in the sense of a formal, systematic "code"). The *anagrapheis*, then, were a special commission appointed by the state to perform this task; their term was originally set at four months, and was then extended as the nature of their job expanded and was clarified. On the speech Lys. 30, see Todd 1996 with bibliography.

[46] See Dow 1963, 38; Stroud 1968, 25; Ostwald 1986, 418; Todd 1996, 108.

[47] See N. Robertson 1990, 45; Sickinger 1999, 98. But it must be pointed out that there is no evidence that anyone else was required to validate the *anagrapheis'* collected texts (see also Rhodes 1991, 93).

[48] See Beauchet 1976 [1897], 463–64 in the context of public slaves.

[49] Attic Stele VI, lines 31–46; see Pritchett 1953, 271.

discretion: since they were probably not under the direct supervision of their master or even an overseer, privileged slaves could have a say over the precise nuts and bolts of the work, provided that it yielded a suitable outcome. Some privileged slaves, especially bankers, were entrusted with considerable discretion over transactions involving large sums of money. Others, like Nikomakhos, were granted discretion over matters of great significance to the running of the city. Finally, privileged slaves' capacity for movement particularly distinguished them from baser chattel slaves: since they generally lived, and certainly worked, outside the home, they were automatically granted more control over their daily movement.

A privileged slave might also have power over other slaves' labor and movement. Slave managers (whom we might call moderately privileged) often oversaw the lower-ranking slaves of a given household. Moreover, there is some evidence for privileged slaves owning their own slaves, de facto if not de jure: In the *phialai exeleutherikai* records (mentioned above), a certain *dēmosios* named [. . .]leides (his full name is not preserved) charges his freedwoman Krateia for "deserting" him (*IG* II² 1570.78–79), implying that Krateia had once been his slave.[50]

Privileged slaves, like their baser counterparts, were susceptible to all kinds of corporal punishment, including whipping.[51] Likewise, they were afforded the same protections from abuse. In fact, Nick Fisher points out that the very few cases where *hubris* charges were brought (or almost brought) on behalf of a slave deal exclusively with privileged slaves.[52] Privileged slaves, in turn, would have more opportunities than their baser counterparts to exercise authority over other slaves through punishment, for example as foremen (Xen. *Oik.* 13.4), or even as "owners" (see [. . .]leides, above).

The juridical privileges of the privileged slave were essentially equivalent to that of the average chattel slave. Although Pittalakos is said to have brought a suit (*dikēn lankhanei*) for *hubris* against Hegesandros and Timarchus for trashing his house and whipping him (Aesch. 1.62), probably someone else brought the case on his behalf.[53] The only occasion on which a slave could try or be tried in a case seems to have been the maritime suit (*dikē emporikē*), a procedure that arose in the mid-fourth century. While it appears that men of any legal status could bring a *dikē emporikē*, the slaves most likely to be involved in such a case would have been

---

[50] See also Todd 1995, 194, who concludes from the case of [. . .]eides that "public slaves did have an exceptional status, including certain independent rights of ownership." Cf. Meyer 2010, 73n210.

[51] In addition to Ag. Inv. I 7180, lines 13–16 (discussed above), see Ag. Inv. I 7180, lines 30–32; *IG* II² 333.6–7; *IG* II² 1013.5, 45–49.

[52] Fisher 1995, 69–70.

[53] As suggested by Hunter 2006, 6.

privileged ones. Another possible venue in which a slave, especially a privileged one, might have been able to bring a suit was in cases before the polemarch, the magistrate in charge of noncitizens' legal affairs. But even that is speculation, based on the fact that [. . .]leides (see above) apparently filed a *dikē apostasiou* (a suit brought before the polemarch) against his freedwoman Krateia. It is, however, possible that someone else prosecuted Krateia on [. . .]leides's behalf.[54]

"Privileged" slaves were not allowed to marry,[55] but given that they often resided outside of their master's house, it is certainly conceivable that one could live with a partner. The nurse in Dem. 47 (see chapter 1) is said to have had a husband, but the implication seems to be that she only married him *after* she was manumitted (*sunōikēse de andri, epeidē apheithē eleuthera*; 47.55). Lampis has a wife and children (*ousēs d'autōi gunaikos … kai paidōn*; Dem. 34.37), but, as noted above, his status is not entirely clear. The issue is further complicated by the fact that a slave might consider his or her partner a "wife" (*gunē*) or "husband" (*anēr*), even if they had not conducted a formal marriage. Whether privileged (and especially public) slaves could dispose of their "property" as they saw fit is also a matter of debate.[56] Since this propery was not legally recognized as their own, on the one hand it was not theirs to bequeath; on the other, it is certainly possible that informal (de facto) bequests were made.

A further way in which privileged slaves were distinguished from their baser chattel slave counterparts is that they had a much greater chance of being freed. Manumission was more likely to come to privileged slaves for a variety of interrelated reasons: they could prove they had the skills to work on their own; they were in a position to become close with their masters, almost as colleagues, and certainly as employees; and they had the resources both to pay their masters for their worth (if the masters required that)[57] and to support themselves with food and shelter without the assistance of a master. Pasion and Phormion are of course particularly exceptional cases, since they acquired citizenship as well as their freedom. This certainly was not the norm, but it does seem reasonable to suggest that a privileged slave, on average, was much more likely than a baser slave to be manumitted. Moreover, among those who were manumitted, those working in lucrative fields like banking, who

---

[54] Cf. Hunter 2006, 6, who calls this an "unequivocal instance of a public slave instituting a suit before the polemarch on his own behalf."

[55] Cf. Beauchet 1976 [1897], 464, who argues that public slaves could conduct valid marriages; there is, however, little evidence to support this assertion.

[56] Beauchet 1976 [1897], 463 argues that *dēmosioi* could dispose as they chose of their "patrimony," but as Jacob 1928, 151n2 points out, no ancient evidence supports this claim.

[57] Cf. Dio's *Fifteenth Discourse*, in which a slave who appears to be relatively privileged says to his interlocutor, an Athenian citizen, "Do you not think I could liberate myself?" The Athenian replies, "Yes, if you should raise the money somewhere to pay your master with" (15.22).

could make generous donations to the Athenian state, would be the most likely to be given citizenship (see chapter 8).

Downward mobility for privileged slaves was presumably also possible, although it is rarely attested. The closest we come is domestic slaves in comedy being sent to work in the mill, a sort of demotion to lower-status slavery (Lys. 1.18; Men. *Her.* 2–3). One would imagine that a slave entrusted with "privileged" tasks was generally obedient enough not to compromise his or her position.

For the most part, privileged slaves were subject to the same restrictions in the religious sphere as were their baser counterparts. There were, however, some areas in which privileged slaves seem to have had greater access to their masters' religion. So, for example, our best evidence for the participation of slaves in the Eleusinian Mysteries (see chapter 1) comes from records attesting to the initiation specifically of *dēmosioi*, paid for by the city (*IG* II² 1672.207, 1673.24). In addition, the Eleusinian temple accounts record the cost of a sacrificial victim, jugs, and two measures of wine for *dēmosioi* at the Choes ("Drinking Vessels") festival in honor of Dionysus, paid for on behalf of the *dēmosioi* by the city (*IG* II² 1672.204–5). Other slaves were privileged in that they acted as temple servants (*hierodouloi*), devoted to serving a deity and his or her temple.[58] Finally, in terms of their autonomous religious activity (as opposed to their participation in their masters' religious practices), privileged slaves, particularly those who were rich, were more likely to be able to afford dedications than were their baser counterparts—although it should be noted that even the basest slaves, those working in the mines, could afford to make dedications if they pooled their resources (see chapter 1).

Privileged slaves were excluded from the political sphere: no slave, no matter how privileged, could hold any sort of office. They did, however, have the *potential* to attain political rights. Those who were especially wealthy (like Pasion and Phormion) could make donations to the state, thereby earning citizenship and with it political power (see chapter 8). In addition, privileged slaves had the capacity, once freed, to become more engaged than their baser counterparts in the military sphere. So, for example, if a rich slave was manumitted, he might make contributions to the state to fund the military (as Pasion did), or even serve as a hoplite or member of the cavalry.[59] There was, however, probably no distinction between privileged and less-privileged slaves in terms of conscription in times of emergency. One possible exception depends on

[58] The most famous example of a temple slave is a fictional one, the title character of Euripides's *Ion*. See recently Lape 2010, ch. 3, for a reading of the *Ion* in light of Athenian citizen identity.

[59] In exceptional circumstances, some slaves may have served in these capacities even before manumission, but only as substitutes for their masters. This practice is better attested in Sparta than Athens: see, e.g., Xen. *Hell.* 3.4.15.

how we take the passage of Demosthenes cited above, in which the *khōris oikountes* are called upon to man the fleet. For those who take this phrase to mean privileged slaves, this would imply that privileged slaves were drafted separately from other slaves. If, however, we interpret *khōris oikountes* as either freed slaves or some other intermediate status (a more plausible reading, to my mind), this passage is less useful for determining the military role of privileged slaves.

Privileged slaves, then, were on the cusp of freedom: they held a number of rights, and manumission was actually attainable for them, given sufficient accumulated income. Socially, they possessed more honor than the basest chattel slaves, though as chattel, they were still in many ways "socially dead" (see chapter 1). Moreover, the economic status of (at least some) privileged slaves clearly was a source of frustration for citizens, as seen in the Old Oligarch passage quoted above. By possessing more wealth and privileges than poor, juridically free citizens, these slaves must have implicitly called into question the value of "freedom," a concept assigned tremendous importance by the Greeks.[60] In this way, their very existence challenged any neat ideas about free versus slave status.

[60] See Raaflaub 2004.

CHAPTER 3

FREEDMEN WITH CONDITIONAL FREEDOM

TWO MAJOR SUBTYPES OF FREED SLAVE EXISTED IN CLASSICAL ATHENS.[1] THIS chapter focuses on slaves freed with strings attached; in the following chapter I will turn to unconditionally freed slaves, as well as freeborn resident aliens, with whom they share a very similar status. I would like to begin, however, with some basics on how manumission worked in classical Athens. Slaves in Athens could be freed in a number of different ways.[2] Sometimes a master freed his own slaves. He could do so through a simple verbal declaration,[3] as well as posthumously, through a will.[4] He could even free his slave through proclamation by a herald, a practice that seems to have involved a performative utterance delivering the slave into freedom.[5] Often this was conducted in front of a large audience at the City Dionysia—at least until the middle of the fourth century BCE, when public announcements in the theater apparently became so common (and so distracting) that "some legislator" (we are not told who) forbade this practice (Aesch. 3.41–2).[6]

Slaves could also be freed through "purchase" by a third party, a procedure known as "sale for the purpose of freedom" (*prasis ep' eleutheriai*).[7] This sale was, however, something of a fiction: it was a means of manumission whereby a third party, ostensibly buying the slave, actually paid for the slave's freedom. It most commonly happened in the case of men buying the freedom of their slave beloveds, whether high-class prostitutes or attractive slave-boys.[8] The *hetaira* Neaira (see chapter 2) once again provides a good example. Because she was a slave and lacked the legal standing to pay for her own freedom (even with money she herself

---

[1] On the status of freedmen in Greece, see, e.g., Harrison 1968, 181–86; MacDowell 1978, 82–83; Klees 2000; Zelnick-Abramovitz 2005, ch. 6; Dimopoulou-Piliouni 2009.

[2] The most recent comprehensive work on manumission in ancient Greece is Zelnick-Abramovitz 2005. The description of manumission modes that follows here can also be found in Kamen 2009, 52–54.

[3] See Rädle 1969, 10–12; Zelnick-Abramovitz 2005, 74.

[4] See Rädle 1971, 361–64; Zelnick-Abramovitz 2005, 74–75.

[5] See Rädle 1971, 361–64; Zelnick-Abramovitz 2005, 71–72; Mactoux 2008, 437–51.

[6] Cf. Zelnick-Abramovitz 2009, 305–6, who argues on the basis of this passage that manumission in the theater could still take place after this law, provided that the Council and Assembly gave approval.

[7] See Zelnick-Abramovitz 2005, 81–82.

[8] See Weiler 2001, who argues that, because of prostitution and concubinage, female slaves had more opportunities than male slaves to be manumitted. For an example of an attempted "purchase" of a slave boy, see Hyp. 3.

collected from her former lovers),[9] she had to make use of a third-party buyer, turning to yet another former lover, the Athenian citizen Phrynion. She entrusted him with the collected money, to which he added the difference and "bought" her (for the purpose of freedom: *ep' eleutheriāi*) from her owners. The latter agreed to the purchase, stipulating only that Neaira no longer prostitute herself in Corinth ([Dem.] 59.32).

In addition to such instances of masters manumitting their own slaves, we also find cases in which the Athenian polis itself freed both privately and publicly owned slaves. These instances, although somewhat rare, could entail the manumission of large numbers of slaves and generally occurred in times of crisis. So, for example, slaves were sometimes freed for their service in wartime. The earliest attested example is the freeing of slaves who fought for Athens in the Battle of Marathon (490 BCE).[10] However, perhaps the best-known case of military manumission took place during the Peloponnesian War, before the large naval battle between Athenian and Spartan fleets at Arginousai in 406/5 BCE. Because their fleet was numerically weaker in this endeavor, the Athenians not only drafted slaves but also freed them and granted them and other foreigners who took part citizenship.[11] Similar measures were taken by Thrasyboulos after the battle of Mounikhia ([Arist.] *Ath. Pol.* 40.2) (see chapter 5), and by Hyperides after the battle of Chaeronea (Plut. *Mor.* 849a) (see chapter 8). As mentioned in chapter 2, the polis also periodically freed slaves who offered up information in particular types of lawsuits.[12] In Athens, these were cases primarily pertaining to religious offenses, transgressions the polis took very seriously.[13] For instance, after the Mutilation of the Herms and Defamation of the Mysteries in 415 BCE, the polis rewarded anyone who came forward with information: money was offered to free people, and freedom was offered to slaves.[14] Thus we find manumission offered by the polis in extraordinary circumstances—namely, when the polis' interests were threatened, whether it was in wartime or in the case of some sort of religious transgression that might pollute the entire city.

The freed slave's new freedom was guaranteed in a few ways.[15] One crucial mode of protection was the presence of witnesses. In one of his

---

[9] On this restriction, which was often circumvented in practice, see Todd 1995, 187–88.

[10] See Hunt 1998, 27n5 for bibliography.

[11] See Hunt 2001; Tamiolaki 2008.

[12] An owner might also manumit his own slaves for offering up information beneficial to his (the owner's) case: Mirhady 2000, 64 with n1 suggests that this may be the case with the (now) free person who had testified under torture on Euxitheos's behalf (Ant. 5).

[13] See R. Osborne 2000.

[14] See Thuc. 6.27.2; Andoc. 1.12–18, 27–28.

[15] On publicity as a crucial means of protecting the freed slave's new status, see Rädle 1969; Zelnick-Abramovitz 2005.

speeches against his former guardian, Aphobos, Demosthenes speaks of his

> female slaves, who remember that my father on his death-bed set this man [Milyas] free [*apethenta touton eleutheron einai*]. Besides this, my mother was ready to call to her side my sister and myself, and swear . . . that my father when he was about to die had set this man free [*apheinai*], and that Milyas was regarded by us as free thereafter. (Dem. 29.25–26; translated by A. T. Murray)

Potential witnesses to this manumission thus included a number of individuals—the female slaves, Demosthenes, his sister, and his mother—and as witnesses, they could have testified in court to Milyas's manumission (and hence his free status, the point at issue here; if Aphobos's claim had succeeded, Milyas would have been tortured for testimony as if he were a slave [Dem. 29.14 and *passim*]). Another mode of protection was testamentary. Not only were witnesses likely present for the making of a will,[16] but the document itself served as "witness" to the slave's manumission.

The entire polis could also, at least notionally, serve as a witness in Athens. Before the heralding of manumissions at theaters was banned, attendees of tragedy, comedy, and other ritual events would have been default witnesses to such proclamations. In fact, that was the point of making the proclamation at the theater: to guarantee the largest possible audience and therefore the largest pool of witnesses. Indeed, Aeschines says that such proclamations had "all Hellas as witness" (*marturas tous Hellēnas*; 3.42). Hyperbolic, perhaps, but at least the whole city (or a representative portion thereof), plus a fair number of foreign visitors, would have known that a given slave was now freed. Proclamations made at altars could likewise secure a large audience, comprised of those who happened to be conducting religious activity on the spot. I would argue further that both of these modes—heralding in the theater and at altars—involved not only the witnessing of large groups of Athenian citizens, but also the gods themselves, who were conceptualized as being "present" in these locations. So, for example, Dionysus, a statue of whom was carried into the theater in an elaborate procession, was thought to oversee the proceedings of the City Dionysia.

Although all of these practices succeeded in guaranteeing witnesses, they nonetheless lacked a secure form of documentation. We have no way of knowing how often oral proclamations were backed up with written documentation: clearly there was no written record of Milyas's manumission, hence the plausibility of Aphobos's claim that Milyas was still a slave. Wills, while more reliable than oral testimony by eyewitnesses,

---

[16] On the importance of witnesses in proving the validity of a will, see, e.g., Is. 9.7–8; Dem. 28.5.

were nonetheless insecure documents, regularly challenged in court as composed under the influence of madness, drugs, women, or senility.[17] There was also a general suspicion of individual wills as forgeries.[18] Theater proclamations likewise garnered publicity, but this publicity was ephemeral.

One consequence of this is that if freed slaves were unjustly claimed as slaves, by their master or someone else, they had no concrete ways of proving their status. This danger is well illustrated by Dio Chrysostom's *Fifteenth Discourse (Slavery II)*, which, though written during the Roman Empire, harks back to classical Athens, where the dialogue is set. One of the interlocutors, a slave, asks:

> Do you think that all those who are in a state of servitude [*douleuontes*] are slaves [*douloi*]? But are not many of these, although free men, yet held unjustly in servitude? Some of them have already gone before the court [*eis dikastērion*] and proved that they are free [*apedeixan eleutherous ontas heautous*], while others are enduring to the end, either because they have no clear proof of their freedom [*ouk ekhontes apodeixai phanerōs peri tēs eleutherias*], or else because those who are called their masters are not harsh with them. (Dio Chrys. 15.13; translated by J.W. Cohoon)

Although this passage does not refer specifically to the plight of freed slaves—as opposed to free men wrongfully enslaved—it seems highly probable that they would be the people most likely to find themselves in such a situation. In Athens in particular, I would argue, freedmen faced a real risk of being carried off as slaves by someone alleging to be their master.

A legal countermeasure, however, was available, for the benefit of anyone wrongly enslaved, including wrongly enslaved freedmen. This was the *aphairesis* (or *exairesis*) *eis eleutherian* ("taking away into freedom"), whereby anyone who wished (*ho boulomenos*) could intervene to defend the alleged slave, furnishing sureties before the polemarch (the magistrate in charge of noncitizens' affairs) for the appearance of the latter in court. In turn, the alleged master could then bring a private lawsuit called a *dikē aphaireseōs* (or *exaireseōs*) against the slave's (or alleged slave's) defender.[19] As Harpocration defines this *dikē*,

> whenever someone carried off [*agoi*] someone on the grounds that he was a slave, [and] then someone else removed [*exairoito*] him on the grounds that he was free,

---

[17] See the law in Dem. 46.14. Other partial quotations of, or allusions to, this law: Is. 2.13, 19; 6.9, 21; Hyp. 3.17–18; [Dem.] 44.68; [Arist.]*Ath. Pol.* 35.2.

[18] For this suspicion, see, e.g., Is. 1.41; 4.12, 23; 9.12; Arist. *Prob.* 950b3. For a discussion of Athenian attitudes toward wills, see Thompson 1981.

[19] For a discussion of these procedures, see Harrison 1968, 178–80, 221; MacDowell 1978, 80; Todd 1995, 187, 192; Maffi 1997 (on Athens and Gortyn); Zelnick-Abramovitz 2005, 292–300.

it was allowed that the one laying claim to the man as a slave file a *dikē exaireseōs* against the one removing [*exairoumenōi*] him into freedom. [For example,] Isaeus in the removal of Eumathes into freedom. (Harp. s.v. *exaireseōs dikē*)

From Harpocration and Dionysius of Halicarnassus we have two preserved fragments of Isaeus's *dikē exaireseōs* (frr. 18 and 19), the only such *dikē* from which direct speech remains. Corroborating evidence for this practice includes brief descriptions in other court speeches.[20] For example, after the newly freed Neaira was abused by Phrynion (the man who "bought" her), she packed up and moved to Megara, where she became involved with the Athenian citizen Stephanos. Phrynion then removed her by force (*ēgen*), essentially reclaiming her as a slave, and Stephanos in turn successfully "removed her to freedom" (*aphairoumenou ... eis eleutherian*) ([Dem.] 59.40).

The existence of the *aphairesis eis eleutherian* thus provided enslaved freedmen with a means of recovering their freedom. But there were limitations to this protection: not only was the vindicator not rewarded for his deed (unless one counts the freed slave's gratitude), he also had no assurances of immunity. In [Dem.] 58, *Against Theokrines*, the speaker asks the clerk to read "the law which declares that anyone who is adjudged to have wrongly asserted the freedom of a slave [*eis tēn eleutherian aphelesthai*] shall pay half the penalty assessed into the public treasury" (58.21). Given this risk, the incentives to defend a freedman must have been negligible. If, however, there were sufficient grounds to make a case in favor of the freedman's status—for example, documentary evidence or eyewitnesses to the act of manumission—the risks for the defender would have been lessened and the protection for the freedman therefore increased.

Not all manumission was absolute. For some it was conditional, and these individuals are the subject of the rest of this chapter. Commenting on Aristotle's statement that "the condition of the free man is that he does not live under the constraint of another" (*Rhet.* 1367a32), Finley says that "manumitted slaves were free men, if we ignore ... conditional manumissions and minor obligations towards the ex-master."[21] But conditional manumission is a big thing to ignore: it is hard to imagine that the difference between a conditionally freed slave and an unconditionally freed one was not a significant one. In fact, Zelnick-Abramovitz has argued convincingly that freed slaves who had continuing obligations and those who were free from obligations represented distinct status groups.[22]

---

[20] See Lys. 23.9–11; Aesch. 1.62–63; Isoc. 17.11–17. The title of another speech (Hyperides's *Against Aristogoras*) is preserved in Harp. s.v. *aphairesis*.

[21] Finley 1981 [1964], 122.

[22] She also argues, less convincingly, that the terms *apeleutheros* and *exeleutheros*, respectively, designate these two categories (see Zelnick-Abramovitz 2005, 99–126), a theory criticized by Meyer 2010, 55n154; for

Before I turn to our (limited) evidence for conditional manumission in classical Athens, it might be helpful first to address the more plentiful evidence provided by Hellenistic manumission inscriptions from other Greek poleis, in which ex-slaves' continuing obligations are often spelled out.[23] Delphi provides one of our richest sources of evidence for manumission, in the form of over a thousand manumission inscriptions dating from 201 BCE to c.100 CE. At Delphi, manumission was nearly always conducted through the fictive sale of a slave by his or her owner to Apollo. It was, however, the slave who paid, under the guise of "entrusting the sale" to the god. These manumissions fall into two distinct categories: those granting full freedom, and those offering only conditional release. Close to three-quarters (72 percent) of slaves freed in the second century BCE were given full freedom. Over time, however, fewer slaves were given full freedom at Delphi—the percentage decreased to 48 percent by the end of the first century BCE—and those who were paid increasingly higher prices for this privilege.[24]

A large number of slaves, then, were freed conditionally. The most striking feature of conditional-freedom manumission inscriptions is a so-called *paramonē* clause, mandating that the freedman remain and serve his or her former master. *Paramonē* seems to have been invented as a technical term in the third century BCE, referring to any legal obligation to "remain" with someone, whether under surety, in contracts for services, or in contracts of loan.[25] In the case of Delphic manumission, the *paramonē* clause states an obligation to remain (*paramenein*) with the manumittor, generally until the latter's death. So, for instance, one inscription reads "Let Nikaia and Isthmos remain [*parameinatō*] by Sosias as long as Sosias lives, doing everything possible that Sosias orders, in a manner unworthy of reproach" (*GDI* 1689). The *paramonē* clause also often includes sanctions, whether bodily punishment, sale, or invalidation of manumission, in the case of failure to perform *paramonē* service. Next generally follows a provision of payment to obtain early release (*apolusis*). Before or after the release clause is a security clause, which protects the freedman from being arbitrarily arrested or enslaved, and ensures that the sale to the god is secure.

Although these manumissions involving *paramonē* do not specify particular duties, we do get a sense of the rights they granted freedmen. For instance, as seen from the frequent phrase "doing whatever he wants and

---

the conventional view, that these terms are basically synonymous, see Zelnick-Abramovitz 2005, 103n79. For yet another interpretation (that *exeleutheroi*, unlike *apeleutheroi*, were born free), see Dimopoulou-Piliouni 2009, 36–38.

[23] On *paramonē*, see most recently Zelnick-Abramovitz 2005, 222–48.

[24] One of the best accounts of Delphic manumission is still Hopkins 1978, ch. 3.

[25] Samuel 1965.

going wherever he wants" (*poiōn ho ka thelēi kai apotrekhōn hois ka thelēi*), most freedmen—both those who were "fully free" and those under *paramonē*—had the right to do as they wished and go where they pleased. This implies that *paramonē* does not necessarily mean that one must stay in the ex-master's home, only that one should remain close enough to carry out obligations. In his study on *paramonē*, A. E. Samuel points out that because freedom of motion and action is a characteristic attribute of free men (*eleutheroi*), not of slaves, manumission, however conditional, provided one with the rights of *eleutheroi*.[26] In addition, freedmen, according to these inscriptions, could not be enslaved or sold, a right one associates with free men. Finally, in a small (but not negligible) number of inscriptions, there are provisions for the judgment of disputes, implying that the freedman would be protected against arbitrary decisions made by his former master.[27]

In classical Athens, we can get a sense of "*paramonē*"[28] obligations from the philosophers' wills recorded by Diogenes Laertius, in which conditionally freed slaves are required to remain (*paramenein*) and work for the family of the deceased, generally for a fixed number of years. So, for example, the will of Lykon stipulates:

> Mikros I set free [*aphiēmi eleutheron*], and let [my younger brother] Lykon raise him and educate him for the next six years. And Khares I set free [*aphiēmi eleutheron*], and let Lykon raise him. And I give him two mnas and my published books. . . . And I set free [*aphiēmi . . . eleutheran*] also the mother of Mikros, as well as Noëmon, Dion, Theon, Euphranor, and Hermias. And Agathon should be set free [*apheisthai eleutheron*] after "remaining" [*parameinanta*] two years, and the litter-bearers Ophelion and Poseidonios after "remaining" four years.[29] (D. L. 5.73)

Mikros's mother, Noëmon, Dion, Theon, Euphranos, and Hermias are all freed unconditionally—or at any rate, no conditions are stipulated. Agathon and the litter-bearers, by contrast, are freed but are required to "remain" (*parameinanta*) in some capacity for fixed lengths of time.[30] We might also compare, with caution, the evidence of Plato's *Laws*:

> And a man may lead away [*agetō*] a freedman [*apeleutheron*], if he does not serve [*therapeuēi*], or does not sufficiently serve, those who have freed him [*apeleutherōsantas*]. And the service [*therapeia*] consists in the freedman

---

[26] Samuel 1965, 270; see also Westermann 1946.

[27] See, e.g., GDI 1832, 2072. See also Samuel 1965, 278.

[28] I am using quotation marks because there is no evidence that this noun was in use as a technical term prior to the third century BCE. In fact, this lack of attestation leads Gernet to suggest that *paramonē* was not a legal obligation before this time (1955, 172n4). However, even if *paramonē* as a formal term did not exist, *paramonē*-like obligations certainly did.

[29] For other freedmen in Lykon's will, see D. L. 5.72–74.

[30] For other manumissions in the philosophers' wills: D. L. 3.42; 5.14–15, 55; 10.21.

[*apeleutherōthenta*] visiting three times a month the hearth of the man who freed him, promising to do whatever is necessary of those things which are just and at the same time possible, and concerning marriage to do what seems good also to his former master [*tōi genomenōi despotēi*]. (Pl. *Laws* 915a; see further 915b–c)

Even if we do not accept Plato's laws as authentically Athenian,[31] they may lead us to suspect that some such obligations were similarly defined for freedmen in Athens.[32]

Moreover, we know that if conditionally freed slaves in Athens did not perform their remaining obligations, they faced the possibility of a lawsuit, the *dikē apostasiou*.[33] It is the record of the verdicts in these cases that we find preserved in the *phialai exeleutherikai* inscriptions (chapter 2). From the pseudo-Aristotelian *Athenian Constitution* we learn that cases of *apostasis* were brought before the polemarch ([Arist.] *Ath. Pol.* 58.3). Harpocration describes this kind of *dikē* as

a private suit [*dikē*] allowed to manumittors [*apeleutherōsasin*] against their freedmen [*apeleutherōthentōn*], if they stand apart from them [*aphistōntai*], or enroll another as *prostatēs* [patron], or fail to do the other things required by the laws. Those found guilty have to become slaves, whereas those who have won the suits become completely free [*teleōs eleutheros*] at once. It occurs often [*pollakis*] in the orators, as in Lysias's *Against Aristodemos* and Hyperides's *Against Demetria, for Apostasis*. (Harp., s.v. *apostasiou*)

The first violation for which manumittors could charge their freedmen, under this *dikē*, was "standing apart" from them.[34] Presumably this situation arose when an ex-slave claimed that he or she did not need a patron (*prostatēs*). All free resident aliens in Athens had to have *prostatai*, whose precise role was ill-defined but who were required nonetheless.[35] Such a claim was therefore only relevant if the ex-slave was a citizen, or trying to pass as one.[36] It appears that metics had free choice in selecting their patrons; freedmen, on the other hand, were required to enroll their ex-masters as *prostatai*. The second violation for which freedmen might be charged with a *dikē apostasiou* was seeking legal protection (*prostasia*) from someone besides their manumittor. The third charge, failure to "do the other things required by the laws," is quite vague. Since we are not in possession of any Athenian "freedmen laws" (though we are

---

[31] On the relationship between Plato's laws and Athenian law, see, e.g., Morrow 1960.

[32] On Plato's freedman laws, see Rädle 1972.

[33] For a recent discussion of the *dikē apostasiou*, see Zelnick-Abramovitz 2005, 274–92.

[34] See also Ammon. 60 and Hesych. s.v. *dikē apostasiou*.

[35] On the role of the *prostatēs*, see Whitehead 1977, 89–92; Zelnick-Abramovitz 2005, 248–52.

[36] On slaves passing as free or even as citizens, see Vlassapoulos 2009.

told that some existed[37]), we cannot say precisely what these violations entailed.

Thus, like the threats of punishment found in the Hellenistic manumission inscriptions, the *dikē apostasiou* can be interpreted, at least in part, as a way for a master to guarantee that his freedman fulfilled certain obligations to him. The threat of a lawsuit was one way to circumvent the sticky legal status of the slave: qua slaves, they were not legally permitted to sign contracts, and therefore could not pledge before manumission that they would fulfill their obligations after manumission. But how could one trust newly freed slaves to sign such a contract *after* manumission, prolonging their service to their former master?[38] Therefore, without resorting to contracts, what bound freedmen to their *paramonē* duties may well have been fear of prosecution, not to mention conviction, in a *dikē apostasiou*.

Let us now try to summarize the bundle of privileges and disabilities constituting the status of the conditionally freed slave. Since they were legally free, they could own property, though as noncitizens, they still could not own land (see further chapter 4). Their freedom of labor continued to be restricted, since their former master mandated at least part of their work (namely, the *paramonē* service). And though they did this work as "free people," they were presumably not paid and their labor was still conceptualized as servile. This conception is best exemplified by Hellenistic manumission inscriptions, where we find phrases like "let [these freed slaves] remain in *paramonē* service . . . doing servile labor [*doul(eu)ontes*] and doing everything ordered blamelessly,"[39] and "let her remain in *paramonē* . . . doing everything ordered like a slave [*hōs doula*]."[40] In addition, conditionally freed slaves' freedom of movement was curtailed in that they needed to remain close enough to their former masters to perform any lingering obligations. If freedom of movement is a defining feature of status,[41] then the very fact of their restricted movement also makes conditionally freed slaves closer to servile than free.

As we saw in chapter 1, a further key difference between slaves and free men was that "slaves are liable with their body [*sōma*] for all offences, while free men, even in the worst circumstances, can protect this [i.e., the body]" (Dem. 22.55; see also Dem. 24.167). But corporal punishment, at least in the Hellenistic manumission inscriptions, was also held

---

[37] See Poll. 3.83, who says that Demosthenes speaks of freedman laws: *exeleutherikous nomous kai apeleutherikous nomous*. See Zelnick-Abramovitz 2005, 301–6 and 2009 for "laws on manumitted slaves."

[38] Gernet 1955, 168–69.

[39] FD 3.3.294, lines 8–10. See also FD 3.3.337, lines 2–3.

[40] FD 3.3.329, lines 4–5.

[41] See Westermann 1945b.

out as a threat to conditionally freed slaves.[42] The implication of this threat is that if conditionally freed slaves did not fulfill their obligations, there was a sense in which their body—if not their legal status—slipped back into servile mode.

Conditionally freed slaves did have some limited legal personality (see further chapter 4), though whether they were officially considered metics (resident foreigners) is unclear.[43] Nevertheless, like the requirement of a patron, many of their legal rights and privileges and disabilities in the area of family were similar to those of unconditionally freed slaves and freeborn metics (as we will see in the next chapter).

In addition, they were often granted the opportunity to acquire unconditional freedom and thus move up the status ladder. This opportunity could arise in a variety of different ways: either automatically after their former master died, or after the allotted period of time for *paramonē*, or if they paid for an early release (*apolusis*) from their obligations. Social mobility, however, worked both ways for the conditionally freed slave, since downward mobility was also a real danger. In the Hellenistic manumission inscriptions, it is sometimes explicitly stated that freedom could be revoked if a conditionally freed slave did not perform his or her *paramonē* services properly: a fictive sale of a slave to the god could be declared null (*atelēs*) and void (*akuros*) by court action,[44] or a former master could, among other things, sell the (disobedient) conditionally freed slave back into slavery.[45] Such threats are not explicitly found in classical Athens, but we have seen that if freed slaves were claimed as slaves (by either their former master or anyone else)—and if no one vindicated their freedom through an *aphaireisis eis eleutherian*, or if they had insufficient documentation to prove their free status—they could fairly easily fall back into slavery. Moreover, the fate of a freedman convicted in a *dikē apostasiou* was quite grim. In the passage quoted earlier, after listing the charges under which a freedman could be prosecuted with this *dikē*, Harpocration relates the results of both conviction and acquittal: the convicted return to slavery, the acquitted are released from all remaining obligations.[46] A final form of downward mobility, at least in the fourth century, resulted if a freed slave (like any alien) was caught married to an Athenian citizen; if prosecuted and convicted in a *graphē xenias* (a public

---

[42] See, e.g., *GDI* 1716, 1729.

[43] Klees 2000 argues that only the unconditionally freed slave was assimilated to metic status.

[44] See, e.g., *GDI* 1819, 1944; *FD* 3.3.6.

[45] See, e.g., *FD* 3.3.175, 3.3.329, 3.3.337.

[46] Scholars have debated whether convicted, re-enslaved freedmen were handed back to their ex-masters (see, e.g., MacDowell 1978, 82) or were sold publicly (see, e.g., Klees 1998, 334–54). Hans Klees interprets a law of the fourth-century Athenian statesman Lycurgus (Plut. *Mor.* 841f–842a) as stating that anyone could buy a convicted, re-enslaved freedman: he simply had to obtain permission from the latter's former master, who was presumably reimbursed for his loss of property.

suit against foreigners posing as citizens), he or she could be sold into slavery ([Dem.] 59.16) (see further chapter 4).

Conditionally freed slaves could, in theory, participate in any religious rites open to other noncitizens (see further chapter 4), though the restrictions on their movement may have meant that they participated no more than slaves did. There is, however, some epigraphic evidence for slaves or freed slaves consulting the oracle at Dodona about *paramonē*,[47] so we might imagine conditionally freed slaves praying to the gods for an end to their remaining obligations. If, for example, they had been freed under the auspices of a god, they might be inclined to turn to this particular deity for further assistance. Finally, like other non-citizens, a conditionally freed slave had no political voice (see further chapter 4), but he could be drafted to perform military service (see further chapter 4)

On the spectrum of statuses, the conditionally freed slave falls somewhere between slave and free, more servile than an unconditionally freed slave (chapter 4), but less so than a slave.[48] Various scholars have tried to define this intermediate status.[49] William Westermann, for instance, proposes that the status of the freedman under *paramonē* was similar to that of Spartan helots, or of indentured servants—that is, a sort of "limited slavery" or "bondage service."[50] Another interpretation, one stressing the fact that the freedman was juridically free, is that the freed slave possessed "half freedom."[51] To my mind, neither of these descriptions fully conveys the complicated, tension-ridden nature of the conditionally freed slave's status.[52] Paradoxically, conditionally freed slaves were neither free nor slave, but in some ways *both*.[53] They too, like privileged slaves, destabilized the neat ideological dichotomy of slave versus free. Though nominally located on opposite sides of a clear-cut line dividing free people from slaves, both status groups threatened the clarity of that distinction by combining elements of slavery and freedom.

[47] See Eidinow 2012.

[48] Cf. Garlan 1988 [1982], 79, who says "The juridical situation is confused, and the concrete circumstances belong somewhere in between slavery and liberty, evidence that manumission never ceased to be considered as a de facto as well as a de jure matter."

[49] For a brief description of the debate on how to define this status, see Garlan 1988 [1982], 78–79; and more recently Zelnick-Abramovitz 2005, 244.

[50] On manumission under *paramonē* as "bondage service," see Westermann 1945a, 218 (also for "limited slavery"); 1945b, 6, 9.

[51] Stressing their juridical freedom: Bömer 1960, 39–40n4. Emphasizing half freedom: Koschaker 1931, 41, 43 (with n3); cf. Sokolowski 1954, 174.

[52] Cf. Hopkins 1978, 144.

[53] Neither slave nor free: Koschaker 1931, 40.

CHAPTER 4

METICS (*METOIKOI*)

IN THIS CHAPTER WE TURN TO *METOIKOI*, FOREIGNERS WHO, UNLIKE *XENOI*, were official residents of Athens, rather than just passing through.[1] In its broad sense, the term *metoikos* encompassed two subcategories of resident alien, distinguished from each other not only legally but also (more significantly) socially: 1) freeborn foreigners (*metoikoi* or metics in the narrow sense); and 2) freed slaves, most likely those who were not (or who were no longer) bound to their previous masters.[2] It is unfortunately unclear to us whether freed slaves became metics (in the broad sense) automatically after being released from remaining obligations to their former master,[3] or whether this was a separate registration process.[4]

These two subcategories of metic share a number of traits, the most obvious of which was their non-Athenian origin. In fact, freed slaves were almost always non-Greek: in the Attic Stelai inscriptions, only three of the forty-five slaves listed are explicitly stated to be *oikogeneis* ("homeborn"), and of those remaining, only one is identifiable as Greek.[5] Freeborn metics too were, by definition, non-Athenians, although most of them were Greek. Another similarity between the two groups was the special tax they were required to pay. Harpocration (s.v. *metoikion*) tells

---

[1] For definitions of the term *metoikos*, see Whitehead 1977, 6–10. Scholars debate the etymology of *metoikos*: either it denotes one who has changed his or her home (*meta* = change) or one who lives with the Athenians (*meta* = with). On metic demographics, see Németh 2001.

[2] On the status of metics, see, e.g., Clerc 1893; Harrison 1968, 187–99; Gauthier 1972, 107–49; Whitehead 1977 (with Whitehead 1986b); MacDowell 1978, 76–78; Hansen 1991, 116–20; Todd 1995, 194–99; Hunter 2000a, 15–23; cf. Niku 2007 (on the status of metics in Hellenistic Athens). On the status of freedmen, see, e.g., Harrison 1968, 181–86; MacDowell 1978, 82–83; Klees 2000; Zelnick-Abramovitz 2005, ch 6.

For the view that freedmen were assimilated to metics in Athens, see, e.g., Clerc 1893, 282; Beauchet 1976 [1897], 481 and *passim*; Foucart 1896, 50; Calderini 1908, 307 and 372; *NDI* IX s.v. *liberti* and *NDI* X s.v. *manumissio*; Diller 1937, 149; *DAGR* s.v. *apeleutheroi*; Whitehead 1977, 16–17, 114–16; MacDowell 1978, 82; Finley 1998 [1980], 165; Biscardi 1982, 95 ("in un certo senso"); Garlan 1988 [1982], 80 ("if not identical, at least very similar"; but cf. p. 82: "The situation of freedmen was not identical on all counts to that of metics. It was more precarious"); Gauthier 1988, 29; E. E. Cohen 1992, 109–10; Andreau 1993, 180; Klees 2000, 6 (with some qualification); E. E. Cohen 2003 [2000], 150; Fisher 2008, 125–26; Hermann-Otto 2009, 102.

For the view that freedmen were distinct from metics: Harrison 1968, 181–86; Bearzot 2005, 79–85; Zelnick-Abramovitz 2005, 308–19; Gärtner 2008; Dimopoulou-Piliouni 2009. On freedmen as a subcategory of metic, see, e.g., Whitehead 1977, 116; Hansen 1991, 119; Lape 2010, 47.

[3] See Klees 2000, 6.

[4] Zelnick-Abramovitz 2005, 310 argues that until a freed slave was enrolled as a metic, he or she was legally defined as an *apeleutheros* or *exeleutheros*; see also Dimopoulou-Piliouni 2009, who argues that this step was not automatic but a special promotion that only some freedmen attained.

[5] Pritchett 1956, 280.

us that both types of metic paid the *metoikion* (metic tax): twelve drachmas each year for men, six for women.[6] In addition to the *metoikion*, both groups were, if sufficiently wealthy, liable to the *eisphora*, a high property tax paid by both citizens and noncitizens of means (see also chapter 10) (Dem. 22.61).[7] Freeborn and freed-slave metics also shared a lack of citizenship, despite their residence in the city as free men. Indeed, as Aristotle says, "a citizen [*politēs*] is not a citizen by living in a certain place (for metics and slaves share this habitation)" (*Pol.* 1275a6–8). Yet both subgroups of metic had many of the rights and obligations of citizens. They were expected to obey the city's laws[8] and were obligated to perform military service. The corollary of this was that they were granted a number of legal privileges. The polemarch, the magistrate in charge of noncitizens' affairs, heard

> charges of [freedmen] acting without their *prostatēs* [patron] [i.e., *dikai apostasiou*] or of [freeborn metics] lacking a *prostatēs* [i.e., *graphai aprostasiou*], and cases pertaining to estates and heiresses; and in all other actions that in the case of citizens are brought in by the [eponymous] archon, the polemarch handled these things for metics [*metoikois*]. ([Arist.]*Ath. Pol.* 58.3)

Here freeborn and freed-slave resident foreigners are lumped together as *metoikoi* under the jurisdiction of the polemarch.

Despite these similarities, however, freedman metics seem to have represented a status group—that is, a group with its own cluster of rights, privileges, and so on—separate from freeborn metics, the latter of whom were often indicated exclusively (and confusingly, at least for us) by the term *metoikoi*. Although both paid the *metoikion*, freed slaves also paid an additional sum: again, according to Harpocration (s.v. *metoikion*), "Menander in *Anatithemenē* and in *Didymai* says that in addition to the 12 drachmas, they also paid a triobolon, perhaps to the tax-collector." While it is uncertain whether this small amount was paid only once, or annually, the difference nonetheless seems significant—psychologically, if not materially.[9] This special tax marked them as somehow distinct from freeborn metics.

Furthermore, although both freeborn metics and freedmen were required to have patrons (*prostatai*), freedmen were assigned their former master (or the latter's heir) as *prostatēs*, whereas freeborn metics had free choice.[10] Indeed, according to Isocrates, the Athenians "judge the

---

[6] On the *metoikion*, see Whitehead 1977, 75–77.

[7] For a discussion of how much metics and freedmen were expected to pay for *eisphora*, as compared with citizens, see Whitehead 1977, 78–80.

[8] See, e.g., Lys. 22.5: "Tell me, sir, are you a resident alien? Yes. Do you reside as an alien to obey the city's laws or to do just as you please? To obey."

[9] For the view that this extra tax might have had a psychological significance, see Harrison 1968, 185.

[10] Gernet 1955, 171; Harrison 1968, 185; Garlan 1988 [1982], 77.

character of our [freeborn] resident aliens by the kind of patron they select to represent them" (Isoc. 8.53). In addition, freedmen, unlike freeborn metics, had limited license in bequeathing their estates. If they died childless, all of their property went to their former master. This is well illustrated in an oration of Isaeus: in order to get their hands on a certain deceased Nikostratos's money, Ktesias and Kranaos go so far as to pretend that he is their freedman (Is. 4.9). Freeborn metics, on the other hand, could presumably leave their estates to whomever they wanted; at any rate, we have no evidence to the contrary.

Finally, we cannot pass over the fact that there apparently existed laws specifically targeting freedmen, which were irrelevant to freeborn metics.[11] According to Pollux, Demosthenes spoke of "freedman laws" (*exeleutherikous nomous, kai apeleutherikous nomous*) (3.38)—laws which Yvon Garlan believes pertain to the *dikai apostasiou* and *aphaireseōs* (on these *dikai*, see chapter 3).[12] If so, these may have been *nomoi* established to protect the interests both of freed slaves and of their former masters. Moreover, A.R.W. Harrison suggests that the existence of such laws indicates "some statutory regulation of the status" of freedmen, though the details are hard to recover.[13]

In addition to these differences,[14] certain texts clearly distinguish between freeborn metics (*metoikoi* in the narrow sense) and freedmen. In his discussion of Athenian working people (*banausoi*), Aristotle asks how they can be classified if not as citizens—after all, they are neither foreigners (*xenoi*) nor metics (*metoikoi*). But then again, he says, "slaves are not in one of the aforementioned [constituent parts of the city (*merē*), i.e., foreigners and metics], nor are freedmen [*apeleutheroi*]" (*Pol.* 1278a1–2). This statement shows that Aristotle, and probably others as well, distinguished between *apeleutheroi* and (freeborn) metics, at least in certain contexts. The same conclusion can be drawn from [Xen.] *Ath. Pol.* 1.10: "if it were legal for a free man to strike a slave, or a metic, or a freedman [*ē ton metoikon ē ton apeleutheron*], an Athenian would often have been struck under the mistaken impression that he was a slave." The separation of slave, metic, and freedman here indicates a perceived status distinction between the groups.[15] Indeed, we find this terminological differentiation made occasionally in other poleis as well.[16] Finally,

---

[11] On "freedman laws," see Zelnick-Abramovitz 2005, 301–6 and 2009.

[12] Garlan 1988 [1982], 82.

[13] Harrison 1968, 181.

[14] For a survey of differences between freedmen and (freeborn) metics, see Dimopoulou-Piliouni 2009.

[15] Cf. Whitehead 1977, 115, who says: "Logically this makes no more sense than 'fruit or apples', but I suspect that it reflects a common (and perfectly natural) distinction in everyday speech and thought." I think, rather, that it was a distinction made *in law*, observed in "everyday speech and thought" only in certain contexts.

[16] E.g., a third-century law from Keos specifies that a feast be given "to the citizens, and to those whom the city invited, and to the metics [*metoikous*], and to the freedmen [*apeleutherous*]" (*LSCG* 98). For more epigraphic examples from outside of Athens, see Dimopoulou-Piliouni 2009, 47–49. One could argue, however, that a distinction was made in other cities, but not in Athens: see, e.g., Gauthier 1988, 29.

further evidence may come also from Demosthenes's comment about the Athenians' manning ships with both metics and *khōris oikountes* (Dem. 4.36), the latter of whom may have been freedmen (see chapter 2).

Let us now briefly sum up the rights and privileges constituting these two status groups, which, for the sake of convenience, I will collectively call "metics." In terms of claims to property, it seems that the only restriction, for both subgroups of metic, was on owning immoveable property (Xen. *Poroi* 2.6): they could not own land, unless granted the special right of *enktēsis* (see further chapter 6), or of course if they were granted citizenship. This also meant they could not lend money on the security of land or a house. They did, however, have complete power over moveable property.

Metic labor was considered necessary for keeping the Athenian economy afloat ([Xen.] *Ath. Pol.* 1.12; Xen. *Poroi* 2.1).[17] In theory, metics had power over their labor—Xenophon calls them "self-supporting" (*hautous trephontes*) (Xen. *Poroi* 2.1)—but certain practical factors compromised this power. Freed slaves likely performed whatever work they had done as slaves (as the *phialai exeleutherikai* inscriptions perhaps suggest[18]), wherever they had done it. Freeborn metics, on the other hand, while they had free choice, tended to work in certain sectors of the economy, for example as traders and craftsmen, and accordingly clustered in certain neighborhoods (namely, the Peiraieus and Kerameikos).[19] Apparently, they had to pay a special fee if they wanted to set up a stall in the Agora (Dem. 57.34).

Both fully freed slaves and freeborn metics seem to have had the right to move wherever they wished. They were designated by the deme where they lived (i.e., *oikōn en* or "living in," paired with the name of the deme), which seems to have been a more precise reflection of their actual habitation than a citizen's demotic,[20] since the latter remained the same even if a citizen moved to another deme. Presumably if metics moved, they would change their *oikōn en* formula accordingly.[21]

Metics of both kinds could own slaves whose labor they controlled, as is attested in the *phialai exeleutherikai* and elsewhere (e.g., Lys. 5). Like any masters, they could punish the slaves they owned with physical abuse. Metics

---

[17] See Németh 2001 on metic professions.

[18] But cf. Meyer 2010.

[19] Cf. Németh 2001: 336, who calculates that of the metics whose occupations we know, only 9.2 percent were traders and craftsmen, whereas a much larger percentage (39.4 percent) were artists and intellectuals. Our evidence, however, is biased in favor of elite metics.

[20] Cf. Wilamowitz-Möllendorff 1887, esp. 213–15, who argued that metic "demotica" indicated official membership in a deme akin to citizen demotica. This point was adopted, in turn, by Clerc 1893 (see esp. 236–59).

[21] Whitehead 1977, 72–75, though he concedes that we do not have the evidence to prove this.

themselves were not corporally punished, but at the same time, unlike citizens, they were not conceived of as legally or ideologically untouchable (see chapter 10). If someone were to abuse a freed slave or freeborn metic physically, his or her *prostatēs* could file a suit (on which more below); servile treatment of a free man or woman would certainly constitute *hubris*. This is not to say, however, that it was always prosecuted as such. While Demosthenes criticizes his opponent Aristogeiton for forcefully dragging the metic Zenobia to the auction house as if she were a slave, he does not mention any legal action taken specifically on her behalf (Dem. 25.57).

The privileges and liabilities of the metic in judicial proceedings are a matter of some debate. As mentioned above, metics were required to have a *prostatēs*, but it is unclear precisely what the role of the *prostatēs* was. One view, now discredited, is that the *prostatēs* was selected for only one task: to supervise the metic's enrollment in a deme.[22] Nowadays, the (generally) accepted interpretation is that the relationship between the metic and *prostatēs* was a permanent one, lasting beyond the metic's enrollment.[23]

The question then becomes: what did this permanent relationship entail? It has been argued by some that during the fifth and early fourth centuries BCE metics could bring cases only through representation by their *prostatēs*. This changed, however, in the fourth century, when the *prostatēs* was no longer required for trial; he may have been needed, however, for preliminaries to the trial (e.g., the preliminary hearing or *anakrisis*).[24] The role of the *prostatēs* in court does seem to be implied by (the somewhat vague) statement by Aristotle: "In many places [*pollakhou*] metics do not even completely share in these things [i.e., the right to sue and be sued], but it is necessary for them to select a *prostatēs*" (*Pol.* 1275a7–14). However, it is, first of all, not entirely clear whether Athens was one of those many places, and moreover, we have no firm evidence for any Athenian trial in which a metic is represented by a *prostatēs*.[25] Whitehead and others have argued that even in the fifth century, the *prostatēs* was not *required* for trial, but merely assisted the metic whenever the latter needed legal help (e.g., in the preliminary hearing, or during the trial as a witness), and that in the fourth century, when the metic's status became more formalized, the *prostatēs* had little if any role to play.[26] On either of these two interpreta-

---

[22] Wilamowitz-Möllendorff 1887, 232, followed by Clerc 1893, 266–70 and *RE* s.v. *metoikos*.

[23] Whitehead 1977, 91 points out that the requirement of enrolling a metic in a deme is, while plausible, purely speculative.

[24] See, e.g., Harrison 1968, 189–93.

[25] The only possible exception is the reference to Lysias in the third person by the speaker of *P. Oxy.* 13.1606, which Harrison 1968, 191 takes as evidence that metics required their *prostatēs* to speak for them. Cf. Whitehead 1977, 91, who argues that the speaker is just as likely to be a co-pleader (*sunēgoros*), with further bibliography for both interpretations on 106n145.

[26] Whitehead 1977, 90–91, following Gauthier 1972, 126–36.

tions (I tend to side with Whitehead and others on this question), the *prostatēs'* role became little more than symbolic by the fourth century.

Assuming that a *prostatēs* might have, but need not have, spoken on behalf of a metic in court, let us now investigate the metic's capacities in private lawsuits *(dikai)*.[27] Metics could both sue and be sued in private procedures, but their trials were in general heard by different courts than those of citizens. Thus, if either the defendant or plaintiff were a metic, the case would (in most but not all instances) first be brought before the polemarch, who divided his list of cases into ten portions, assigning each portion by lot to one of the ten tribes for trial ([Arist.] *Ath. Pol.* 58.2–3). If the case was a *dikē apostasiou* (see above), or one concerning estates or heiresses, the polemarch handled it himself, presiding over the court trying the metic in question ([Arist.] *Ath. Pol.* 58.3). If the metic was the defendant in a *dikē*, the plaintiff could demand sureties (of three citizen guarantors) up to the sum involved in the dispute (Isoc. 17.12); these sureties were necessary since metics could not own land. If, however, metics could not produce sureties, they were thrown in prison. In this way, the metic was distinguished legally and symbolically from the citizen, since the latter was not required to produce sureties.

The distinction between metics and citizens is seen also in cases of murder. If metics were killed, their relatives were responsible for bringing charges (a *dikē phonou*) against the killer.[28] Whereas a master could bring a case against the killer of his slave, a former master was not entitled to bring a case against the killer of his freed slave; this fell to relatives alone, as in the case of other metics (Dem. 47.68–73).[29] *Dikai phonou* were passed, via the Basileus, to a court called the Palladion ([Arist.] *Ath. Pol.* 57.3). The Palladion heard cases dealing with the unpremeditated homicide of citizens, as well the killing (premeditated or not) of both slaves and foreigners. The penalty for the convicted killer of a metic was exile, regardless of whether the killing was premeditated; by comparison, the premeditated killing of a citizen was punished with death.[30] It is hard to determine what happened when a metic was charged with murder, since we have no evidence for cases of this sort. Finally, at least after 350 BCE, metics could prosecute in *emporikai* and *emmēnoi dikai* (commercial and "monthly" cases, respectively; see Dem. 32–35, 56), cases that apparently did not take into account the status of the participants.[31] These trials were most likely held in the popular courts.[32]

---

[27] On metics' rights in *dikai* (excluding *phonou*), see Gauthier 1972, 136–41; Whitehead 1977, 92–93.

[28] On metics' rights in *dikai phonou*, see Gauthier 1972, 141–44; Whitehead 1977, 93–94.

[29] On this passage of Dem. 47, see Grace 1975.

[30] On the equivalence in penalty between the premeditated murder of a metic and the unintentional homicide of a citizen, see, e.g., Whitehead 1977, 93 (with Whitehead 1986b, 147); Todd 1995, 274; Allen 2000, 108; C. Patterson 2000, 100.

[31] On these types of *dikai*, see E. E. Cohen 1973 and Lanni 2006, 149–74.

[32] See Lanni 2006, 152–53; cf. E. E. Cohen 1973, 93–95, who speculates that these cases were judged not by regular dikasts but by those knowledgeable about commercial matters.

We are even less certain about metics' rights in public suits (*graphai*).[33] Metics were likely excluded from the "anyone [of the Athenians] who wishes" (*hoi boulomenoi*) who could bring *graphai*, although there is at least one possible instance of a foreigner doing so (Epainetos of Andros: [Dem.] 59.64–66). On the other hand, metics could be, and often were, indicted in *graphai*. In the fifth century, the polemarch dealt with all *graphai* involving metics, but in the fourth century most of these cases were handled by the same officials who oversaw other *graphai* involving citizens.[34] One of the *graphai* remaining under the jurisdiction of the polemarch was the *graphē aprostasiou* ([Arist.] *Ath. Pol.* 58.3), a public charge that a metic did not have a *prostatēs*.[35]

Metics faced a number of other legal liabilities as well. So, for example, the Boule may have had rights of summary execution over metics in *graphai* (see Lys. 12 and Isoc. 17),[36] a right they did not have over citizens ([Arist.] *Ath. Pol.* 45.1). In addition, metics were subject to summary arrest (*apagōgē*) and delivery to the *pōlētai*, the public officials who sold state property, if they did not pay the *metoikion* (Harp. s.v. *metoikion*).[37] Metics, like citizens, had the right to offer testimony as witnesses, but their testimony may have been less valued by the citizen jurors.[38] It is also possible that metics—like slaves, and unlike citizens—could be tortured to provide testimony in public and private cases (Lys. 13.27, 54, 59).[39] Torture probably was not necessary for them to produce evidence, however. Finally, Cynthia Patterson has convincingly argued that although the Athenian court system provided "equal access" to metics, their rights were in practice limited by a number of factors: they could not own land; they had few family connections in Athens, and therefore few supporters; and they faced anti-metic sentiment from the citizen jurors.[40] Another way of putting this is that their social status hindered them in ways that their legal status did not.

Another repercussion of not owning land is that metics could not pass down an estate to their heirs, though they could bequeath their moveable property. As mentioned above, it was the polemarch who heard their cases about estates or heiresses ([Arist.] *Ath. Pol.* 58.2). After Pericles's citizenship legislation (451/0 BCE) stipulating that to be a citizen

---

[33] On metics' rights in *graphai*, see Gauthier 1972, 144–49; Whitehead 1977, 94–96; Todd 1995, 196.

[34] MacDowell 1978, 223; Rhodes 1981, 652 (on [Arist.]*Ath. Pol.* 58.2).

[35] Harp. s.v. *aprostasiou: tōn prostatēn mē nemontōn metoikōn.* See Kapparis 2005, 106–10 and Meyer 2010 on the *graphē aprostasiou.*

[36] See Gauthier 1972, 146–48.

[37] This seems to have been the only form of *apagōgē* used uniquely against metics: see Hansen 1976, 30; cf. Lipsius 1966 [1905–1915], 326–27.

[38] See Whitehead 1977, esp. 95; Todd 1995, 96–97; Allen 2000, 105.

[39] Whitehead 1977, 95 with n167; Hansen 1991, 118.

[40] C. Patterson 2000.

one had to be born to two citizens (*astoî*), metics were no longer able to produce citizen children, even with a citizen spouse.[41] Marriage between metics and citizens, on the other hand, seems not to have become illegal until a law was passed sometime in the fourth century BCE.[42] After the passage of this law, such a marriage became a crime for which violators could be prosecuted with a *graphē xenias*.[43] A metic (or any foreigner) accused of marrying an Athenian citizen woman would be indicted before the Thesmothetai (the six junior archons); if convicted, he and his property would be sold, with one third of the value going to the prosecutor. If, in turn, a foreign woman married an Athenian citizen, the latter had to pay a fine of one thousand drachmas ([Dem.] 59.16). Conventional wisdom holds that this fourth-century law was passed in order to prevent the children of mixed unions from attaining Athenian citizenship. Geoff Bakewell has recently argued that the law may, in addition, represent an attempt by Athenians to prevent their male relatives from marrying into the large pool of nubile metic women.[44]

Metics had various avenues of social mobility open to them. In the next chapter we will examine privileged noncitizens like *isoteleis*, *proxenoi*, and others: that is, metics who were granted one or more rights that set them apart from (and higher than) the average metic. Naturalization was not terribly common, but it was a possibility for metics, particularly if they were wealthy enough to make a large donation to the state; that is, economic status clearly provided one of the keys to mobility. In addition, though exact numbers are impossible to gauge, I imagine that freeborn metics were more likely to be naturalized than freed-slave metics. Since freeborn metics were generally Greek, and freed slaves generally non-Greek (see chapter 1), the latter had to overcome two hurdles—not only being foreign but also being an ex-slave—whereas the former had to overcome only one. In preserved naturalization decrees, citizenship does seem to be granted much more often to freeborn foreigners than to former slaves.[45]

Metics could also move down the status ladder more readily than citizens (although, as we will see in chapter 10, even the status of citizens

---

[41] Cf. E. E. Cohen 2003 [2000], 58–61, who argues that a metic, if an *astos* (to Cohen, a "local"), could produce a *politēs* ("citizen") child through union with another *astos*. For the view that metics should not be considered *astoi*, see Whitehead 1977, 60–61.

[42] For a discussion of this law, Kapparis 1999, 198–206. Its date is disputed. Kapparis 1999, 201–2 argues that it dates to sometime between 403 and 340, most likely in the 380s BCE. For the view that it was instead Pericles's law in 451/0 that rendered marriage between an Athenian and a foreigner illegal, see, e.g., MacDowell 1978, 87. See also Walters 1983, 320–21, who stresses that it was not marriage per se but the fraudulent pretense of legal marriage between two Athenians that was made illegal by Pericles's legislation.

[43] Most scholars assume that the suit one would bring against a violator of this law was a *graphē xenias*. But cf. Kapparis (2005, 76–95), who argues that that the *graphē xenias* (a suit, he says, introduced in the fifth century) should not confused with the suits stemming from this fourth-century law.

[44] Bakewell 2008/9.

[45] On naturalization decrees, see M. J. Osborne 1981–1983.

was not beyond challenge), both because of the types of offenses for which they could be tried and also because they lacked the support network enjoyed by most citizens. As mentioned above, if a resident foreigner was convicted in a *graphē xenias*, he was sold into slavery ([Dem.] 59.16, Dem. 24.131, Dem. *Ep.* 3.29; etc.). The penalty for conviction in a *graphē aprostasiou* or a *dikē apostasiou* was sale into slavery by public auction (Phot. and Suda s.v. *pōlētai*; see also Harp. s.v. *apostasiou*). Metics of all stripes could be sold into slavery if they failed to pay the metic tax (Dem. 25.57; Harp. s.v. *metoikion*).[46] Though both types of metic could fall into slavery, freed slaves faced a greater danger of downward mobility since they could more credibly be claimed as a slave by their former master (or anyone else, for that matter; see chapter 3). Certain measures were in place to remedy this danger: the *aphairesis eis eleutherian*, and, at least for a brief window of time in the late fourth century, the results of (possibly fictive) *dikai apostasiou* recorded and prominently displayed on the Acropolis. If anyone were to challenge the free status of a freedman—at least of one made "completely free" (*teleōs eleutheros*) through a *dikē apostasiou*—the inscriptional record could presumably have been cited as evidence in the latter's favor.

Metics were barred from holding religious office (*hierosunē*) (Dem. 57.48) and were excluded from any cult observances of organizations open only to citizens (that is, tribes; phratries [clans]; and *genē*, noble kin groups claiming descent from a shared mythical ancestor).[47] They could, however, perform sacrifices in their own homes and make dedications at most public sanctuaries. Moreover, they were allowed some limited participation in deme and polis ceremonies, as seen in a set of laws from the deme Skambinodai (*IG* I³ 244C.4–10). At the Panathenaia, metics were probably not included in the ritual sacrifices—a decree about the organization of the festival mentions only Athenian citizens (*IG* II² 334)—but they did have a place in the procession to the altar, for which they wore red chitons (Phot. s.v. *Skaphas*; Suda s.v. *Askos en pakhnēi*). Their role in the procession was considered "the metics' liturgy" or public service (Bekk. *Anec.* 1.304.28; 1.280.1). Male metics were *skaphēphoroi* (Hesych. s.v. *Skaphēphoroi*), carrying basins called *skaphai* which held objects needed for the sacrifices (Bekk. *Anec.* 1.304.27).[48] Female metics could be either *hydriaphoroi* (carrying water jugs) or *skiadelphoroi* (carrying parasols) (Harp., Suda s.v. *Skaphēphoroi*). The Roman author Aelian believed that these roles were one way in which the Athenians committed *hubris* against metics (Ael. *VH* 6.1), leading many nineteenth-century

---

[46] See further Meyer 2010.

[47] Metics' role in civic religion: Clerc 1893, 148–77; Whitehead 1977, 86–89; Parker 2005, 170–71; Wijma 2010.

[48] On *skaphēphoroi*, see further Suda, Harp., Phot., s.v. *metoikion*.

scholars to conclude that these were servile, humiliating tasks. However, as Clerc pointed out over a hundred years ago, there is nothing inherently shameful about carrying things in a religious procession. Quite the opposite, these jobs were considered an honor.[49] The most likely interpretation is that metics' service in the Panathenaia fell somewhere between *hubris* and *timē*: it granted metics the right to participate in civic religion (an honor), but the fact that they were marked as "other" was inevitably stigmatizing, even if the tasks were not themselves humiliating.

It is likely that many metics, since they were foreign-born, had their own gods and cults, either gods particularly sympathetic to slaves and freedmen in the case of freed-slave metics, or in the case of all metics, gods from their own home cities or countries (for Greek metics, of course, their gods would have been largely the same). Athens was relatively tolerant of the worship of foreign gods by its foreign population.[50] So, for example, sometime in the fourth century the demos allowed Egyptians in Athens to found a sanctuary to Isis (*IG* II[2] 337, lines 42–45).[51] Moreover, some foreign cults were actually folded into Athenian civic religion. A good example is the (originally private) cult of the Thracian goddess Bendis,[52] possibly introduced into Athens by metic Thracian merchants.[53] Unfortunately, it is not clear when exactly the cult was established in Athens, but we do know that it was recognized as a state cult by 429/8 BCE (*IG* I[3] 383, line 143). It was presumably around this time that the Athenian demos granted the Thracians the right to acquire land (*enktēsis*) on which to found a shine to Bendis, and to conduct a procession from the hearth of the *prytaneion* to the Peiraieus (*IG* II[2] 1283, lines 1–7).[54] This procession of Thracian worshippers, along with a separate procession of Athenians (Pl. *Rep.* 327a), was to be part of a civic festival called the Bendideia, which also entailed a torchlit race on horseback and a night festival (Pl. *Rep.* 328a; *IG* I[3] 136, line 27). By the time the state cult was established, both Thracians and Athenians could and did join *orgeones* (cult groups) of Bendis, but these *orgeones* were segregated. This meant that, apart from at the Bendideia, metics worshipped separately from citizen Bendis-worshippers.[55]

---

[49] On the role of metics in the Panathenaia, see Clerc 1893, 154–65; and more recently Wijma 2010, 27–84.

[50] On metics and foreign cults: Clerc 1893, 118–47, Whitehead 1977, 88–89.

[51] *IG* II[2] 337 (RO 91) is dated to 333/2 BCE. This inscription's main purpose is to grant merchants from Kition the right to acquire land (*enktēsis*) on which to found a sanctuary to Aphrodite; the cited precedent of a grant to the Egyptians is "probably recent" (according to Rhodes and Osborne 2003, 456).

[52] On the introduction of Bendis to Athens: Simms 1988; Garland 1992, 111–14; Parker 1996, 170–75. On the involvement of metics in this cult, see Wijma 2010, 243–309.

[53] See, e.g., Simms 1988, 68; Parker 2011, 237. On the uncertainty about whether the Athenians or the Thracians first introduced the cult to Athens, see Parker 1996, 172.

[54] One of the shrines to Bendis was in the Peiraieus on the hill of Mounikhia (Xen. *Hell.* 2.4.11).

[55] See Simms 1988, 68–73.

The most significant difference between metics and citizens, of course, was the fact that the former possessed no political rights. As Aristotle says, a metic is excluded from all *timai* belonging to citizens (*Pol.* 1278a38), including magistracies, priesthoods, juries, and participation in the Boule and Ekklesia (Dem. 57.48). Metics, however, did have a number of political obligations. I mentioned above the *metoikion*, which, in addition to providing revenue to the state, also marked the metic socially as "not a citizen."[56] If sufficiently wealthy, metics were also expected to perform liturgies along with the richest Athenian citizens (Dem. 20.18–21), including, for example, funding choruses (Lys. 12.20).[57] There do, however, seem to have been some limits to the liturgies they could perform: we do not hear, for instance, about metic trierarchs (that is, metics funding warships), probably because military service was so closely linked to civic identity.[58] Finally, as mentioned above, metics were expected to pay the special *eisphora* tax, provided that they were sufficiently wealthy.

Metics were part of the Athenian military but most likely fought in segregated units.[59] While those well off enough to afford hoplite armor could serve as infantry—in the mid-fifth century, the 13,000 heavy-armed infantry included citizens and "however many metics were hoplites" (*metoikōn hosoi hoplitai ēsan*) (Thuc. 2.13.7)[60]—it seems that no metics were eligible to serve in the cavalry, which was reserved for the wealthiest citizens (Xen. *Poroi* 2.5). The poorest metics were able to play a role as rowers in the navy ([Xen.] *Ath. Pol.* 1.12; Dem. 4.36–37).[61] Because of a fear that metics might move back home in order to dodge the draft, a law was instituted preventing metics from leaving town during wartime (Hyp. 3.29, 33).

Although freeborn metics and freed slaves shared similar political and legal rights, these rights were not identical, and the differences, while small, were often symbolically important. Perhaps even more significant, I would argue, was the distinction in their *social* status. Freedmen, unlike freeborn metics, were always, inescapably, former slaves—especially, but

---

[56] Whitehead points out this *social* significance of the *metoikion*: for metics, it was "the stamp of metic-status, and a constant reminder of the citizen/metic divide" (1977, 76).

[57] On metic liturgies, see Whitehead 1977, 80–82.

[58] For this point, see Whitehead 1977, 81. But cf. E. E. Cohen 2003 [2000], 73–4n164, who cites a few examples of what he identifies as metic trierarchs.

[59] On segregated units, see Whitehead 1977, 83–84 (with bibliography).

[60] For evidence that Athenian infantry troops were drawn from citizens and metics, see also Thuc. 2.31.1; 3.16.1; 4.90 (where *xenoi* are also mentioned); Lycurg. 1.16 (Athenians and "others living [*oikountōn*] at Athens"); Xen. *Poroi* 2.2 (metics are obligated to serve in infantry along with [*sustrateuesthai*] citizens). On metics in the army, see further Whitehead 1977, 82–84.

[61] On metics in the navy, see Whitehead 1977, 84–86.

not exclusively, in the eyes of their former masters.[62] In an oft-cited but somewhat cryptic statement, the third-century BCE Stoic philosopher Khrysippos is reported to have said that "a slave [*doulon*] differs from a domestic servant [*oiketou*] in that freedmen [*apeleutherous*] are still slaves [*doulous*], whereas those who have not been released from ownership are domestic servants" (Athen. 267b). Unfortunately, it is unclear what, precisely, Khrysippos meant by this. Perhaps he was referring to the obligations freedmen often owed their former masters (what was later called *paramonē*), or perhaps he was referring to the lingering stigma of servility attached to freed slaves.

Either way, it is evident that freedmen were in fact thought of, in many contexts, as "still slaves." This phenomenon is particularly well attested in Attic oratory, where freed slaves are sometimes explicitly referred to as *douloi* or slaves.[63] Attic oratory also contains extended attacks using what I call "servile invective"—accusations or insinuations of servile history—designed to play on the jury's prejudices against freed slaves.[64] Perhaps the best-known examples can be found in the speeches of Apollodoros, himself the son of a freed slave, against Phormion, his father's former slave. In these speeches, Apollodoros repeatedly refers to Phormion as a slave and vividly calls to mind Phormion's purchase day (see especially Dem. 45).[65] No matter how far Phormion advanced financially and politically, he was always, in some sense, the slave of Apollodoros's father. For the freed slave, then, there was a gap between his *legal* status (metic) and the way he was often viewed by Athenian society (always servile).

[62] As Demosthenes says in his speech *Against Timokrates*, "Those who have become free, you know, gentlemen of the jury, are never grateful to their masters for their freedom, but hate them most of all men, since they [i.e., the masters] share in the knowledge that they had been slaves" (Dem. 24.124).

[63] See, e.g., Is. 6.49; Dem. 20.131–33.

[64] See Kamen 2009.

[65] For this sort of invective, see also Lys. 13 and 30.

CHAPTER 5

PRIVILEGED METICS

THE STATUS GROUP I AM CALLING "PRIVILEGED METICS" IS SOMEWHAT MOTLEY; in fact, there is no one word or phrase in Greek for this category. However, I find it useful to categorize together, for heuristic purposes, all metics who possessed rights superior to the average metic. Within this rubric, each subcategory of "privileged" metic was distinguished from the next by a particular privilege or bundle of privileges.[1] Some of these privileges, in turn, conferred more honor (*timē*), and therefore a higher social status, than others.

One such privilege was *enktēsis*, the right to own real property.[2] Most of our evidence for *enktēsis* is epigraphic, derived from inscriptions granting this special privilege to groups or individuals. Such grants of *enktēsis* are made, for the most part, for secular purposes, though we do occasionally find examples of grants made for specific religious purposes. Jan Pečírka, author of what is still the definitive study on *enktēsis*, divides the recipients of *enktēsis* into three main categories: gods (in which case *enktēsis* is granted to their noncitizen worshippers for building a shrine); groups of political exiles (for whom *enktēsis* is granted for only a fixed length of time); and individual foreigners who rendered service to Athens (the majority of our examples), in which case *enktēsis* is granted either alone or (in most cases) in conjunction with *proxenia* or *isoteleia*, rights I will discuss further below.[3] The earliest securely dated example of *enktēsis* granted to individuals for secular purposes is *IG* I³ 102, from 410/9 BCE.[4] In this inscription, those who aided the city by assassinating Phrynikhos, one of the leaders of the oligarchy of the Four Hundred in 411 BCE, are rewarded with *enktēsis* (lines 30–32), as well as protection by the Boule and its presiding officers, the *prytaneis*.[5]

---

[1] For a brief summary of privileges granted to foreigners in Athens, see MacDowell 1978, 78–79.

[2] On *enktēsis* in Attica, see Pečírka 1966. See also Henry 1983, ch. 7 on the formulae found in *enktēsis* grants.

[3] Pečírka 1966, 148.

[4] See Pečírka 1966, 18–21, 137. In addition to this inscription, there are four other possible fifth-century instances of *enktēsis* from Attica (some may be earlier than *IG* I³ 102, but their dates are not secure), and thirty-four from the fourth century (for these numbers, see Pečírka 1966, 138).

[5] *Enktēsis* was in fact often combined with other awards: see Henry 1983, 210–11. Other variations in the *enktēsis* inscriptions include the addition of *Athēnēsi(n)* (and *oikounti Athēnēsi*) (Henry 1983, 211–13); the addition of *kata ton nomon* (though it is unclear exactly what this law is; the earliest example is dated to 325/4 BCE) (214–15); and in at least one example, the fact that *enktēsis* was granted in response to an application (*aitēsis*) (215–16).

Alan Henry, in his work on honors and privileges in Athenian decrees, divides the formulae by which secular instances of *enktēsis* are granted into two types: one in which the value of the property is not expressed, the other (considerably less common) in which it is.[6] In the former case, we occasionally find grants for possession solely of a house (*oikias enktēsis*),[7] a restriction implying enough land to build a house on, but not enough to allow for farming.[8] This type of *enktēsis* was a lesser privilege than a grant of house *and* land, and was particularly suitable for political exiles temporarily living in Attica,[9] like the Akarnanians who had fought alongside the Athenians at Chaironea in 338 BCE (*IG* II[2] 237, lines 24–25).[10] Much more commonly, we find grants of a house and land (*gēs kai oikias enktēsis*).[11] Such *enktēsis* is sometimes said to pass on to the descendants (*ekgonoi*) of the grantee, but more often there is no mention of *ekgonoi*. Unlike Pečírka, who finds the notion of non-hereditary ownership of property unlikely,[12] Henry argues that unless the grant of house and land is explicitly said to be hereditary, the right belonged only to the grantee. Clearly, Henry says, the Athenians could conceive of temporary, non-hereditary *enktēsis*, since they granted it to political exiles. He contends, therefore, that in cases where the grant is not said to be inherited, heirs could inherit only the money from the sale of the property and not the property itself.[13] Pečírka's interpretation strikes me as more plausible; on a practical level, I think it would have been difficult, and needlessly intrusive, for the state to enforce the sale of a property, forcibly removing from their home the heirs of someone whom the state had deemed worthy of the honor of *enktēsis*.

Another privilege granted to foreigners was *isoteleia* (equal taxation).[14] Put most simply, this privilege—in Harpocration's words, "honor" (*timē*)—involved exemption from the *metoikion* or metic tax (Harp. s.v. *isotelēs kai isoteleia*) (on the *metoikion*, see chapter 4). This exemption was primarily symbolic, since anyone granted *isoteleia* was presumably sufficiently well off to afford the yearly twelve-drachma tax (roughly the equivalent of one or two weeks' pay for a manual laborer). The "honor" was that *isoteleia* brought them conceptually closer to citizen status, in that they were responsible for paying only the same taxes as citizens (Hsch. s.v. *iso-*

---

[6] For the former, see Henry 1983, 205–16; for the latter, 216–21.

[7] For grants of a house alone, see Henry 1983, 205–7.

[8] See MacDowell 1978, 134; Todd 1995, 199.

[9] See Pečírka 1966, 147; Henry 1983, 205.

[10] See also Rhodes and Osborne 2003, 382.

[11] For grants of a house and land, see Pečírka 1966, 147; Henry 1983, 207–16.

[12] See Pečírka 1966, 149.

[13] See Henry 1983, 208–10.

[14] On the rights of *isoteleis*, see Whitehead 1977, 11–13; Henry 1983, 246–49.

teleis; Bekk. *Anec.* 1.267.1). Moreover, again according to Harpocration, *isoteleis* also had exemption from "the other things that metics did" (*tōn allōn hōn epratton*). Interpretations of the particular rights and exemptions here referred to once fell into one of "two extreme camps" (in David Whitehead's words): a minimizing camp, stating that *isoteleia* represents exemption only from the *metoikion*; and a maximizing one, arguing that *isoteleia* includes *enktēsis* and also other legal rights, including the right to fight alongside Athenians and to pay the *eisphora*—a heavy property tax—along with citizens.[15] Whitehead himself wisely stakes out a middle ground, arguing that *isoteleia* entails exemption from all of the taxes to which noncitizens were subject: the *metoikion*, the market tax (on which see chapter 4), and possibly other taxes obscure to us now.[16] Greater privileges might have been implied in grants of *ateleia* (complete tax exemption), but our evidence for such grants is relatively sparse.[17]

A well-known example of *isoteleia* in classical Athens comes from the aftermath of the reign of the Thirty Tyrants in 403 BCE. After the democrat Thrasyboulos and his band seized Phyle, marched to the Peiraieus, and defeated the troops of the Thirty at Mounikhia (403 BCE), he led his men back to Athens and restored the democracy (Xen. *Hell.* 2.4.2–42). At this point, he proposed a bill "admitting to citizenship all those who had come back from Peiraieus, some of whom were clearly slaves" ([Arist.] *Ath. Pol.* 40.2). But after the proposal was passed by the Assembly (Plut. *Mor.* 835f), a rival politician named Arkhinos brought a successful *graphē paranomōn* (a lawsuit against the proposer of an illegal decree) against Thrasyboulos (Aesch. 3.187).[18] Epigraphic evidence attests to the privileges that were ultimately granted to three distinct groups of Thrasyboulos's men.[19] The first, those who came down with Thrasyboulos from Phyle, were the core group and were most certainly given citizenship.[20] The second group, those who fought with Thrasyboulos at Mounikhia, and the third group, those remaining at the Peiraieus (the only group for which a heading remains on the inscription), were likely given identical privileges: their exact nature is disputed but it probably entailed

[15] See Whitehead 1977, 11–12 with bibliography.

[16] Whitehead 1977, 12.

[17] On *ateleia*, see Henry 1983, 241–46. He divides the examples of *ateleia* in Athenian decrees into four categories: undefined *ateleia* (241–43); *ateleia* of the *metoikion* (244–45); exemption from military service and garrison-duty (245); and total *ateleia* (*pantōn*) (245–46).

[18] On the *graphē paranomōn*, see Hansen 1974, 28–65; Yunis 1988.

[19] For the most recent edition of these inscriptions, see RO 4. On *IG* II² 10, see further M. J. Osborne 1981, 37–41; 1982, 26–43 (D6). On the additional fragments, see Hereward 1952, 111–13 and Walbank 1994, 169–71, #2. That there were three groups is argued by Hereward 1952, 111; see also M. J. Osborne 1982, 27. Cf. Krentz 1980, 302–3, who suggests that there were probably four.

[20] See M. J. Osborne 1982, 32–33.

isoteleia.[21] In any event, those recipients who were originally slaves would have experienced a tremendous leap in status from slave to *isotelēs*, and possibly even to citizen.[22]

Yet another honor granted to noncitizens was *proxenia*—that is, the title of *proxenos*, roughly translated as "ambassador"—which was most often coupled with the title "benefactor" (*euergetēs*). According to a scholiast, the "most honored" (*protimōmenoi*) foreigners were *proxenoi*, followed by *isoteleis*, and lastly by those metics who paid the *metoikion* (Bekk. *Anec.* 1.298.27). In the fifth century, the title *proxenos* was reserved for diplomatic liaisons to Athens, who were not necessarily metics nor resident in Athens. The *proxenos'* main duty was looking after the interests of Athens and its representatives in his home city, and in return he was given the honorific title of *proxenos* and a set of privileges (see further below). Early on, these individuals tended to remain, for the most part, in their home cities and had little or no need to make use of their newfound rights in Athens. By the fourth century, however, *proxenoi* began to spend more time in Athens, and the title was increasingly bestowed on foreigners who were more or less permanently resident in the city. With these developments, *proxenoi* became more likely to exercise their special rights.[23]

While the title of *proxenos* was itself mainly honorific, it often came packaged with other (more specific) rights and privileges. Michael Walbank catalogues the most common privileges granted alongside proxeny in fifth-century Athenian decrees, including the following: protection of the *proxenos* (and often his family) in Athens from civil wrong,[24] usually coupled with an injunction to state officials to watch over his interests (*epimeleia*) (with severe penalties against wrongdoers),[25] or with a clause enabling the *proxenos* to seek redress in Athens at the polemarch's court;[26] and the right, if needed, to receive *prosodon* (the

---

[21] For *isoteleia* as the privilege here, see M. J. Osborne 1982, 33–34. Cf. Whitehead 1977, 158, who argues that all participants were given citizenship.

[22] In addition to the testimony of [Arist.] *Ath. Pol.* 40.2 (see above), the names in the inscriptions (some of which are foreign or servile) and the humble occupations paired with these names lend support to the view that at least some slaves were granted privileges.

[23] On the status of *proxenoi*, see Whitehead 1977, 13–14. On the institution of *proxenia*, see M. B. Wallace 1970 (focusing on the evidence for early proxeny); Gauthier 1972, 27–61; Marek 1984 (catalogue of all known proxenies); Herman 1987, 130–42 (discussion of *proxenia* and *xenia*). See also Walbank 1978, on fifth-century BCE proxeny decrees from Athens; and Henry 1983, ch. 4, on formulae used in grants of *proxenia* and *euergesia*. Although there is no comprehensive work on fourth-century proxeny decrees, on fourth-century Athenian decrees awarding proxeny to individuals from Asia, see Gastaldi 2004; and on Athenian decrees awarding proxeny and euergesy from 352/1–322/1 BCE (as well as those awarding citizenship), see Lambert 2006.

[24] See Henry 1983, ch. 5 on formulae for protection granted in honorary decrees; for specific protection provisions in the sphere of jurisdiction, granted especially to *proxenoi*, see Henry 1983, 163–71.

[25] On general protection (*epimelesthai*, *epimeleia*), see Henry 1983, 171–81.

[26] On the right of access to the polemarch's court, see Henry 1983, 164–68.

right to present one's case to the Boule and Ekklesia without intermediaries), often with a clause stating that the *proxenos'* business is to take precedence over all other business on the agenda.[27] Other privileges frequently paired with *proxenia* include *isoteleia*;[28] *enktēsis*; *asylia* (freedom to import and export without violation); entertainment at the *prytaneion*;[29] and even citizenship.[30]

Sometimes coupled with *proxenia*, but characteristic more broadly of honorary decrees, are the following privileges: the right to pay the *eisphora* tax and serve in the military alongside citizens instead of in a separate metic division (these two generally show up in conjunction);[31] the award of front-row seats at the city's festivals (either permanently or for one particular festival); the award of statues, set up most commonly in the Agora;[32] as well as other unspecified benefits.[33] Of these privileges, *eisphora* is perhaps the most striking, since the "right" to pay a heavy property tax does not appear at first glance to be a privilege so much as an obligation. However, the right to pay this tax has symbolic value, in that it aligns privileged metics conceptually with the richest citizens, at least in terms of economic status if not of legal or social status.

To illustrate the range of privileges a metic might receive, it helps to look more closely at one example.[34] An inscription, dated to 330/29 BCE, preserves a decree proposed by Lycurgus, part of which reads:

> Since he [Eudemos] first offered to give 40 drachmas to the demos for war, if there should be need, and now has given 1000 carriages for the construction of the stadium and the Panathenaic theater, and sent all these things before the Panathenaia, it was resolved by the demos to praise Eudemos son of Philurgos of Plataia and crown him with a crown of olive because of his good will to the demos of the Athenians, and for him to be among the benefactors [*euergetai*] of the demos of the Athenians, both him and his descendants, and for him to have

[27] See Henry 1983, ch. 6 on formulae in decrees granting preferential right of access to the Boule and Ekklesia.

[28] Whitehead 1977, 13 argues that *isoteleia* first appears alongside *proxenia* in individual grants (e.g., *IG* II² 83), but by the mid-fourth century, if *IG* II² 288 is correctly restored, it was granted to all *proxenoi* as a matter of course.

[29] Henry 1983, ch. 9 discusses the two main types of entertainment at the *prytaneion* extended in honorary decrees: 1) invitations to *deipnon/xenia* for a particular occasion (262–75); and 2) (not attested before 314/3 BCE) grants of permanent *sitesis* (275–78). The evidence demonstrates that, at least in principle, citizens were invited to *deipnon*, noncitizens to *xenia*.

[30] The entire list that precedes is drawn from Walbank 1978, 5–7.

[31] See Henry 1983, 249–50.

[32] On the award of seats and statues, see Henry 1983, ch. 10.

[33] On "unspecified benefits," see Henry 1983, ch. 11.

[34] One can find many examples of individuals receiving multiple privileges: see Pečírka 1966, esp. chart on 152–59; see also Walbank 1978, esp. chart on 9–23.

enktēsis of land and house, and to perform military service and pay the *eisophora* together with the Athenians. (*IG* II² 351, lines 11–32)[35]

For his contributions (mainly financial) to the city, Eudemos was richly rewarded with a packet of honors: a crown, the title of *euergetēs* for himself and his descendants, *enktēsis*, and *eisphora* and *strateia* (military) rights.

Let us briefly take stock of the legal and social status of privileged metics like Eudemos. A metic granted *enktēsis* was given the right to own property, unlike a "regular" metic. This right, however, could be limited in a number of ways (see discussion above): it could be temporary; it could be limited to a house, rather than a house plus land for farming; and its value could be capped. Moreover, as mentioned above, there remains debate about whether property owned by a metic with *enktēsis* was inheritable by his heirs; I imagine that it in most cases it was.

A privileged metic, like a "regular" metic, had power over his labor and movement, as well as that of any of his slaves, whom he had the right to punish.[36] In the judicial realm, the privileges and liabilities of privileged metics seem to have been identical to those of their less-privileged counterparts. It is unclear whether privileged metics were granted any special marriage rights. The Euboians were granted *epigamia* (the right to intermarry with Athenian citizens) (Lys. 34.3), but this was exceptional and designed primarily to benefit Athenians living in Euboia. Otherwise, our only evidence for *epigamia* is the word *enguēsis* ("pledge," "betrothal") in the inscription granting rewards to Thrasyboulos's men (RO 4, line 9; see above). However, while some take this word as equivalent to *epigamia*, others interpret it as referring to an earlier promise (mentioned in Xen. *Hell.* 2.4.25) that these men would secure *isoteleia*.[37]

Privileges such as those outlined in this chapter appear to have been cumulative, meaning that a metic with one privilege was more likely than an unprivileged metic to accumulate more rights.[38] For instance, Eudemos, discussed above, may already have been an *isotelēs* when he was given the additional privileges detailed in the decree. Privileged metics were not given special rights in the sacral sphere, though it is possible to consider the rights of, for example, Thracian worshippers of Bendis privileged in that they were granted *entkēsis* to build a temple

---

[35] See also Pečírka 1966, 68–70 for a discussion of this inscription.

[36] I use male pronouns in this chapter, since most (if not all) privileged metics were male.

[37] Contrary to the majority view, M. J. Osborne 1982, 34–35 takes *enguēsis* to mean pledge, followed tentatively by Rhodes and Osborne 2003, 21. I agree with M. J. Osborne that the recent renewal of the Periclean citizenship laws, as well as their recent application in the decree of Theozotides on orphans, "are enough to render it virtually incredible that the Athenians on this occasion, while refusing to grant citizenship, should have given permission for intermarriage on the grand scale" (1982, 34).

[38] As Whitehead says, "inherent in any privilege was potential candidacy for the next, more prestigious one" (1977, 14).

and allowed to form *orgeones* (see chapter 4).[39] Some privileged metics did have special political rights, including *prosodon* and equal taxation with citizens. Militarily, they could in some circumstances be granted the right to serve alongside Athenian citizens, as Eudemos was.

Legally, then, the privileged metic was in various respects superior to his less-privileged peers. Socially, too, privileged metics represented a distinct, higher-ranking status group. (The fact that most were likely Greek, unlike the average nonprivileged freed-slave metic, probably granted them additional social standing.) Take, for example, the *isotelēs*, who was distinguished from the average metic in that he paid taxes equivalent to the Athenian citizen. This privilege obviously had financial ramifications, but (as mentioned above) its significance was primarily symbolic: insofar as a metic (*metoikos*) was *defined* as someone who paid the *metoikion*, someone who did not have to pay this tax was in some sense *not* a metic. As Whitehead says about *isoteleis*: "Juristically, of course, *isoteleis* remained noncitizens, and no doubt the *polites* would always think of them as foreigners, *xenoi* in the loose sense; but in fact they filled a small yet precise niche in the status-structure of Athenian society."[40] We might say something similar about *proxenoi*. As the scholiast cited above says, *proxenoi* were the most honored within the privileged metic hierarchy; in Whitehead's words, they were "a favored minority."[41] Finally, given that any metic granted privileges was (ideologically, at least) being rewarded for services rendered to the city, he was implicitly more favored and more embraced by the citizens of Athens than were "regular" metics—and in some cases, more so than "regular" (that is, not euergetic) citizens. He was not a citizen, to be sure, but legally and socially he edged ever closer.

---

[39] That this was a privilege is argued by Simms 1988, 68. See also Parker 1996, 174, who points out that the metics who provided horses for the festival's horse races must have been particularly wealthy.

[40] Whitehead 1977, 12–13.

[41] Whitehead 1977, 14.

CHAPTER 6

BASTARDS (*NOTHOI*)

THE STATUS OF *NOTHOI* HAS LONG BEEN A VEXED QUESTION.[1] AT LEAST AS early as Solon's legislation (594/3 BCE), a *nothos* was defined as the child of two parents who were not legally married, hence the term's standard translation: "bastard."[2] After Pericles's citizenship legislation in 451/0—referred to as a law "on *nothoi*" (Plut. *Per.* 37.2)—the status of *nothoi* became a bit more complicated, with repercussions for their entitlement to citizen status. Moreover, this new post–451/0 status can be divided into two distinct sub-statuses of illegitimate children (see, e.g., LSJ s.v. *nothos*): 1) a child born to a citizen and a noncitizen (also called a *mētroxenos* if the mother was the foreigner, as was most often the case); and, likely a much smaller subcategory, 2) a child born out of wedlock to two Athenian citizen parents.[3]

I will start with the first type of *nothos*, considered by some to be the primary meaning of *nothos* in our period. The legal status of these bastards is fairly clear-cut: at least after 451/0, they were in general not citizens, since by the terms of Pericles's legislation those not born from two *astoi* (citizens) are to have no share in the polis, that is, are not to be citizens ([Arist.] *Ath. Pol.* 26.3).[4] It is true that this law seems to have fallen into abeyance sometime in the second half of the fifth century, meaning that some individuals defined as bastards by Pericles's legislation nonetheless received citizenship during this time (Dem. 57.30).[5] However, Pericles's law was reenacted in 403/2, ensuring that from that point on only those born from two citizens (*astōn*) had a share in the city ([Arist.] *Ath. Pol.* 42.1). In fact, two further measures guaranteed the noncitizen

---

[1] On the status of *nothoi*, see, e.g., Harrison 1968, 61–68; Humphreys 1974; MacDowell 1976; Rhodes 1978; C. Patterson 1990. The most thorough treatment of the status of *nothoi* is Ogden 1996. On *nothoi* in Greek literature, see Ebbott 2003.

[2] On Solon's bastardy laws, see Ogden 1996, 37–44.

[3] C. Patterson 1990, who surveys the history of the word *nothos* in early Greek literature and law (47–54), concludes that *nothos*—even in the classical period—refers only to "the paternally recognized offspring of a mismatched or unequal union" (62). Contrast Ogden 1996, 15–17, who argues that at least by the mid-classical period, *nothos* encompasses all extramarital children. On the significance of the bastard's relationship to his mother, see Ogden 1995.

[4] On Pericles's law, see C. Patterson 1981. For various interpretations of the purpose of this legislation, see Boegehold 1994; Ogden 1996, 64–69 (with bibliography); and more recently Blok 2009 and Lape 2010, 19–25 (and *passim*). [Arist.] *Ath. Pol.* chalks it up to the (large?) number of citizens at this time (26.3).

[5] See Ogden 1996, 70–77 on the relaxing of Pericles's citizenship law during this time; he in fact argues (77) that the law was revoked in 411 BCE, though we have no concrete evidence for this theory.

status of mixed marriages: Aristophon's proposal that anyone not born from an *astē* was to be a *nothos* (Athen. 577c), and Nikomenes's proposal that children born after 403/2 would not have citizenship unless born to two citizens (Schol. Aesch. 1.39).[6] Therefore, with the exception of those born during the short period of time during which Pericles's law was relaxed or suspended, bastards of this stripe were *not* citizens. However, this does not mean they had exactly the same status as metics. I will come back to this point shortly.

Less clear is the legal status after 451/0 of the second type of *nothos*— that is, "bastard" in the sense of an illegitimate child born to two citizens out of wedlock.[7] Some scholars believe that such bastards were citizens, whereas others believe that they were not.[8] The argument in favor of these bastards' citizenship status has been supported by a number of pieces of evidence. First, it has been argued that although *nothoi* were excluded from the circle of heirs called the *ankhisteia* (Aristoph. *Birds* 1649–68; Is. 6.47; Dem. 43.51) and could not belong to their fathers' phratries (clans) (Aristoph. *Birds* 1669–70; Dem. 57.54) or *genē* (noble kin groups) ([Dem.] 59.60), these factors did not necessarily entail their exclusion from Athenian citizenship.[9] Second, Pericles's citizenship law, as cited in [Arist.] *Ath. Pol.* 42.1, does not explicitly mention the necessity of marriage. Third, Plutarch tells us that the descendants of the oligarchs Arkheptolemos and Antiphon, *both bastard and legitimate*, were rendered *atimoi* (disenfranchised) by a decree of 411 (Plut. *Mor.* 834a–b), which seems to imply that bastards were, in the normal course of events, citizens.[10] Fourth, Raphael Sealey has argued that children born to citizen concubines and citizen men—although conceived outside the context of formal marriage—were in fact citizens. Because Draco's law preserved in Dem. 23.52 states that a man can legally kill anyone he catches in adultery with his wife, mother, sister, daughter, or concubine (*pallakē*) "kept for begetting free [*eleutheroi*] children," and because *eleutheros* seems to mean "citizen" in [Arist.] *Ath. Pol.* 42.1 ("a young man can be admitted to his father's deme if both parents are citizens, and if he is free [*eleutheros*] and born according to the laws"), Sealey contends that a child born to a citizen concubine must have been a citizen.[11]

---

[6] But cf. Walters 1983, 322, who argues that these are two completely separate decrees, one dealing with citizenship, the other with legitimacy.

[7] As Todd 1995, 178 points out, "there is very little evidence formally to resolve this question, and most of it is capable of varying interpretations."

[8] For bibliography on these two camps, see Ogden 1996, 151n1; Ogden himself (1996, 151–74) argues against their citizen status.

[9] Harrison 1968, 64 with n1.

[10] For both of these points, see MacDowell 1976, 89 and 1978, 68.

[11] Sealey 1984, 113–14.

The fifth piece of evidence is Isaeus's speech *On the Estate of Pyrrhos* (Is. 3), for which a little background is necessary. A certain Pyrrhos died, leaving a will in which he adopted his nephew Endios. When Endios died, a man named Xenokles stated in an affadavit that the estate was not adjudicable, since Pyrrhos had left behind a legitimate daughter, namely Xenokles's wife Phile. Endios's mother denied the legitimacy of Phile, and her son successfully prosecuted Xenokles for perjury in his affadavit. Then, in Is. 3, the son prosecuted Nikodemos, the brother of Phile's mother, on the ground that he had perjured when he stated that he had formally betrothed his sister to Pyrrhos. Because this son refers repeatedly in the speech to Phile as a *nothē*, and her marriage to Xenokles is not being disputed (just her mother's to Pyrrhos), it has been argued that bastards must have been citizens, since at the time of this speech marriage between citizens and noncitizens was not allowed ([Dem.] 59.16, 52).[12]

Those who hold that extramarital bastards were *not* citizens have, I think, convincingly challenged each of these arguments. First, it has been argued that phratry membership was indeed necessary for entry into demes, and so exclusion from phratries necessarily entailed exclusion from citizenship.[13] Second, we should be wary of making any positive arguments from the silence about marriage in [Arist.] *Ath. Pol.* 42.1.[14] Moreover, as just mentioned, [Arist.] *Ath. Pol.* 42.1 next states that a young man can enter his father's deme only if he is "born according to the laws," a phrase which in other contexts of legitimacy is equivalent to *gnēsios*, "born through marriage."[15] Third, the punishment of *atimia*, in the context of the descendants of Arkheptolemos and Antiphon, might not refer to a stripping of citizen rights: it could instead refer to total outlawry (the sense of *atimia* especially in early Athens), and therefore, illegitimate children need not have been citizens in order to be declared *atimoi*.[16] In addition, the lateness of this account (first century CE) means that it is not necessarily the most reliable source for the practices of classical Athens. Fourth, the argument that the children of an Athenian concubine were citizens has also rightly been challenged, since the *eleutheros* of Dem. 23.52 must be understood in its historical context (that is, the seventh century BCE). In that context, the term *eleutheros* means "free" only in the sense of "not a slave," not in the sense of "citizen."[17] Therefore, this law—even though it was still in effect in Demosthenes's day—is

---

[12] Harrison 1968, 66; MacDowell 1976, 89–90 and 1978, 68.

[13] Ogden 1996, ch. 2. On citizenship and phratry membership, see Lambert 1993, 31–43.

[14] Rhodes 1978, 89; Todd 1995, 178.

[15] Ogden 1996, 41.

[16] Rhodes 1978, 90; see also C. Patterson 1990, 46n25; Todd 1995, 178; Ogden 1996, 156.

[17] See C. Patterson 1990, 54; Ogden 1996, 33–34.

not terribly useful for determining the status of *nothoi* in the period after 451/0 BCE.

Finally, we have to use Is. 3 with caution, for a number of reasons.[18] To begin with, since accusations of illegitimacy are a common tactic in inheritance disputes,[19] we should not take the speaker at his word that Phile was a *nothē*. Moreover, there are problems with the line of argumentation on which his claim is based: the speaker says that since Nikodemos did not object to the adjudication of the estate to Endios, Phile must have been excluded from the *ankhisteia*—and therefore must have been a *nothē*. But there may have been other legitimate reasons why Phile acted as she did.[20] It is also not entirely clear whether her marriage to Xenokles was technically legal; the speaker never says that it was illegal, but if it had been, it would not have been in his interest to emphasize this fact, given that it was his own brother (Endios) who gave Phile in marriage.[21] The issues at hand, then, are quite fuzzy: if Phile had unquestionably been a legally married *nothē*, we would know that *nothoi* were themselves citizens;[22] if she had unquestionably been an illegally married *nothē*, we would know that they were not. But since we do not even know for certain whether she was a *nothē*, no such generalizations can be made, and Is. 3 cannot be used as evidence for the citizenship status of bastards.

To step back for a moment, we might ask: what kinds of people would have fallen into the subcategory of *nothoi* born to two citizens out of wedlock? Ogden lists the following circumstances under which such a bastard would have been produced: "1. [B]y an Athenian concubine (*pallakē*); 2. by an Athenian courtesan (*hetaira*); 3. by the rape of an Athenian woman; 4. by adultery with an Athenian woman; 5. by incest with an Athenian woman."[23] For circumstances #3–5, Ogden argues that the children of these sorts of unions would likely either not have been raised, or would have been passed off as the legitimate offspring of the woman and her husband. And #1 and #2, he argues, are unlikely situations to

---

[18] For the problems involved in using this speech to determine the citizen status of *nothoi*, see C. Patterson 1990, 70–73; Ogden 1996, 163–65.

[19] See, e.g., Lape 2010, ch. 2.

[20] Perhaps Phile was too young when Pyrrhos died to gain possession of the estate, and so was passed over in favor of Endios, and later, since Endios did not marry (and had no children to whom the estate would be passed down), she and Xenokles might not have objected to waiting to make their claim (Wyse 1904, 276; C. Patterson 1990, 72–73). Moreover, if they had reported Phile as an heiress, Xenokles would have had to abandon her to her next-of-kin, which was standard practice for *epiklēroi* (heiresses). Alternatively, perhaps the citizen status of her maternal family was in dispute, and she was waiting until the issue was settled before attempting to make a claim (C. Patterson 1990, 73).

[21] Wyse 1904, 279; Rhodes 1978, 91; C. Patterson 1990, 72; Ogden 1996, 164.

[22] But cf. Rhodes 1978, 92, who argues that since Pericles's law was meant primarily to exclude foreign blood, a woman who was illegitimate but still Athenian may have been allowed to marry as if she were a citizen, even if she was not technically a citizen herself.

[23] Ogden 1996, 157.

begin with, since it is nearly impossible to find definitive evidence for citizen *pallakai* or *hetairai*.[24] In this respect, he disagrees with Sealey, who argues for the existence of lawful concubinage between Athenian citizen *pallakai* and citizen men, based in part on a statement in Is. 3.39 ("Even those who give their women-folk into *pallakia* first reach agreements about the benefits to be furnished to the *pallakai*").[25] However, as Ogden correctly points out, there is no indication that the subject of this statement is necessarily Athenian *citizens* and their daughters. Moreover, the statement is contradicted by evidence from New Comedy, in which it is said to be paradoxical for a concubine to be given any kind of dowry, however small.[26] Is. 3.39 is therefore an insecure basis for asserting the existence of Athenian citizen *pallakai*. All in all, then, Ogden says that the number of people falling in this category—that is, those *recognized* as born to two citizen parents who were not married—"would have been extremely tiny, and possibly non-existent."[27] Those who did exist would likely not have been citizens themselves, since the evidence, on balance, suggests that recognized *nothoi* (of all stripes) were not granted citizenship.

Let us survey, then, the legal and social status of *nothoi*. Detlef Lotze well describes bastards as "between metics and citizens."[28] Legally, they were most akin to metics. A *nothos*, like a metic, could own property but not land or a house. Also like metics, *nothoi* had complete control over their own labor and movement, as well as their slaves', and they could punish any slave they owned. Whether they themselves were susceptible to corporal punishment is harder to determine: since they were of less-than-citizen status, their bodily integrity would not necessarily have been a concern to the Athenian demos, but societal constraints—including the social status of their citizen parent(s) within the community—might have made it unacceptable to lay a hand on them. Given their legal status as noncitizens, their privileges and liabilities in judicial proceedings would have been similar to that of metics. We might suppose, however, that they had more support than metics did from citizen friends and relatives in the courtroom.

The legal exclusion of *nothoi* from the *oikos* is one of their most distinctive attributes. Because they were not enrolled in their father's phratry—an enrollment that was fundamental to recognition as a citizen (see

---

[24] Ogden 1996, 158–63.

[25] Sealey 1984, 116–17 claims that particularly poor Athenian citizen families who were unable to afford a large dowry gave their marriageable daughters as *pallakai*.

[26] For these objections, see C. Patterson 1990, 60n80; Ogden 1996, 159.

[27] Ogden 1996, 151; see also Kapparis 1999, 200. This point was made as early as Wyse 1904, 278.

[28] Lotze 1981.

chapter 10)—they were overtly marked as "not legitimate." At least by the middle of the fourth century (and possibly earlier), bastards, qua noncitizens, were not allowed to marry Athenian citizens.[29] And, as mentioned above, they were not part of their family's *ankhisteia* and therefore could not normally inherit. One difficulty here is how to interpret the puzzling "law of Solon," as cited in Aristophanes's *Birds*: "There is no *ankhisteia* for the bastard if there are legitimate children (*gnēsiōn*); but if there are no legitimate children, the next-of-kin share in the property" (*Birds* 1660–66). Clauses from two distinct laws seem to be stuck together here.[30] The first is likely from a very early law of intestate succession, stipulating that if there were no legitimate children, *nothoi* had the first claim. The second is from a law that is later—but certainly earlier than the late fifth century, and possibly dating back to Solon—which banned any and all inheritance by *nothoi*.[31] That is, if there were no legitimate offspring, the property went to the next-of-kin rather than to any illegitimate offspring. Even with these restrictions, however, it appears that fathers could still bequeath limited sums to their *nothoi* offspring—the so-called "bastard's portion" (*notheia*)—which was either 500 or 1000 drachmas.[32]

A *nothos* was (nearly) always a *nothos*. It was an impossible status to shake, unless, hypothetically, a father who had not previously acknowledged his (legitimately born) son decided at some later point to recognize the boy as his own, in which case the *nothos* would be reclassified as *gnēsios* and have all the rights of a citizen.[33] Alternatively, in some contexts a *nothos* could be adopted by his father, thus *becoming* his legitimate heir.[34] In fact, granted the right to do so by the demos, Pericles adopted Pericles the Younger, his *nothos* son with the *hetaira* Aspasia, after his legitimate children died (Plut. *Per.* 37).[35] Moreover, just like other noncitizens, *nothoi* might try to pass themselves off as citizens, but if they were caught, they were punished severely. Apparently after Pericles's citizenship law was passed, prosecutions against *nothoi* pretending to be citizens were frequent: according to Plutarch (again, admittedly a source we should take with a grain of salt), nearly 5,000 *nothoi* were convicted and sold into slavery (Plut. *Per.* 37.4)!

---

[29] But cf. Rhodes 1978, 91.

[30] See Humphreys 1974, 89n5.

[31] That this later law was Solonian is argued by C. Patterson 1990, 51n46; Ogden 1996, 36. Cf. Harrison 1968, 67–68, who proposes (on the basis of Dem. 43.51 and Is. 6.47, stating that *nothoi* are to be deprived of *ankhisteia* "from the archonship of Eukleides") that the law was passed in 403/2.

[32] Schol. Aristoph. *Birds* 1655; Harp. s.v. *notheia*; Suda s.v. *epiklēros*.

[33] That one could not legitimize *known* bastards is argued by Harrison 1968, 68–70.

[34] Harrison 1968, 68 grants this possibility.

[35] Cf. Carawan 2008, who argues, innovatively, that Pericles's citizenship law was actually amended in 430 BCE to allow fathers to adopt their *nothoi* if they had no surviving legitimate children.

In religious rites, *nothoi* presumably could have played the same role as metics in city festivals and cults, though at least formally they would have been excluded from their family's religious cults (Dem. 43.51; Is. 6.47). In terms of political rights, the *nothos'* exclusion from phratry and *genos* membership most likely entailed exclusion from deme membership, and thus from citizenship (although as I note above, there is disagreement on this point). Militarily, again, the *nothos* presumably would have had the rights and liabilities of a metic.

Possibly shedding some light on the *nothos'* privileges in the sacral, political, and military spheres is the somewhat mysterious gymnasium for *nothoi* at Kunosarges, just outside the city walls of Athens.[36] Unfortunately, our sources for this institution are few and far between. Plutarch tells us that Themistocles exercised at this gymnasium—which was sacred to the *nothos* Heracles, and where *nothoi* were "enrolled" (*suntelountōn*)[37]—because his mother was a foreigner (Plut. *Them.* 1). Athenaeus records a decree proposed by Alcibiades and located in the Herakleion at Kunosarges, prescribing that a priest is to sacrifice monthly offerings with the *parasitoi* (fellow diners), appointed from the *nothoi* and their sons according to tradition (Athen. 234e);[38] and Demosthenes mentions someone who is enrolled (*suntelei*) among the *nothoi* at Oreos, just as the *nothoi* in Athens were "at some point" (*pote*) enrolled at Kunosarges (Dem 23.213).

It is unclear, however, what precisely the nature of this gymnasium was or even when it became associated with *nothoi*. Some scholars believe that the association may have gone all the way back to the time of Solon.[39] Sally Humphreys, on the other hand, has argued that Plutarch's account (our main evidence for the cult existing before 451/0) is anachronistic, and that the gymnasium became an official meeting place for *nothoi* only *after* 451/0. In fact, she suggests that the cult at Kunosarges was designed for (and by) "upper-class boys" disenfranchised by Pericles's legislation—that is, those not yet old enough in 451/0 to have been enrolled in the demes—who took pride in being born from a mixed marriage characteristic of their aristocratic forebears. Humphreys views the cult as a voluntary political and religious organization offering membership separate from, but akin to, that in phratries or demes, and requiring its members to participate in and contribute to the cult of Heracles centered at the gymnasium. It was, however, a relatively short-lived

[36] On the *nothoi* of Kunosarges, see, e.g., Humphreys 1974; C. Patterson 1990, 63–65; Ogden 1996, 199–203 and *passim*; Bearzot 2005, 85–91.

[37] On the connection with both Heracles and *nothoi*, see also Suda s.v. *Es Kunosarges* and *Eis Kunosarges*; and Phot. s.v. *Kunosarges*.

[38] See also the fragmentary inscription *IG* I³ 134, which may be another attestation of the involvement of Alciabides in the cult at Kunosarges.

[39] See, e.g., C. Patterson 1990, 64; Ogden 1996, 199.

institution, dying out by the mid-fourth century if not earlier (Dem. 23.123).[40] Cinzia Bearzot has proposed further that the membership lists at Kunosarges served as the city's official record of those who had been "bastardized" by Pericles's legislation. Through this official recognition, *nothoi* after 451/0 were assured not only a religious role in the city (as part of the cult of Heracles), but also a civic and military role.[41] Indeed, Bearzot's argument runs, the lists of *nothoi* were used for calling up supplementary troops.[42] This is an attractive suggestion, but the notion that membership was actually enforced by the city for its record-keeping may be too hard to substantiate from our scraps of evidence. If, however, *nothoi* were in fact associated with the cult after 451/0—whether for the first time (as Humphreys suggests) or dating all the way back to the period of Solon (or at least of Themistocles?)—this association may have granted them political and religious rights distinct from those of metics, not to mention a collective social identity.

The social status of *nothoi*, like their legal status, changed over time. Their complete exclusion from the *ankhisteia* had not only legal repercussions (outlined above), but also social ones, especially within the context of the family. One can easily imagine a tense relationship existing between a *nothos* (especially a male *nothos*) and his legtimate half-siblings, as well as a constant awareness of his inequality, most clearly symbolized by their inequality in inheritance. Also potentially difficult was the relationship between the *mētroxenos* bastard and his father's legitimate wife, a dynamic that frequently plays out in tragedy. So, for example, in Euripides's *Andromache*, Neoptolemos and the slave-captive Andromache have a son named Molossos, whose status as a *nothos* is repeatedly alluded to in negative terms (636, 912, 928, 942). Like many bastard children in tragedy (and especially in Euripides), Molossos is hated by his father's wife Hermione, who cannot bear her own children.[43] The *nothos'* debased status within his family, coupled with his lack of privileges in the city, led him to possess, in Cynthia Patterson's words, "an ambiguous social position at the margins of Athenian society."[44] It was, to be sure, a less clear-cut status (both socially and legally) than that of slave, metic, or citizen. Bearzot suggests that this status was most comparable to that of freedmen (*apeleutheroi*), on the basis of a number of (to my mind) superficial

[40] Humphreys 1974.

[41] See also C. Patterson 1990, 63, who argues that the cult at Kunosarges allowed *nothoi* to "participate in civic organization and perhaps recruitment."

[42] Bearzot 2005, 89–91, with bibliography.

[43] See also, e.g., Euripides's *Ion*, in which Kreousa hates Ion when he is thought to be her husband Xouthos's bastard, but loves him when she knows he is her own; cf. Phaedra's passion for her bastard stepson in Euripides's *Hippolytos*.

[44] C. Patterson 1990, 41.

similarities, but also, most interestingly, the fact that the Suda (s.v. *Es Kunosarges*) says that the Athenians called *apeleutheroi* "*nothoi*."[45]

We should also not overlook the possibility that a distinction in social status existed between the two types of *nothoi* described above: *nothoi* born to unmarried Athenian parents and *nothoi* born to an Athenian and a foreigner. In the case of the (admittedly few) recognized bastards born to two unmarried citizen parents, their pure Athenian blood presumably gave them a higher status than that of most mixed-blood *mētroxenoi*.[46] At the same time, however, at least in the immediate aftermath of Pericles's legislation, it may have been the case (as Humphreys suggests) that some *mētroxenoi* took pride in their aristocratic pedigree, not to mention the fact that they followed in the footsteps of Heracles, a famous bastard "honored equally to the gods" (see Suda, s.v. *Eis Kunosarges*).[47] For the most part, however, mixed-blood bastards were likely stigmatized for their impure ancestry, especially in the fourth century, when the ideology of the pureblooded Athenian became most prominent and most strongly policed (see also my Conclusion). The fact that the cult at Kunosarges had disappeared by Demosthenes's day suggests that one's identity as a *nothos* was no longer something that one was willing to advertise.

[45] Bearzot 2005, 85–91 supports this theory with the following arguments: *nothoi* and *apeleutheroi* both had freedom without citizen rights, resided in Athens, represented an intermediate category between metic and citizen, and had a relationship with the Kunosarges gymnasium.

[46] See also Lape 2010, 133.

[47] On membership in the Kunosarges as a source of pride, see Humphreys 1974.

CHAPTER 7

DISENFRANCHISED CITIZENS (*ATIMOI*)

In determining the legal and social status of *atimoi*, I must first define what I mean by *atimia*. I am concerned in this chapter only with *atimia* in its classical sense—"disenfranchisement"—as opposed to its archaic sense of outlawry (i.e., deprivation of all protections of the law).[1] But even in the classical period, *atimia* came in many different forms. First of all, it could be total or partial. Total *atimia*, depending on the offense warranting it, was either temporary or permanent,[2] and entailed being deprived of the rights to take part in the Assembly or Council; to serve as a juror, act as prosecutor in public and private suits, and give evidence; to hold magistracies; to enter sanctuaries; and to enter the Agora.[3] Partial *atimia*, on the other hand, could involve any of the preceding deprivations, in addition to some others (see below).[4] Another distinction to be noted is that between "automatic *atimia*"[5] and *atimia* by sentence.[6] In the latter case, the penalty of *atimia* was inflicted on someone who had committed particular offenses (see further below) and was then prosecuted and sentenced. In the former case, an individual who had committed specific offenses—including prostituting himself— was subject immediately (that is, even without trial) to the restrictions of *atimia*. Finally, some individuals were treated like *atimoi*, but were not technically *atimoi*: the most notable example of these is homicides and possible homicides (see further below).

One of our best sources for *atimia* is a passage from Andocides's *On the Mysteries* (1.73–79).[7] The context is a listing of all the *atimoi* who gained amnesty by the decree of Patrokleides, enacted after the battle at Aigospotamoi in 405 BCE. The first category Andocides lists (1.73) is

---

[1] On *atimia*, see Paoli 1974 [1930], 304–39; Harrison 1971, 169–76; MacDowell 1978, 73–75; Hansen 1976, 55–90; Sealey 1983; Todd 1995, 142–43. See Hansen 1976, 75–82 for the shift in meanings of *atimia*; he suggests (79) that the shift occurred around 510–507 BCE.

[2] On the distinction between temporary and permanent *atimia*, see Hansen 1976, 67–70.

[3] On total *atimia*, see Hansen 1976, 61–63, with citations.

[4] On partial *atimia*, see Hansen 1976, 63–66, with citations.

[5] Scholars refer to those punished in this way in various ways: "ἄτιμος incensurato" (Paoli 1974 [1930], 327–34); automatically *atimos* (Harrison 1971, 171–72; Hansen 1976, 55–98 *passim*); "treated as ἄτιμος" (MacDowell 1962, 138); *atimos* if they actively served in politics (Todd 1995, 107n5, 116n15); "unconvicted or potential *atimos*" (R. W. Wallace 1998).

[6] On automatic *atimia* vs. *atimia* by sentence, see Hansen 1976, 66–67.

[7] On Andoc. 1.73–79, see MacDowell 1962, 106–19 and Hansen 1976, 82–90.

the state debtors, whose property was confiscated to pay off their debts if they did not pay up within eight prytanies (roughly ten months).[8] In this category are those found guilty at the examination of their conduct (*euthunē*) performed when they vacated their offices, thus owing a fine to the state treasury; those found guilty in an ejectment suit (*dikē exoulēs*) on the grounds that they were holding property that belonged to someone else, thus having to restore the property to the owner and pay the state a fine equal to the property's value; those found guilty in certain types of public suits requiring money to be paid to the state treasury; those owing fines (*epibolai*) imposed by magistrates;[9] those who had farmed taxes and then defaulted, not paying the treasury the amount they had promised to collect; and those who had served as sureties for a tax-farmer who defaulted.

The second category Andocides lists (1.74) are those *atimoi* who retained possession of their property, but who were (unlike state debtors) permanently disenfranchised (*kathapax atimoi*).[10] First in this category are those individuals convicted of theft or of accepting bribes, for whom the penalty of *atimia* extended also to their descendants. Although some scholars believe that this subcategory of *atimoi* actually belongs in 1.73 and was accidentally transposed to 1.74, the evidence for this theory is, to my mind, not conclusive.[11] Andocides also includes in this category those who deserted on the battlefield; those found guilty of evading military service, of cowardice, or of withholding a ship from action while serving as trierarch; those who threw away their shields; those who were convicted three times of giving perjured evidence; those convicted three times of either falsely procuring summons-witnesses or falsely witnessing a summons; and those found guilty of mistreating their parents.

Finally, Andocides's third category (1.75) includes those who were partially *atimoi*, unlike those in the first two categories, both of which entailed total *atimia*. Andocides includes in this category soldiers who were discovered (after the fact) to have remained in Athens during the reign of the Four Hundred in 411 BCE; these men were banned from speaking in the Assembly and becoming members of the Council. Others condemned to partial *atimia* were deprived of one or more of the following citizen rights (1.76): prosecuting public suits, bringing a written denunciation (*endeixis*), sailing up the Hellespont or crossing to Ionia, and entering the Agora.

---

[8] On the punishment of state debtors in Athens, see Hunter 2000b.

[9] This is how this sentence is generally interpreted; cf. MacDowell 1962 *ad loc.*, who believes it might also refer to fines imposed by juries.

[10] For the term *kathapax atimoi* (not actually used in Andoc. 1), see Dem. 21.32, 87; Dem. 25.30; [Arist.] *Ath. Pol.* 22.8.

[11] That this subcategory was accidentally transposed was a view argued by Paoli 1974 [1930], 304–7 and adopted by MacDowell 1962. Cf. Hansen 1976, 86–88 for a defense of Andocides's text as it stands.

Drawing on Andocides (our most complete ancient source on the topic) as well as other material, Mogens Hansen offers the following classification of offenses punishable by *atimia*: "offences of omission" (that is, neglect of civic duties);[12] third-time offenses;[13] serious offenses warranting hereditary *atimia* as an additional penalty;[14] and miscellaneous other offenses, including squandering one's patrimony and prostituting oneself.[15] From his exhaustive survey, Hansen concludes that *atimia* was the punishment that citizens incurred not in their capacity as private individuals, but in their capacity as citizens.[16] I agree with Hansen's assessment, but with a qualification. The Athenians clearly viewed most of these offenses, like deserting in war or misconduct in office, as civic offenses. I would argue that other offenses, like prostitution or squandering one's patrimony, were considered civic offenses *by analogy*. That is to say, the underlying principle behind the disenfranchisement of certain offenders was that they had committed offenses *analogous* to, and thus potentially leading to, civic offenses. So, for example, if a citizen mistreated his own body, his parents, or his inheritance, he would (by analogy) also mistreat his city.[17] This logic is made most overt in Aeschines's speech *Against Timarchus* (see esp. Aesch. 1.28–30), in which Timarchus is prosecuted for having spoken in the Assembly despite being a prostitute (and thus subject to automatic *atimia*). The allegation that Timarchus has sold his body is taken as evidence that he would readily sell out his city for the sake of financial gain (Aesch. 1.29 and *passim*).[18]

Let us turn now to the legal and social status of *atimoi*. State debtors lost their claims to property (Andoc. 1.73), whereas other *atimoi*—those with permanent *atimia* (Andoc. 1.74) and those with partial *atimia* (Andoc. 1.75–76)—did not. However, even those with permanent *atimia* were at

---

[12] Hansen 1976, 72–73: "not appearing when called up . . . not obeying the general's order or for desertion from the army . . . cowardice . . . not taking part in a naval battle . . . desertion from the navy . . . not serving as an arbitrator in one's sixtieth year . . . not bestowing old age provision on one's parents . . . not carrying through a public action . . . not divorcing [an adulteress] . . . non-payment of debts to the state or to the gods."

[13] Hansen 1976, 73: "false evidence (in general) . . . false evidence given by witnesses to the summons . . . unconstitutional proposals . . . habitual idleness."

[14] Hansen 1976, 73: "treason and attempts to overthrow the democracy . . . attempts to abolish certain laws . . . theft (of public property?) . . . bribery (in public affairs?)."

[15] Hansen 1976, 73–74: "a citizen who squandered his patrimony . . . a prostitute or a person who for gain induced a citizen to be a prostitute . . . a citizen who married off a foreign woman pretending she was an Athenian . . . a citizen who adopted a descendant of [a *kathapax atimos*] . . . a prosecutor who brought a public action but at the hearing obtained less than one-fifth of the votes of the jurors . . . an arbitrator for misconduct in office . . . an official for misconduct in office . . . a citizen who obstructed public officials in the exercise of their office . . . an ostracized citizen who did not respect the temporary exile but was found within an area delimited by Cape Skyllaion and Cape Geraistos."

[16] Hansen 1976, 74.

[17] I use male pronouns in this chapter, since most (if not all) *atimoi* were male.

[18] For a similar argument, see Halperin 1990, ch. 5.

a disadvantage regarding property ownership: because they could not enter the Agora and the courts, they were unable to protect their rights of ownership.[19] *Atimoi* of all stripes had control over their own labor, but their movement was greatly restricted. Those with total *atimia* were banned from all civic spaces, including the meeting places of the Boule and Ekklesia, sanctuaries—on all of which see further below—and even the Agora.[20] (Similar restrictions also held for individuals accused of, but not yet sentenced for, homicide.[21]) Moreover, imprisonment—that is, complete restriction of movement—could sometimes be imposed in the case of state debtors who defaulted on their payment ([Arist.] *Ath. Pol.* 48.1; cf. Dem. 24.39–40) and of *atimoi* who, having violated the restrictions of their *atimia*, were ordered to pay a fine they could not afford (Dem. 24.105).[22] While *atimoi* were permitted to continue living in Athens, the restrictions on their freedoms may have incited many to leave the city and live elsewhere.[23] Unlike citizens who were ostracized,[24] however, *atimoi* had free choice as to where they went. Finally, some under partial *atimia* faced further restrictions to their movement, including those banned from sailing up the Hellespont or crossing to Ionia (Andoc. 1.76).

Disenfranchised citizens continued to have power to punish those of lesser status, including their own slaves. However, if they were stripped of their property (as state debtors were), they might not have had slaves left to punish. *Atimoi* technically could not be physically punished, since they were still citizens. However, if they *were* physically attacked, and were under total *atimia*, they could not bring a suit against their attacker. Moreover, we know that adulteresses—the closest thing to female *atimoi*[25]—could be physically attacked if they entered certain public spaces, with only one condition: that they not be killed ([Dem.] 59.87).

One area in which *atimoi* were particularly disadvantaged was in the realm of judicial privileges. An individual with total *atimia* could not speak in the law courts, which meant that he could neither bring cases nor act as a witness. Some under partial *atimia* were deprived of the right to bring *graphai* (Andoc. 1.76), but could presumably continue to bring *dikai*. Moreover, in the case of many but not all *atimoi*,[26] if they infringed

---

[19] Harrison 1968, 236.

[20] For banning from the Agora, see, e.g., Lys. 6.9, 24; Dem. 22.77, 24.60, 103, 126; Aesch. 1.164, 3.176. Allen 2000, 230 calls the banning of *atimoi* from public spaces "internal exile."

[21] They were barred from the Agora (Dem. 20.158, 23.80, 24.60; Aesch. 2.148; [Arist.] *Ath. Pol.* 57.4; Ant. 6.36) and temples (Dem. 20.158, 23.80; [Arist.] *Ath. Pol.* 57.4; Lys. 13.81) until their case was heard (see also Hansen 1976, 70 for this comparison). For Athenian homicide law, see also MacDowell 1963.

[22] On imprisonment in classical Athens, see Allen 1997 and 2000, *passim*.

[23] See also Todd 1995, 142.

[24] On ostracism, see Forsdkye 2005. I do not discuss ostracized citizens in this book, since only a couple of ostracisms are attested for our period (Forsdyke 2005, 168–75), and the practice fell into disuse after 415 BCE.

[25] Todd 1995, 279; Kapparis 1999, 357; Glazebrook 2005, 47.

[26] See Hansen 1976, 90–94.

upon any of the prohibitions of their *atimia*, they were subject to one of the following legal actions: an *apagōgē*, the arrest of an offender by the prosecutor himself; an *endeixis*, a written denunciation, which could be, but was not always, followed by an *apagōgē*; or an *ephēgēsis*, in which the prosecutor denounced the offender to magistrates, who in turn arrested the offender.[27] *Endeixis* is by far the most commonly attested procedure used against *atimoi* who violated the terms of their *atimia*. Sometimes the trials following *endeixis* were *agōnes atimētoi*, that is, trials for which the sentence was mandatory death penalty; other times *endeixis* and *apagōgē* were followed by *agōnes timētoi*, that is, trials for which the jurors decided the penalty.[28] If the penalty was a fine, the convicted individual was imprisoned until he was able to pay (see above).

Homicides, and homicide suspects, were similar to *atimoi* in that they were also deprived of some of their civic rights. Specific legal actions could be taken against four classes of possible homicides: 1) If someone was accused of homicide by the family of the deceased, and that person exercised his civic rights or entered public places before his trial, anyone could bring an *apagōgē* against him. If convicted of this offense, the offender had to pay a fine determined by the jurors. 2) If someone *suspected* of homicide exercised his civic rights or entered public places, anyone could arrest or indict him, and if convicted, he was sentenced to death. 3) If someone was arrested or indicted on the grounds that he was a *kakourgos* (a certain class of criminal)[29] as well as a homicide, he could be put to death without trial if he confessed to the murder. 4) Finally, exiled homicides were nearly *atimoi* in the archaic sense of "outlaws": if they set foot in Attica they could be killed by anyone with impunity; alternatively, they could be pursued by an *apagōgē*, *endeixis*, or *ephēgēsis*.[30]

As I already mentioned, *atimia* was in some instances hereditary. This was the case for state debtors (until the debt was paid off) and for the following types of *atimoi*: those guilty of treason or attempting to overthrow the democratic constitution; those convicted of bribery or theft (presumably of state funds); and those who had proposed the abolition of particular laws. Of all of these *atimoi*, only state debtors were allowed to have their children (or at least some of them) adopted into other families, in order to spare them hereditary *atimia*.[31] Such *atimoi* technically retained their rights of marriage and inheritance, but these rights were inevitably limited by the fact that they themselves (if under total *atimia*) could

---

[27] See Hansen 1976, ch. 3 on *apagōgē*, *endeixis*, and *ephēgēsis* against *atimoi* (esp. 90–98).

[28] Hansen 1976, 96–97.

[29] On *kakourgoi*, see Hansen 1976, ch. 2.

[30] For (1), see Hansen 1976, 99–100; for (2) 100–103; for (3) 103–7; for (4) 107–9. See also MacDowell 1962, 130–40.

[31] See Hansen 1976, 71–72 on hereditary *atimia*.

not speak in court. That is, although they could presumably still marry Athenian women and produce Athenian children, their rights as legal guardians were curtailed, as were the rights of their offspring. In addition, they could not claim inheritances in those instances where it was necessary to come before the archon or the court; they were restricted to *embateusis*, that is, direct inheritance by an heir.[32]

Social mobility was available primarily to those under temporary *atimia*, such as state debtors, who recovered their rights as soon as they paid off their debts (Isoc. 12.10, Dem. 21.99). Even *kathapax atimoi*, as well as state debtors before they paid off their debts, could have their *atimia* reversed if they applied to the Assembly for a reprieve. In this procedure, no less than 6,000 citizens had to give an affirmative vote by ballot (Dem. 24.45). There were also some exceptional cases of general amnesty during our period, in which rights were restored to all (or nearly all) *atimoi*, possibly in return for fighting on behalf of Athens (see further below): so, for example, after the Battle of Marathon in 490 BCE (Andoc. 1.77); the battle at Aigospotamoi in 405 BCE (Andoc. 1.77–79); the occupation of Athens in 404 BCE (Andoc. 1.80); the restoration of the democracy in 403 BCE (*Ath. Pol.* 39); and the defeat at Chaironea in 338 BCE (Hyp. fr. 33).[33]

Aristophanes's *Frogs*, performed shortly before the Battle of Aigospotamoi, gives us access to some of the motivating factors behind the amnesty of 405 BCE. Of particular interest is a choral passage responding to two fairly recent events: the disenfranchisement of those who partook in the oligarchy of the Four Hundred in 411 BCE (one of whose leaders was a man named Phrynikhos), and the enfranchisement of the slaves who participated in the Battle of Arginousai (406/5) (see chapter 3). The Chorus leader declares:

> We think that all the citizens should be made equal [*exisōsai*], and their fears removed, and if anyone was tripped up by Phrynikhos's holds, I say that those who slipped up at that time should be permitted to dispose of their liability and put right their earlier mistakes. Next I say that no one in the city should be disenfranchised, for it's a disgrace [*aiskhron*] that veterans of a single sea battle should forthwith become Plataians, turning from slaves into masters; not that I have any criticism to voice about that—indeed I applaud it as being your only intelligent action . . . (Aristoph. *Frogs* 687–96; translated by Jeffrey Henderson, with slight modification)

In the eyes of the Chorus—whose words were presumably designed to appeal to the polis as a whole—the natural-born citizens who were involved in Phrynikhos's oligarchic coup lost their citizenship unjustly

---

[32] See Hansen 1976, 63 for these restrictions on the *atimos*' family and inheritance rights.

[33] For these examples of *atimoi* regaining their rights, see Hansen 1976, 68–69.

(or at least deserved to recover it), whereas the slaves fighting at Arginou-sai were unjustly—or at any rate disgracefully (*aiskhron*)—freed and natu-ralized.[34] In the interests of "making all citizens equal" (*exisōsai*), the Cho-rus proposes restoring Phrynikhos's men to citizenship, and conceding to the Arginousai slaves their newfound rights. After the disastrous Bat-tle of Aigospotamoi, Patrokleides apparently took the Chorus leader's advice and proposed the decree discussed above (Andoc. 1.77–79).

Short of an amnesty, an *atimos* could try to "pass" as an enfranchised citizen, but this was a risky endeavor. Disenfranchised citizens, like enfranchised citizens, were monitored by the "policing" of their fellow Athenians:[35] if an *atimos* was caught exercising his civic rights, anyone could bring an *endeixis* or an *apagōgē* against him for violating the terms of his *atimia*. In one instance, a state debtor named Pyrrhos, clearly strapped for cash, was indicted by *endeixis* for serving on a jury (a task for which he would be paid) (Dem. 21.182). It would be relatively easy to detect someone like Pyrrhos, who had been sentenced to *atimia*, but "automatic *atimoi*" were a different story. Strange as it might sound, an automatic *atimos* might not have been aware that he was *atimos* (since he had not been sentenced), nor would others necessarily have known.[36]

Total *atimia* entailed serious restrictions on participation in the sacral sphere, since *atimoi* were banned from sanctuaries and public worship (see, e.g., Aesch. 3.176; Lys. 6.9, 24). The adulteress, too—our female "*atimos*"—was banned from public worship ([Dem.] 59.87, Aesch. 1.183), which was in effect her primary civic role (see further chapter 9). The total *atimos* was perhaps most gravely compromised in his political rights, since he could not speak in the Assembly, one of the primary markers of citizenship. One of the best-attested examples of this deprivation can be found in Aeschines's *Against Timarchus* (see above), since it was by speak-ing in the Assembly that Timarchus violated the restrictions imposed by his *atimia*.[37] The *atimos*, therefore, did remain a citizen—he was not struck from the deme or phratry rolls—but in practice he was denied the right to do most things characteristic of citizens, leaving him in a kind of sta-tus limbo.

As citizens, *atimoi* could presumably still be called upon to provide military service.[38] There might have been some reluctance to recruit them on the part of the city (which had disenfranchised such individuals), not

---

[34] On the significance of the naturalized slaves being called "Plataians" rather than citizens, see Tamiolaki 2008.

[35] On "policing" by citizens in Athens, see Hunter 1994. See also Allen 2000, 203: "the *polis* as a com-munity enforced *atimia*."

[36] R. W. Wallace 1998, 75.

[37] For the prostitute not getting to speak, see Aesch. 1.3, 14, 20, 40, 46, 73, 119, 154, 195; Dem. 22.29–32. See Halperin 1990, ch. 5 on the civic ideology underlying this punishment for prostitutes.

[38] See also MacDowell 1978, 74.

to mention reluctance to participate on the part of the *atimoi* themselves (feeling less connection to and perhaps decreased loyalty to the city), but it is plausible, to my mind, that amnesty was promised to *atimoi* in exchange for military services. Although such a promise is not explicitly attested, it would make sense given both that slaves were promised freedom (see chapter 3) and foreigners were promised citizenship (chapter 8) for participation in warfare, and that a number of general amnesties did in fact take place after major battles (see above).

The very word *atimos*, meaning both "deprived of civic offices" (*a* + *timai*) and "deprived of honor" (*a* + *timē*), encapsulates both the degraded political status and the degraded social status of such individuals.[39] How a given *atimos* was viewed socially likely depended at least in part on the type of offense he had committed (the more egregious the offense, the lower his honor), as well as the type and degree of *atimia* he suffered: partial versus total, temporary versus permanent, and perhaps especially whether he was *atimos* automatically or by sentence. As Robert Wallace points out, although the legal status of potential or unconvicted *atimoi* (his term for automatic *atimoi*) was clearly defined, their status in practice varied "depending on a range of extra-legal factors including the degree of suspicion that attached to them, the number and vigilance of their enemies, their public behavior, and other questions such as their personal status and utility (or danger) to the *polis*."[40] Escaping social stigma—not to mention the legal repercussions of one's *atimia*—may therefore have been easier for some *atimoi* than for others, and was no doubt affected by an individual's wealth and social standing prior to *atimia*.

[39] See also Hansen 1976, 60, who argues that *atimia* entailed "socially a loss of honor" in addition to its legal disadvantages.

[40] R. W. Wallace 1998, 77. Hunter 2000b makes a similar argument about public debtors.

CHAPTER 8

NATURALIZED CITIZENS

IN THIS CHAPTER, I ARGUE THAT NATURALIZED CITIZENS, WHILE NEARLY THE equal of natural-born citizens in the eyes of the law, were markedly different in social status. In order to flesh out this complex status, it is useful first to outline the basics of how naturalization worked.[1] The institution was practiced on an ad-hoc basis as early as Solon, who was said to have naturalized refugees and other foreigners who came to Athens to practice a trade (Plut. *Sol.* 24.4). We are also told that the Athenian statesman Cleisthenes introduced many foreigners and slaves into the civic body, but, as with the reforms of Solon, this too seems to have been a one-time measure (Arist. *Pol.* 1275b36–37; [Arist.] *Ath. Pol.* 21.4).[2] The procedure for naturalization (described in [Dem.] 59.88–92) was not formalized until the classical period, probably sometime in the middle of the fifth century.[3] At this point, it became illegal to grant individuals or groups citizenship unless they had demonstrated *andragathia* (manly excellence) to the Athenian people ([Dem.] 59.89).[4] *Andragathia* here refers not to military courage (as it often does) but to state benefaction: as Apollodoros puts it, citizenship is a "gift" granted to benefactors (*euergetousi*) (59.89).[5] Thus, noncitizens could make a benefaction to the state, for which they were given the gift of citizenship.[6] For those opposed to

[1] The most comprehensive work on naturalization in Athens is still M. J. Osborne's four-volume *Naturalization in Athens*, including epigraphic material (vol. 1) and commentary (vol. 2), testimonia with commentary (vol. 3), and a laying-out of the history and procedure of naturalization in Athens (vol. 4). For a generally positive review (except for a criticism of the term "naturalization" as anachronistic), see Gauthier 1986. On naturalization in Athens, see also MacDowell 1978, 70–73; Henry 1983, ch. 3 (on formulae in naturalization decrees); Todd 1995, 174–76; Lape 2010, ch. 6. For a study of citizenship decrees (as well as decrees granting proxeny and euergesy) from 352/1–322/1 BCE, see Lambert 2006.

[2] See, e.g., Kagan 1963 on Cleisthenes's enfranchisement of slaves and foreigners.

[3] On the procedure for naturalization, see M. J. Osborne 1983, 155–70; Kapparis 1999 *ad loc.* I am not discussing here means by which one might try to sneak into the citizen body, whether through bribery or otherwise. For an insinuation (probably unsubstantiated) that the politician Kleophon acquired his citizenship through dishonest means, see Aesch. 2.76.

[4] M. J. Osborne 1983, 144 suggests that this law was part of Pericles's citizenship legislation of 451/0. On *andragathia* in this context, see Whitehead 1983, 69–70; Kapparis 1999, 364–65.

[5] The concept of citizenship as a "gift" (*dōron* or more often *dōreia*) from the polis, in exchange for services rendered, is a common one in Athenian classical discourse. See, e.g., Dem. 23.23, 64, 65, 89 (*dōreia*); Dem. 26.12 (*dōreia*); Dem. 36.30 (*dōreia*); Dem. 45.35 (*dōreia*); Dem. 46.13 (*dōreia*); [Dem.] 59.2, 13, 90 *bis*, 91 *bis* (*dōreia*); [Dem.] 59.89 (once as *dōreia*, once as *dōron*). See also von Reden 2003 [1995], 93 on the distinction between *dōron* and *dōreia*.

[6] See further Gauthier 1985 on the interconnectedness of benefaction and citizenship (as well as other honors).

the practice, naturalization was considered less a gift exchange than the sale of a commodity. The speaker of [Dem.] 13 says scornfully that nowadays, the Athenians "make citizens [*poieisthe politas*] of scum and home-born slaves born of home-born slaves, taking payment for it as for any other goods for sale [*ōniōn*]" (13.24).

If someone demonstrated *andragathia* to the polis, any Athenian citizen could make a proposal granting this individual citizenship. The proposal then had to be approved by the Assembly ([Dem.] 59.89).[7] At a certain point,[8] the requirement of a second vote of ratification at the next meeting of the assembly was added, for which there had to be a quorum of 6,000 ([Dem.] 59.89).[9] The laws also stipulated that anyone who wished could bring a prosecution for illegal proposal (*graphē paranomōn*) if they thought that a particular naturalization decree was unconstitutional; the matter would then be handed to the courts to be settled ([Dem.] 59.90–91).[10] The fact that half of all known *graphai paranomōn* contest honorary decrees (including citizenship grants) demonstrates that such prosecutions did occur with some frequency.[11] In addition, the very real risk of being prosecuted presumably would have discouraged many citizens from proposing grants of naturalization in the first place, even if they felt a particular candidate was worthy.

Once an individual was naturalized, he was enrolled in a deme (which automatically carried with it enrollment in a tribe), as well as in a phratry.[12] The naturalized citizen was likely introduced to his new deme by a sponsor belonging to that deme, probably the same individual who had proposed the decree granting him citizenship. Quite likely, this same sponsor also introduced the naturalized citizen into his own phratry.[13] In the case of mass grants of citizenship, on the other hand, recipients were assigned by the city to demes and tribes but did not enter phratries.[14] Mass grants[15] were made to the Plataian refugees in 427 BCE (Osborne D1; [Dem.] 59.94–106);[16] the slaves, metics, and other foreigners manning the ships at Arginousai in 406/5 BCE (Osborne T10); the Samians

[7] See M. J. Osborne 1983, 155–61; Kapparis 1999, 363–67.

[8] M. J. Osborne argues that this procedure of a second vote was introduced between 388 and 369/8 BCE (1983, 161); Kapparis 1999, 363 suggests the 380s. A third step—a judicial scrutiny—was introduced c. 318 BCE (M. J. Osborne 1983, 164–67), after the period with which this book is concerned.

[9] See M. J. Osborne 1983, 161–64; Kapparis 1999, 363–67.

[10] See Hansen 1974, 28–65; Yunis 1988; Kapparis 1999, 367–71.

[11] Hansen 1974, 62 and 1991, 211.

[12] I generally use male pronouns in this chapter, since we know next to nothing about the naturalization of individual women in Athens (see, e.g., the discussion of Arkhippe below).

[13] On the means of implementing grants of citizenship, see M. J. Osborne 1983, 171–73.

[14] See M. J. Osborne 1983, 181–83.

[15] M. J. Osborne 1983, category E (202–4).

[16] See Kapparis 1995 for a defense of the authenticity of the decree in [Dem.] 59.104, and an explanation for the discrepancies between the decree and what Apollodoros says in the rest of the text. For the interpretation that the decree is a forgery, see Canevaro 2010, with bibliography.

in 405 BCE (Osborne D4–5); and (some of) the heroes of Phyle in 401/0 BCE (Osborne D6).

Grants to individuals, however, were considerably more common than those to groups. Naturalized individuals included, for example, foreign kings and statesmen securing Athenian interests, and those who sought Athenian citizenship for the protection it offered (for example, refugees, or people betraying their city to Athens).[17] Foreign scholars and artists were also occasionally granted citizenship.[18] Finally, some individuals were naturalized who already lived in Athens and wished to take up citizenship.[19] This last category included figures like the younger Pericles, son of Pericles and the *hetaira* Aspasia, whom Pericles naturalized after his legitimate sons died (see chapter 6).[20] It also included freed slaves,[21] foremost among whom were slave-bankers.[22] Because of the vast quantities of money such individuals acquired in their line of work, they were able to aid the polis financially, thereby demonstrating *andragathia* and essentially buying their own enfranchisement. The most famous freedmen-citizens in Athens were the bankers Pasion and Phormion (see also chapter 2).[23] Pasion earned citizenship through his benefactions (*euergesiai*) to the state ([Dem.] 59.2), and after acquiring citizenship he gave the state one thousand shields and served five times as trierarch (Dem. 45.85).[24] Phormion likewise used his money to supply funds to the state (Dem. 36.56–57), and, like Pasion, after attaining the status of citizen continued to perform services as part of the liturgical class (Dem. 21.157), including serving as trierarch twice.[25]

The *anagrapheus* Nikomakhos (on whom see also chapter 2) may also have been a freedman-citizen. After all, he is said to have "become a citizen from a slave" (*anti ... doulou politēs*) (Lys. 30.27). If we are to take the speaker literally, and believe that Nikomakhos was in fact born a *doulos*, we have to assume that he was at some point freed, and either

---

[17] M. J. Osborne 1983, category A (187–92) and category B (192–94).

[18] M. J. Osborne 1983, category D (200–202).

[19] M. J. Osborne 1983; category C (194–200).

[20] On the naturalization of the younger Pericles, see M. J. Osborne 1983, T5 and Carawan 2008.

[21] See Gauthier 1974 for a critique of the idea that Rome is "generous," Greece "greedy," with respect to the naturalization of freed slaves. Cf. Dio 15.7, in which a slave says: "Do you not know the law they have at Athens and in many other states as well, which does not allow the slave by nature to enjoy the rights of citizenship [*metekhein tēs politeias*]?"

[22] Davies 1981, 65; M. J. Osborne 1983, 196; E. E. Cohen 1991 and 1992. The literary record preserves mention of other enfranchised bankers (Din. 1.43; Dem. 36.29, 50; 45.63), but it is impossible to tell whether they were ex-slaves or freeborn metics before their naturalization (see also Trevett 1992, 161).

[23] On Pasion's naturalization, see Dem. 46.15; [Dem.] 59.2. On Phormion's naturalization, see Dem. 46.13; cf. Dem. 36.47.

[24] Trevett 1992, 6, argues that Pasion could have given the shields while still a metic, but must have been a trierarch after he was naturalized.

[25] That he was trierarch twice is attested epigraphically: *IG* II² 1623.246–48; *IG* II² 1629.647–49.

simultaneously or subsequently made a citizen. Nikomakhos is explicitly said to be a citizen: not only in the passage just cited, but also when he is called "the only one of the citizens [*politōn*]" to dare to extend his term (30.5). In addition, he is said to be a member of a phratry, albeit entering his phratry late.[26] Nikomakhos's lawful possession of citizenship, therefore, was probably not in doubt. If the speaker thought that Nikomakhos was unjustly posing as a citizen, he would have prosecuted him in a more effective way (e.g., in a *graphē xenias*).

One complication in defining the legal status of naturalized citizens is that many did not actually exercise their citizen rights in Athens. In fact, the practice of offering honorary citizenship became increasingly frequent over time, as Athenian citizenship became less valuable and as Athens began to seek foreign allies.[27] In a sense, then, we can envision two relatively distinct subgroups of naturalized citizens in the classical period: those like Pasion and Phormion, who lived in Athens and were very much involved in the day-to-day affairs of the city; and others, like foreign kings or statesmen, for whom citizenship was purely nominal. I will focus here on the status of the former type, those with "active" citizenship, rather than the latter, whose citizenship was in a sense "passive." Moreover, since naturalized citizens possessed many of the same rights and duties as the natural-born citizen (see chapter 10), I will touch only briefly here on the things they shared in common, which will receive more detailed treatment below. Like natural-born citizens, they could own property; they had power over their own and others' labor; they could punish others; and they had full rights in judicial proceedings. They could also bequeath their estates to their descendants, who were generally naturalized along with their fathers.[28]

If naturalized citizens were not already married at the time of their naturalization, they could then marry a citizen woman. But if they were already married prior to naturalization, their wives were probably fellow noncitizens (especially in the fourth century, when marriage between citizens and noncitizens was illegal). One might reasonably ask what happened to the status of these wives, if anything, when their husbands were naturalized. Did they become citizens too? If not, was their marriage now invalid? The debate on these questions rests in part on the interpretation of the status of Arkhippe, wife of Pasion, whom Pasion betrothed in his will to Phormion; at that point, Phormion was not yet

---

[26] For the view that phratry membership was not necessary for citizenship, see, e.g., Harrison 1968, 64, who cites [Arist.] *Ath. Pol.*'s silence on phratry membership as a requirement for deme entry (42.1). For the view that it was, see, e.g., Lambert 1993, 31–43. In any event, it is safe to say that most, if not all, citizens were enrolled in phratries.

[27] See M. J. Osborne 1981–1983; cf. Oliver 2007.

[28] M. J. Osborne 1983, 151–52 posits that the extension of citizenship to descendants of naturalized citizens became automatic around 385/4 BCE (along with the renewal of Pericles's citizenship law).

naturalized. Scholars' views are split on this issue: some assert that the wife's status was ambiguous and determined by whomever she happened to be married to,[29] whereas others believe that naturalization did not affect the wife's status at all.[30] Either way, it seems indisputable that pinning down her status was not a huge priority for Athenian law, probably because it had little bearing on the status of her children.

While naturalized citizens could not ascend any higher on the status ladder than "made citizen" (*dēmopoiētos*), their descendants could qualify as full-fledged citizens provided that they were born to an Athenian mother ([Dem.] 59.92). However, as M. J. Osborne has pointed out, not very many children of naturalized citizens would have qualified for full-fledged citizenship on these grounds, since their fathers, by the time they were naturalized, were most likely already married to a noncitizen woman.[31]

Downward mobility (of a sort) was also possible, in that naturalization offered to noncitizens was sometimes quickly revoked or never enacted. We see this, for example, when the orator Hyperides, after the battle of Chaeronea (338 BCE)—in order to arm as many men as possible in defense of the weakened polis—proposed a decree recalling exiles, restoring civic rights to disenfranchised citizens, freeing all slaves who had participated in the battle, and granting citizenship to metics (*tous metoikous politas poiēsthai*) (Plut. *Mor.* 849a).[32] After the Assembly passed the decree (Lycurg. 1.41), an orator named Aristogeiton indicted Hyperides in a *graphē paranomōn*.[33] Hyperides could not deny the legal substance of Aristogeiton's charge—that is, he acknowledged that his decree violated existing statutes—but in the end he was acquitted, convincing the jury with his argument that desperate times called

[29] Whitehead 1986a argues that because Arkhippe was left a *sunoikia* (apartment building) in Pasion's will, and because only citizens could own property, she must have been considered a citizen; and that the statement in Dem. 46.23 that Phormion should have entered his claim for Arkhippe as *epiklēros* (heiress) before the eponymous archon if she was a citizen, but before the polemarch if she was an alien, seems to imply that Arkhippe could be *either* a citizen or a metic, or both by turns. (But cf. Carey 1991, who responds that Pasion may have bestowed the *sunoikia* with a view to sale, not for Arkhippe to own, and that Dem. 46.23 may simply reflect both the general and the specific procedures open to Phormion, rather than implying that Arkhippe could be claimed in either of the two ways.) Like Whitehead, E. E. Cohen 1992, 102–10 also argues that Arkhippe had an ambiguous status, "neither exclusively an Athenian citizen nor exclusively an alien" (105; see also E. E. Cohen 1991, 254).

[30] See M. J. Osborne 1983, 150–54; Carey 1991; Kapparis 1999, 203, 374. Carey 1991 puts forward the following argument for Arkhippe's (unchanging) metic status (and by extension the status of any naturalized citizen's wife): since she had a large dowry, she could have easily found a citizen husband if she had been legally permitted to marry one; Pasion was unconcerned that Arkhippe, still of childbearing age when married off to Phormion, might bear "mixed-status" children; and the rules of eligibility for archonships and priesthoods state that descendants of naturalized citizens were not eligible unless born from a citizen mother ([Dem.] 59.92), implying that the wives of naturalized citizens were not automatically enfranchised.

[31] M. J. Osborne 1983, 174.

[32] Cf. Hyp. fr. 29 Jensen; Lycurg. 1.36, 41; Dio Chrys. 15.21.

[33] On Aristogeiton's indictment of Hyperides, see Hansen 1974, 36–37.

for desperate measures.[34] By this point, however, the gravest danger facing the city had passed (the Athenians had already made peace with Philip), and so the decree never took effect (Dio Chrys. 15.21).

Naturalized citizens, although they shared most of the privileges and duties of natural-born citizens in the sacral, political, and military spheres, differed in a few important respects. Thus, for example, at least as early as 427 BCE (and maybe earlier), a naturalized citizen could not hold an Athenian priesthood[35] or any of the nine archonships ([Dem.] 59.92).[36] His sons, however, faced no limitations on the priesthoods they could hold, provided that they were born from an Athenian citizen mother (ibid.).[37] Moreover, in ca. 334 BCE certain phratries, probably ones with hereditary priesthoods, became closed to naturalized citizens.[38] Apart from these restrictions, however, the naturalized citizen was nearly indistinguishable from the natural-born citizen in his opportunities for the performance of civic roles.[39]

In fact, I would argue that the primary way in which naturalized citizens in Athens were distinguished from natural-born citizens was their *social* status. The citizen was a *politēs* or *astos*; the made citizen was a *dēmopoiētos*.[40] Lurking in the very name of this status group was a difference, reflecting the fact that the people of Athens had *made* him what he was. A paradigmatic example of the prejudices facing the naturalized citizen can be found in Apollodoros, son of Pasion. Since Apollodoros was a minor at the time of his father's naturalization, he was already a citizen by the time he came of age. If, however, his mother Arkhippe remained a noncitizen (see debate above), he would have faced the same legal disabilities as someone naturalized as an adult (namely, restriction from priesthoods and archonships). Nonetheless, Apollodoros did remarkably well for himself in all respects. He was chosen by lot as a member of the Boule, passing the scrutiny (*dokimasia*) and swearing the customary oath ([Dem.] 59.3). He married a woman from a reputable family ([Dem.]

---

[34] Hyp. fr. 28 Jensen; Rutil. 1.19.

[35] Kapparis 1999, 373 suggests that Apollodoros may be exaggerating, and that it is only *hereditary* priesthoods that are not open to naturalized citizens.

[36] On this passage, see Kapparis 1999 *ad loc.* M. J. Osborne 1983, 174–76 posits that this restriction may have been part of the Periclean citizenship law; but cf. Kapparis 1999, 372.

[37] Political rights for the children of naturalized citizens may have become more restricted in the late fourth century: M. J. Osborne 1983, 173–76 interprets [Arist.] *Ath. Pol.* 55.3—on qualifications for holding office (including being asked "who is your father, who is your father's father, etc.")—as meaning that in the Lycurgan period, candidates for archonships had to demonstrate three generations of Athenian birth on both sides. But cf. Kapparis 1999, 372–73.

[38] M. J. Osborne 1983, 176 argues for this date based on the fact that a new clause appears in citizenship decrees at this point. On the restrictions in phratry entry, see M. J. Osborne 1983, 176–81.

[39] See Farenga 2006 on citizenship as a performance.

[40] The naturalized citizen was also referred to as *ho politēs poiētos* ("made citizen") or *ho kata psēphisma politēs* ("citizen by decree").

59.2),[41] and accumulated over forty talents by renting out his father's factory and bank and collecting debts due to Pasion (Dem. 36.36–38). Finally, he performed a number of liturgies, serving as trierarch or syntrierarch (funding warships) at least three times and as *khorēgos* (funding choruses) in the boys' dithyramb contest at the Dionysia, and paying one *proeisphora* (a special tax on the richest citizens).[42]

However, in spite of his achievements, the fact of his base origins haunted him.[43] As a naturalized citizen, Apollodoros felt he had to work harder to prove himself equal to his fellow citizens. Thus, for instance, he says in one speech:

> The things concerning the city and however many things concern you, I do as lavishly as I can, as you know; for I am not ignorant of that fact that for you, citizens by birth [*tois . . . genei politais*], it is sufficient to perform liturgies as the laws demand, but it is fitting for us, made citizens [*poiētous*], to show that we perform them as a way of giving back thanks [*apodidontes kharin*]. (Dem. 45.78)[44]

Self-conscious statements of this sort stem from Apollodoros's fear of seeming to take for granted his family's receipt of citizenship. And for good reason: accusations like this were in fact frequently leveled, both against him and against others (see, e.g., Dem. 45.47). Making lavish contributions to the state—and especially reminding his listeners of these contributions[45]—was therefore a material way of showing his thanks to the polis. It was also a way of proving his suitability for citizen status, in keeping with his displays of knowledge of Athenian military, ritual, and legal matters.[46]

Ironically, however, it was precisely because of his financial and political engagement in the city that Apollodoros attracted negative attention.[47] Thus in one instance, the citizen Polykles, after neglecting to relieve Apollodoros of his trierachic duties, merely laughs off Apollodoros's extra expenses and says, using what was apparently a current aphorism,[48] "The mouse has just tasted the pitch: for he wanted to be an

---

[41] See Davies 1971, 11672 X: "a well-off but rather shadowy family."

[42] Serving as (syn)trierarch in 368/7 ([Dem.] 53.5); at some time between 374 and 366/5 (*IG II²* 1609.83–89); in 362–360 ([Dem.] 50 *passim*); in 356 (*IG II²* 1612.110). Serving as *khorēgos* in the boys' dithyramb at the Dionysia of 352/1 (*IG II²* 3039). Paying the *proeisphora* in 362 ([Dem.] 50.8–10). See Trevett 1992, 39n23 and Davies 1971, 11672 XII.

[43] For psychological readings of Apollodoros, see M. J. Osborne 1983, 48n126, 196; Trevett 1992, 160; Cartledge 2002, 170.

[44] See also [Dem.] 53.18, in which Apollodoros proposes a fine of one talent rather than the death penalty for his opponent so that no one can say that a "citizen by decree" caused an Athenian's death.

[45] For a critique of Apollodoros's bragging, see, e.g., Dem. 36.41.

[46] For military, see, e.g., [Dem.] 50.4–6; for ritual, see, e.g., [Dem.] 59.74–76; for legal, see, e.g., [Dem.] 59.15. See also Lape 2010, 216–39, who argues that this is part of Apollodoros's larger strategy of reframing "citizen" identity as being about one's character, rather than one's birth.

[47] See also Trevett 1992, 177–78.

[48] A proverbial expression, seen also in Theocr. 14.51 and Herod. 2.63. Cf. Diogenian. 2.64.

Athenian" ([Dem.] 50.26). That is, like the overambitious mouse, Apollodoros had gotten himself stuck in a pitch-pot. In fact, Jeremy Trevett argues that Apollodoros's naturalized-citizen status—rather than his servile birth or commercial background—was the most important source of prejudice against him.[49] It is hard to tell, however, whether Apollodoros necessarily faced more discrimination for his *dēmopoiētos* status than for his slave ancestry. We have no preserved attacks on Apollodoros's slave origins on the same scale as his attacks on Phormion (see chapter 4)—but it is precisely from such attacks on Phormion that Apollodoros betrays his consciousness of his own slave ancestry. Put another way, Apollodoros's condemnation of other slaves (or ex-slaves) was a means of distancing himself from his own servile roots. A similar motivation may underlie what Trevett calls Apollodoros's "enthusiasm" for judicial slave torture.[50] This double standard did not go unnoticed. An anonymous pleader for Phormion points out the hypocrisy of Apollodoros—a slave's son—attacking others for their servility (Dem.36.48). In the end, Apollodoros's attempts to gain truly equal footing with full-fledged citizens failed—as, presumably, did those of other naturalized citizens who tried to act "too much like a citizen by birth."[51]

[49] Trevett 1992, 177.

[50] Trevett 1992, 175 cites Dem. 45.61; 49.52, 55; 52.22; 59.120–25.

[51] Lape 2010, 217, in the context of arguing that the prejudice against naturalized citizens only became manifest when they acted in this way.

CHAPTER 9

FULL CITIZENS: FEMALE

I HAVE CHOSEN TO DEVOTE AN ENTIRE CHAPTER TO THE STATUS OF FEMALE citizens (but not to, say, female metics) because female citizenship is sufficiently different from male citizenship to warrant a distinct status category.[1] That is, female citizens are less equal to male citizens than female slaves are to male slaves, female ex-slaves to male, female metics to male, and so on.[2] However, to avoid treating all women in Athens as an "undifferentiated mass,"[3] I will distinguish between different types of female citizens as appropriate below. One of the most distinctive attributes of Athenian women is that although they were citizens (as I will argue), they were also under the supervision of a *kurios* or guardian.[4] As girls, they were under the guardianship of their fathers, and when they married, they entered the guardianship of their husbands. This much is certain, but the precise degree of control the *kurios* had over women and girls is less clear, as we will see.

The question of the power that citizen women had over property is a vexed one. Scholarly discussion of this question often centers on the interpretation of a law found in Isaeus, stating that women (and children) cannot contract for the disposal (*sumballein*)[5] of anything above the value of a *medimnos* (bushel) of barley (Is. 10.10), a measure that was worth approximately three drachmas in the early fourth century BCE. Some scholars have taken this to mean that Athenian women could *never* dispose of more than a *medimnos*;[6] others have taken it to mean that they could, but only through a *kurios*;[7] and yet others (a view with which I agree) have argued that although de jure they were not permitted to dispose of property beyond this value, de facto they could, through vari-

---

[1] On the legal and social status of Athenian women, see, e.g., Gould 1980; Just 1989, ch. 3; Sealey 1990, ch. 2; Cantarella 2009; and many others.

[2] On gender distinctions as more important for citizens than for other statuses, see Todd 1997, 114.

[3] For this phrase, see Pomeroy 1975, 60. On different types of women in ancient Greece, see Pomeroy 1975; see also, more recently, Gilhuly 2009, who traces three ideological categories of woman in the Athenian imagination: prostitute, wife, ritual agent.

[4] On the *kurios*, see, e.g., Harrison 1968, 30–32, 109–15; MacDowell 1978, 83–86; Schaps 1979, ch. 4; Todd 1995, 207–10.

[5] See Wyse 1904 *ad loc.* on the general term *sumballein*, which "covers every kind of contract, purchase and sale, letting and hiring, lending and borrowing, bailment . . . , exchange, partnership, suretyship, etc."

[6] See de Ste. Croix 1970; Sealey 1990, 37–38.

[7] See, e.g., Harrison 1968, 114; Schaps 1979, 54–55.

ous means.[8] In any case, women's expenditures in the ritual sphere—for example, making dedications to the gods—do not seem to have been constrained by this law.[9]

However, even if this law prevented women from entering into contracts, regardless of whether the law was actually followed in practice, it did not necessarily prevent women from *acquiring* property.[10] So, for example, a woman might acquire property through inheritance. The *epiklēros* (conventionally if somewhat misleadingly translated "heiress"),[11] since she had no brothers, "inherited" the entire estate of her father, in the sense that it was "attached to" (*epi*) her. She held on to the estate until she was claimed in marriage by her closest (willing) relative on her father's side; this man then controlled the income from the property and paid for her maintenance out of it. The property was eventually inherited by her sons when they came of age. Apart from the *epiklēros*, other women in the circle of heirs (*ankhisteia*)—which included not daughters but sisters, cousins, aunts, etc.—could inherit from their deceased relatives (Is. 7.20–22, 11.1–3; Dem. 43.51).[12] Another way of acquiring property was through gifts, whether of clothing or jewelry or other moveable goods; often these were given to a woman when she got married (Is. 2.9, 8.8). However, although women could do with this property whatever they wished, if their *kurioi* wanted to intervene in some manner (say, selling off their jewelry), they had only limited means of redress.[13] Yet a third type of property "received" by women was the dowry (*proix*).[14] Dowries generally came with young women when they married, and if they got divorced, the dowry returned to their fathers, or if their fathers were dead, to the closest male kin acting as *kurios*. During the marriage, however, the dowry was (at least nominally) under the management of the husband, who presumably could do what he wished with any interest it generated.

Did women *own* the various types of property they acquired? The answer to this question depends in part on how one defines "ownership." If it is defined narrowly as the power to alienate property,[15] women (according to the law cited in Is. 10.10) clearly were not able

---

[8] See, e.g., Foxhall 1989. That women could de facto dispense with money is indicated by the presence of female moneylenders: Harris 1992 (on a *horos* inscription); D. Cohen 1998 (on Dem. 41).

[9] See, e.g., Schaps 1979, 71–73; Goff 2004, 69–76. On the involvement of priestesses in the city's financial transactions, see Goff 2004, 64–69.

[10] For one interpretation of women's acquisition of property, see Schaps 1979, ch. 2.

[11] On the *epiklēros*, see, e.g., MacDowell 1978, 95–98; Schaps 1979, ch. 3; Todd 1995, 228–231; C. Patterson 1998, 91–106.

[12] On women in Greek inheritance law, see Schaps 1975; Just 1989, ch. 5; Cox 1998.

[13] Harrison 1968, 112.

[14] On the dowry, see Harrison 1968, 45–60; MacDowell 1978, 87–88; Schaps 1979, ch. 4 and appendices I–IV; Foxhall 1989, 32–39; Todd 1995, 215–16.

[15] See, e.g., Harrison 1968, 202 with n1, based on an interpretation of Arist. *Rhet.* 1361a21. On this basis, he calls women's property "quasi-property" (1968, 112–13).

to own property.[16] Lin Foxhall, however, has argued that this definition of ownership is too narrow in the case of classical Athens. The power to alienate, she says, rather than being synonymous with ownership, was instead only *one* of various ways, including management and use, in which a person could be said to own something.[17] Moreover, because property in effect belonged to households rather than to private individuals, women, as a part of the household, inevitably exercised this broadly defined "ownership."[18] Raphael Sealey, in turn, prefers a "negative definition" of ownership: namely, having property to which all others are denied access.[19] By either of these definitions, a woman technically owned her dowry and anything else she acquired, even if she did not have the right to dispose of it directly. Exercising her rights of ownership was a different story: it seems to have been easier to do so within the context of the household than in the public sphere. It is in fact in the former context that we find various women in our sources (see especially Dem. 41) making financial transactions and owning large sums of money.[20]

Since there was a societal expectation that Athenian women would do the weaving in their households, in one sense women did not have control over their labor: it was prescribed for them. However, women did choose *how* they performed this labor, including what products they fashioned and with what materials, and a more skilled weaver presumably garnered more respect than a less skilled one. Poorer citizen women worked outside the home (e.g., as wetnurses, vegetable sellers, and woolworkers) and were in charge of their own labor to the extent that, unlike slaves, they did not have masters.[21] This work, however, was nonetheless stigmatized as servile. Thus in one lawcourt speech (Dem. 57), the defendant Euxitheos has been struck from his deme's rolls for allegedly being of noncitizen stock. One piece of evidence leveled by his opponent is that his mother was a ribbon seller and a wetnurse, with the implication being that she was not a citizen. In his defense, Euxitheos argues that poverty drives even Athenian citizen women to work outside the home.[22]

[16] For the view that women could not own property, see, e.g., de Ste. Croix 1970, 277; Schaps 1979.

[17] Foxhall 1989 and 1996, 142–43. The fact that a woman could divorce her husband and take the dowry with her, Foxhall argues, means that she in effect had veto power over her husband's decisions about the disposal of the dowry (1989, 37–38).

[18] Foxhall 1989. She is responding in part to Schaps 1979 (esp. ch. 1), who argues that there are two types of property ownership in Athenian law: 1) property belonging to the household and controlled by the head of the household; and 2) property belonging to the head of the household alone (that is, private ownership).

[19] Sealey 1990, 45–48.

[20] Foxhall 1989; Hunter 1989a; Cox 1998. Specifically in the context of Dem. 41: D. Cohen 1998, 61; de Ste. Croix 1970, 276. See also Johnstone 2003, who argues that women were hindered in their control of property because they were not part of the "systems of surveillance" characteristic of Athenian public life.

[21] On women's labor in Athens, see Brock 1994.

[22] For an examination of Dem. 57 from this perspective, see D. Cohen 1998; Lape 2010, 203–16.

The question of women's power over their movement has long been the subject of debate. In the nineteenth and early twentieth centuries, scholars generally assumed that the Greeks practiced a sort of "Oriental seclusion," locking women up within their houses.[23] Although Athenian *ideology* does indeed hold that women remained in the house, scholars now believe that for most women, leaving the house was in fact necessary—whether to work (if the family was poor),[24] or to run errands (in addition to or instead of household slaves), or to attend religious festivals or funerals.[25] Moreover, we find depictions of women gossiping or gathering together at water fountains in Greek literature and art, and while these may often be depictions of what men *imagined* went on among women, there is no reason to think that women did not congregate to chat with each other. Women were, however, generally veiled in public, granting them a degree of invisibility vis-à-vis men outside their households.[26]

There is debate, too, about the extent to which women and men were kept separate *within* the house. While many literary sources seem to suggest that there were distinct men's (*andrōnitis*) and women's (*gunaikōnitis*) quarters in the house, other evidence—both literary (e.g., Lys. 1) and especially archaeological—indicates that the division of space may not have been as strictly defined in practice as in ideology.[27] Put another way, the terms *andrōnitis* and *gunaikōnitis* designated fluid social spaces rather than physically defined spaces. Lisa Nevett has plausibly suggested, for example, that the term *gunaikōnitis* may refer to the parts of the house occupied by women when (non-kin) male visitors came to the house, thus temporarily "segregating" women in order to restrict contact between male outsiders and the citizen women of the house.[28]

Women had the power to punish the household's slaves both verbally and corporally. Like male citizens (see chapter 10), they too had bodily inviolability.[29] Assault of a woman, sexual or otherwise, constituted *hubris*, an offense prosecutable with a *graphē*.[30] There was, however, one circumstance in which a citizen woman could be physically punished: if she was a known adulteress who then took part in public sacrifices, any Athenian who wished could assault her ([Dem.] 59.86).

---

[23] This view was first questioned, if not entirely contradicted, by Gomme 1925.

[24] See Brock 1994 on working women as an exception to the ideology of "female seclusion."

[25] See, e.g., Just 1989, ch. 6 and especially the work of David Cohen: see, e.g., D. Cohen 1989 and 1991a, ch. 6.

[26] See Llewellyn-Jones 2003, who compares the Greek veil to a portable house.

[27] See, e.g., Jameson 1990a and 1990b; Nevett 1994, 1995, 1999; Antonaccio 2000; Ault and Nevett 2005, 160–63; Morgan 2010, ch. 5.

[28] See Nevett 1994, 1995, 1999; see also Antonaccio 2000, 532.

[29] Schaps 1998, 167–77 argues that this is one of the many ways in which Athenian women were freer than slaves. I would add that it also distinguished them from noncitizens.

[30] On *hubris* and sexual violence, see D. Cohen 1991b and 1995, ch. 7; Omitowoju 2002, esp. ch. 1.

However, since the adulteress essentially belonged in the category of (unconvicted) *atimoi* (see chapter 8),[31] this punishment was inflicted on her as a quasi-*atimos* rather than as a full citizen.

For the most part, scholars agree that women could not testify in court.[32] Michael Gagarin has correctly argued, however, that women's testimony could nonetheless be invoked in various ways: for example, through women's evidentiary oaths, which were sworn outside of court, and by women's testimony cited or quoted within the narrative portion of a speech.[33] Despite these restrictions on testifying in court, however, female citizens could in some circumstances serve as plaintiffs or defendants. We know, for instance, that female plaintiffs could claim inheritances in court through their *kurios* (Is. 3.2–3, 7.2; Dem. 43.9).[34] Moreover, citizen women, represented by their *kurios*, could apparently be defendants in trials where the penalty was death (Ant. 1; Dem. 57.8),[35] though it is unclear whether any of these women (unlike noncitizen female defendants) actually appeared in person.[36]

Even with these judicial limitations, Foxhall has argued if we define "law" broadly (as, she says, the Greeks did), we see that there are a number of ways in which female citizens were engaged in the legal process: for example, their legal status might be called into question; various aspects of their lives were governed by laws; and many court cases between men began as disputes between or involving women.[37] I would add, as well, that although women could not serve on juries, they might have influenced (directly or indirectly) how their husbands voted in court (see, e.g., [Dem.] 59.110–11), thus affecting the outcome of trials.

Citizen women faced both privileges and limitations in the area of family.[38] After 451/0 BCE (with a few exceptions) they could produce citizen offspring only through marriage with a male citizen (on this debate, see chapter 6). This marriage could take one of two forms (Is. 6.14).[39] In the more common form of marriage, the girl was first betrothed to her intended (in a procedure called *enguē*, arranged by the intended and the girl's father); she was then handed over to him and he became her

[31] Todd 1995, 279; Kapparis 1999, 357; Glazebrook 2005, 47.

[32] For a review of bibliography on this question, see Todd 1990, 26n12. See also Goldhill 1994, 357; Todd 1995, 208; Gagarin 1998.

[33] See Gagarin 1998.

[34] See Sealey 1990, 43–44; Todd 1995, 208.

[35] Sealey 1990, 49; Todd 1995, 208.

[36] So, e.g., Gagarin 1998, 40 argues, on the basis of deictic pronouns, that the stepmother accused of homicide in Ant. 1 was not present in court.

[37] Foxhall 1996, 140–49.

[38] On women's rights in the area of the family (including marriage and succession), see, e.g., Lacey 1968; MacDowell 1978, ch. 6; Just 1989, ch. 4 and 5; Pomeroy 1997; C. Patterson 1998 (esp. ch. 4 on democratic Athens); Cox 1998.

[39] On Athenian marriage and divorce, see Todd 1995, 210–16; Mirhady 2010.

new *kurios* (in a procedure called *ekdosis*). Since the woman was essentially the object of a contract, rather than a party to it, Sealey speaks of the "legal passivity" of women in marriage.[40] The less common form of marriage involved the *epiklēros*, whose marriage to a close relative (see above) had to be ratified by a court hearing (*epidikasia*). It was generally the case, though not required, that a girl be given in marriage with a dowry; if there was no dowry, the validity of her marriage was viewed with suspicion (Is. 3.28–29). It has been argued that if a family were too poor to provide a dowry for their daughter, she might be given as a *pallakē* (concubine),[41] but I imagine this was uncommon, since the children of such a union would probably not have been citizens (see again chapter 6).

A number of measures were in place in the event that a marriage ended. If a husband died, his widow was faced with a couple of options: she could remain in the *oikos* of her late husband and have his heir as her new *kurios*, or she could return to the *oikos* of her original *kurios* (or if he was no longer alive, her closest male kin). If she had no children, she was compelled to take the second option. If she returned to her original *kurios*, the latter (or her late husband, via a will or on his deathbed) could marry her off to a new husband.[42] Finally, if a woman with children died, her children inherited her dowry (Dem. 40.14, 50), but if she did not have children, the dowry returned to her original *kurios* (Is. 3.36).

Marriages could also end in divorce, in which case the wife returned to her original *kurios*, along with her dowry. Divorce could be initiated by the husband (through a procedure called *apopempsis*); by the wife (*apoleipsis*); or even by her original *kurios* (*aphairesis*), provided that she was still childless (Dem. 41.4). If a woman was caught in adultery, her husband was compelled to divorce her, and she was stripped of various civic rights ([Dem.] 59.85–86). In any of these scenarios, if the woman's ex-husband did not return her dowry, he could be prosecuted with a *dikē proikos* (private lawsuit for a dowry), and if he was unable to pay back the entire dowry, he could pay interest on it as a form of alimony; if he did not pay the interest, he could be prosecuted with a *dikē sitou* (private lawsuit for maintenance) for failing to support her.

Since the citizen woman was basically at the pinnacle of the status ladder allowed to her gender, upward mobility was nearly impossible. But we might think, for instance, of the lower-class female citizen who had to work as a ribbon-seller for a living: if she happened to marry a wealthy man (unlikely but not impossible), she could rise in social status. A woman who took up a prominent priesthood would also see a rise

---

[40] Sealey 1990, 28.
[41] Sealey 1984.
[42] On the status of Athenian widows, see Hunter 1989b; Cudjoe 2010, chs. 2–5.

in status.[43] Downward mobility was also possible, if uncommon. So, for example, a citizen woman could be partially disenfranchised, as in the case of the adulteress (see above). She could also be enslaved, although this was nearly impossible in classical Athens. A Solonian law preserved in Plut. *Sol.* 23.2 states that a man could sell (*pōlein*) his unmarried daughter or sister if he found that she was no longer a virgin, which seems to imply that she could be sold into slavery. Allison Glazebrook, however, has reasonably reinterpreted this passage as meaning that the unchaste girl could be prostituted.[44] In either case, her punishment would represent a profound decrease in status.

One of women's most significant roles in Athens was in the realm of religion.[45] At least for some female citizens, this role began in childhood. In a famous passage of Aristophanes's *Lysistrata*, the chorus of women describes the services they took on from a young age: serving as *arrhēphoroi* (a word of uncertain etymology possibly meaning "carriers of secret objects") for Athena at the age of seven; grinding barley for Athena's sacred cakes at the age of ten; at some point thereafter, wearing yellow robes in the festival of the Arkteia for Brauronian Artemis;[46] and, finally, wearing dried figs and carrying baskets in the Panathenaia as *kanēphoroi* ("basket carriers") (Aristoph. *Lys.* 641–47). These roles, however, were honorific and performed by only a small number of girls in the city: for example, only two *arrhēphoroi* were chosen per year "on the basis of good birth" (*di' eugeneian*) (Harp. s.v. *arrhēphorein*).[47] Already of high status, these girls garnered further honor (both for themselves and their families) by undergoing rites on behalf of all the girls of the city.

In adulthood, there were a number of different ways in which women could engage in ritual practices. All female citizens, unless stripped of their rights, could participate in women's festivals like the Thesmophoria (honoring Demeter and Persephone) and Adonia (mourning the death of Adonis).[48] While the agency of women in these contexts inevitably caused some anxiety among men, the festivals were also deemed necessary to promote fertility and the procreation of a new generation of citizens. Some women were chosen to serve as *archousai* ("women leaders"), the female equivalent of the male *archontes* ("leaders," i.e., magistrates),

[43] See Goff 2004, 185–93 and Connelly 2007, ch. 7 on the special privileges and honors given to priestesses.

[44] Glazebrook 2005 with bibliography.

[45] On the significance of women in civic religion, see most recently Dillon 2002; Cole 2004; Goff 2004; Connelly 2007; Reitzammer 2008.

[46] Sourvinou-Inwood 1988 has thoroughly investigated the Arkteia, describing it as a rite of passage before adulthood in which girls make their transition into female citizens.

[47] The process by which these girls were chosen is unclear: see Parker 2005, 220.

[48] On women's festivals, see Dillon 2002, pt. 2; Goff 2004, 203–20; on women's role in the Adonia, see Reitzammer 2008.

in overseeing particular festivals. Thus, in a speech of Isaeus, we hear that the wives of the members of a particular deme chose the speaker's mother, together with another woman, to preside (*archein*) at the Thesmophoria and carry out the ceremonies (Is. 8.19). Finally, select women could also serve as priestesses,[49] the most prominent in Athens being the priestesses of Athena Polias on the Acropolis and of Athena Nike. As mentioned above, women could attain social advancement through the honors and privileges granted to them in this capacity.

Athenian women could not hold any of the traditional "political" offices in the city, nor could they serve in the Ekklesia or Boule or on juries.[50] Moreover, unlike men, women were not enrolled in demes. The evidence for their role in phratries is a little less clear-cut: it is possible that some phratries required that women be *introduced* to, if not *enrolled* into, their father's or husband's phratries.[51] On the basis of this limited political involvement, some scholars have argued that Athenian women were not actually citizens, on the grounds that citizenship necessarily entails the right to participate in the political process of government.[52] Others have called their citizenship "passive" or "latent."[53] I prefer to think of their citizenship as *different* than male citizenship, a notion well explored by Cynthia Patterson. In an important article, she argues that in order to determine whether women were considered citizens, we have to look at the various terms the Athenians themselves used for citizenship.[54] In this way, she demonstrates that the term *Attikos* (feminine *Attikē*) indicates "a native relationship to the land and polis of Athens,"[55] whereas *Athēnaios* has a more public, political charge and is therefore used mostly of men. *Athēnaios*, she finds, is not used in the singular for women (since the name is reserved for the goddess Athena), but it does appear in the plural, *Athēnaiōn* (e.g., *IG* I³ 35). Like *Athēnaios*, *politēs* (the feminine *politis* is rare) has a political charge, denoting a member of the political community, whereas *astos* (feminine *astē*),

---

[49] For a comprehensive look at the priestess in Greek religion, see Connelly 2007. On selection of women for priesthoods, see Goff 2004, 174–85; Connelly 2007, ch. 2.

[50] On women's restricted role in politics, see, e.g., Just 1989, ch. 2.

[51] See Lambert 1983, 178–88 (cf. Gould 1980, 40–42, Pomeroy 1997, 75–82). The possibility that fathers could introduce (*eisagagein*) girls to their phratries is attested in only one classical source, and even in that case, the father is said *not* to have done so (Is. 3.76). The later grammarians attest to introduction (*eisēgen*; Poll. 8.107) and even enrollment (*engraphein*; Suda s.v. *Apatouria*) of both boys and girls. The evidence is slightly better, though still not definitive, for the introduction of women to their husbands' phratries at the *gamēlia* ("wedding feasts"; see Is. 3.76, 79; 8.18, 20; Dem. 57.43).

[52] Perhaps most famously Loraux 1993, 116–23; on p. 119: "There is no such thing as a 'female citizen.'" See also, e.g., Hedrick 1994, 299: "it must be emphasized that women were not citizens."

[53] "Passive": Sourvinou-Inwood 1988, 112; "Latent": Sealey 1990, 14, borrowed (but used slightly differently) by Goff 2004, 164. Cf. Cantarella, who says that women "had the *status*, but not the functions, of citizens" (2005, 245).

[54] C. Patterson 1986.

[55] C. Patterson 1986, 51.

like *Attikos*, refers to a community insider. Patterson concludes from this terminological study that the preferred use of *Attikē* and *astē* for women might reveal a different *type* of citizenship (or membership-in-the-city) for women than for men.[56] This distinctly "female citizenship" consisted of two main components: producing citizen offspring, especially after 451/0 BCE,[57] and playing an important role in civic religion, as described above.[58]

Proving female citizenship was slightly more difficult than proving male citizenship (see chapter 10), because (as mentioned above) women were not inscribed in the lists of phratries and demes. The best way to prove that a woman was a citizen was to summon witnesses who had been present at, and could therefore attest to, her birth to citizen parents, her lawful *enguē* to a male citizen by her *kurios*, and her marriage feast as part of a lawful union.[59] The testimony of these witnesses, however, could always be challenged, and often it was.[60] It was therefore less reliable than an inscribed record, though of course inscribed records could also be challenged or revised.

Athenian citizen women played no official role at all in the military sphere: they were never drafted to fight, nor did they volunteer. The idea of a female warrior was not totally unimaginable to the Athenians—after all, their patroness goddess Athena was a warrior—but such a role seems to have been reserved for divinities rather than mortal women. Nonetheless, the sex strike in Aristophanes's *Lysistrata*, however preposterous it might be, demonstrates that women were thought to care about, and even to have had an indirect influence on, military affairs.

Female citizens, then, held a status distinct from that of male citizens: through their production of citizen offspring and their participation in civic rituals, they played a role of great consequence for the city, albeit one of less importance than men's in terms of governance. Unlike men, who gained honor through public performance of their citizen rights and obligations (see chapter 10), women did so by remaining nearly invisible in all realms but the religious: as Pericles famously states in his Funeral Oration, women attain glory (*kleos*) if they are not spoken of (Thuc. 2.45.2). For other reasons, too, shares of glory or honor were not divided equally amongst female citizens. A wealthy woman, especially one who played a significant role in civic cult, had a much larger share

[56] For further study of the vocabulary of citizenship, see C. Patterson 2005, 268–70; Blok 2005; cf. R. Osborne 2011, 92–105. See also my Conclusion.

[57] On women's developed "citizen identity" after Pericles's citizenship law, see R. Osborne 1997.

[58] On female citizenship manifested in civic religion, see, e.g., Dillon 2002, pt. 1; Goff 2004, esp. ch. 3; D. Cohen 2005 (with Foxhall 2005).

[59] See Lape 2010, 90–91, with bibliography.

[60] On challenges to testimony of this sort, see Scafuro 1994.

of *timē* than did a poor woman who was compelled by her circumstances to work outside the home, and who was probably unlikely to be selected for a leadership role on the deme or polis level. A chaste married woman, moreover, accrued more societal honor than did one suspected of being an adulteress. We must be careful, then, not to view female citizens as a monolithic social status group.

CHAPTER 10

FULL CITIZENS: MALE

JUST AS WITH CHAPTER 9, I BEGIN THIS CHAPTER WITH A DISCLAIMER: I HAVE chosen to dedicate one chapter to male citizens, but in a sense this chapter could also have been split into multiple chapters. In theory, all male citizens were equal in legal status, but this was not the case in practice, and they were certainly not equal in social status. Within the status group of "male citizens," then, there was a range of sub-statuses, varying by wealth and age, among other factors.[1]

The process of integrating male citizens into the civic body began early. Within the first few years of their lives, boys were introduced to their fathers' phratries (Is. 8.19) on the third day of the Apatouria, a yearly festival (Schol. Aristoph. *Ach.* 146; cf. Andoc. 1.125–26). Fathers swore that their sons had been born in accordance with the laws, and a sacrificial victim, either a lamb or a sheep, was placed on an altar as an offering (probably called a *meion*). If the phratry members gave their assent, the animal was sacrificed and portions were shared out amongst them (Dem. 43.82). If, however, someone objected, this individual removed the sacrificial offering from the altar (Is. 6.22; cf. Dem. 43.14). It appears that, at least in some phratries, a second introduction occurred when a boy reached adolescence, with another animal sacrifice (probably called a *koureion*). Once again, the phratry members had to either give their assent or remove the sacrificial victim. If the phratry members gave their assent, the boy was at this point or shortly thereafter officially scrutinized (*IG* II² 1237.13–26) and registered in the phratry (*IG* II² 1237.97–98; Is. 7.16).[2]

Next, at the age of eighteen, young men were inscribed in their fathers' deme register (*lexiarchikon grammateion*), provided that they first passed scrutiny (*dokimasia*) by the members of the deme.[3] The *dokimasia* was an investigation that determined whether they were of age and whether they were free and born according to the laws (*eleutheros ... gegone tous nomous*) ([Arist.] *Ath. Pol.* 42.1). If the deme-members voted that a particular candidate was underage, he was sent back "to the boys," to try again when he actually turned eighteen. If, however, they voted that he

---

[1] On the importance of age divisions among the Athenian citizens, see, e.g., Hansen 1991, 88–90.

[2] On the various steps of admission to the phratry, see Lambert 1993, ch. 4.

[3] On this *dokimasia*, see Rhodes 1981, 495–502; Whitehead 1986c, 97–104; B. Robertson 2000; Lape 2010, 192–98.

was not in fact free (*eleutheron*),[4] he could appeal the decision to a popular court (*dikastērion*). If the court found that he had no right to be enrolled, the state sold him as a slave, but if he won, his fellow demesmen were required to register him ([Arist.] *Ath. Pol.* 42.1). The Boule then scrutinized the lists of newly enrolled young men and if any were found to be under the age of eighteen, the members of that deme were fined ([Arist.] *Ath. Pol.* 42.1). At least by the end of the 330s BCE, and perhaps as early as the 370s (Aesch. 2.167), these young men were then required to serve for two years as military recruits called ephebes ([Arist.] *Ath. Pol.* 42.2–5).[5] After the *ephebeia* was instituted, young men became full citizens only after their term of service, that is, at age twenty.

One's level of wealth affected the degree to which one could exercise full citizen rights. In 594/3 BCE, Solon divided the citizens of Athens into four property classes: the *pentakosiomedimnoi* (500-bushel men, that is, those whose property yielded at least 500 bushels per year), the *hippeis* (cavalry), the *zeugitai* (yokemen), and the *thētes* (laborers).[6] Under this classificatory scheme, *thētes* could not hold office but were allowed to serve in the Assembly and on juries ([Arist.] *Ath. Pol.* 7.3), and even the *zeugitai* were ineligible for selection as archons (this changed in 457/6 BCE: [Arist.] *Ath. Pol.* 26.2). Although these four property classes—and their attendant rights and disabilities—continued to exist throughout the classical period, it appears that by the fourth century, the classes were essentially meaningless and *thētes* could in practice hold any office.[7]

In addition to one's level of wealth, one's age also determined the rights one could exercise. Aristotle calls "citizens in a sense" (*pōs politas*) children who are too young to have yet been enrolled in demes, as well as those men over fifty-nine who have been discharged from political and military service (*Pol.* 1275a14–19). Moreover, since one needed to be at least thirty to be a juror, legislator, or magistrate (see further below), Mogens Hansen posits that "every third Athenian citizen had only limited citizen rights."[8]

Let us now take stock of the status of male citizens. Any male citizen could own property and had complete power over his own possessions.[9] This is not to say, however, that all citizens owned real property. *Thētes*,

---

4 For the view that *eleutheros* means "free" in this context, see Gomme 1934, 130–40; Rhodes 1981, 499–502 (with some reservations); Whitehead 1986c, 101. For the view that it means "of citizen birth," see, e.g., Diller 1935, 308–9n34 and others.

5 On the Athenian *ephebeia*, see Vidal-Naquet 1986 [1981], ch. 5. See also Liddel 2007, 290–93, with bibliography.

6 For an overview of Solon's property classes, see van Wees 2006, with bibliography.

7 See Rhodes 1981, 146; Hansen 1991, 88; van Wees 2006, 367–76.

8 Hansen 1991, 89.

9 On Athenian property law, see, e.g., Harrison 1968, pt. 2; MacDowell 1978, ch. 9; Todd 1995, ch. 12.

for example, were defined as citizens who owned less than 200 bushels' worth of land ([Arist.] *Ath. Pol.* 7.4); presumably some had a small patch of land, but others may have owned none at all. Many of the poorest citizens of Athens rented apartments alongside resident aliens in *sunoikiai*, multi-occupant buildings (Aesch. 1.124). Such citizens, however, would likely have been (socially) stigmatized, since a defining characteristic of the Athenian citizen was his right to own land, however little.[10]

Ideally, a male citizen did not perform labor on behalf of others, since doing so was considered banausic and servile.[11] In fact, Aristotle, who reflects (in his own way) many ideological assumptions of his time and place, thought that in an ideal society, working people would be disqualified from citizenship (*Pol.* 1278a6–8). However, in practice, many poor citizens worked as artisans and laborers. Such citizens were not only looked down upon (though they were that) but also at risk of having their own or their children's citizenship questioned (see, e.g., Dem. 57). Any citizen had legal control over the labor of those employed by him, whether they were slaves, freedmen, or even lower-ranking citizens. Likewise, a citizen had control over his own and his slaves' movement, with some de facto restrictions. A poorer citizen, for example, might have been particularly constrained in his movement: for instance, he might have been tied to his land if he did not have slaves to work it, or tied to his workshop if he did not have employees.

A male citizen had the power to punish those below him, although there were restrictions placed on his capacity to corporally punish slaves who were not his own (see chapter 1). He was himself, qua citizen, characterized by corporal inviolability:[12] at least notionally, he could not be physically violated, and this held for rich and poor alike. This rule, however, must have been enforced more frequently in the case of rich people, who were less likely to be mistaken for slaves. There were also some exceptions to the ideology of the inviolate citizen body: the very worst crimes incurred the penalty of corporal punishment (not to mention execution),[13] and as Mark Golden has pointed out, male athletes—many of whom were from well-off families—were subject to whippings and other bodily punishment at the hands of (slave) referees and trainers.[14]

Unlike all statuses below him, the male citizen had every available privilege in judicial proceedings: he could bring cases of any sort and

[10] For the possibility that in the fifth century, the "truly landless" citizen was not even registered in the deme lists, see Raaflaub 1996, 156, with bibliography.

[11] See, e.g., Cartledge 1993, 163–64 for this ideology; see also Johnstone 1994 on the distinction between banausic labor and (valorized) aristocratic toil (*ponos*). Cf. Wood 1988 and Hanson 1999 [1995] on the laboring peasant-citizen.

[12] See, e.g., Halperin 1990, ch. 5; Hunter 1992.

[13] On the execution and corporal punishment of citizens, see Allen 2000, ch. 9.

[14] Golden 2008, ch. 2.

be taken to court in turn.[15] The only adult citizens not allowed to bring suits (apart from *atimoi*) were ephebes, who could not leave their military service. But even they were allowed to sue or be sued in cases concerning estates or heiresses, and possibly in cases concerning inherited priest-hoods ([Arist.] *Ath. Pol.* 42.5).[16]

Litigation was a big part of what it meant, ideologically, to be an Athenian citizen.[17] One can imagine, however, that a poorer citizen might have been less likely than a richer one to let a case come to court, for a number of reasons. First of all, it was not cheap: speechwriters (*logographoi*) cost money, and writing one's own speech, especially if one was poor and uneducated, was unlikely to yield good results. In addi-tion, there were financial and other costs involved in litigation. One often had to pay court fees in advance of the trial, and in many suits a prosecutor could be penalized if he did not secure a requisite number of votes. So, for example, in most public suits, if a prosecutor did not obtain one-fifth of the votes, he might be susceptible to a hefty fine or *atimia*, and in some private suits, failure to secure one-fifth of the votes compelled the prosecutor to pay one-sixth of the value of his claim to his opponent.[18] These were risks that many were probably reluctant to take, especially if they had little money to start with or had to take time off work and lose income. Moreover, although mass juries in Athens appreciated democratic sentiment in their speakers, they were also par-ticularly well disposed toward citizens who had in some way benefited the polis (through, e.g., payment of liturgies) and acted as "good" citi-zens, something poorer people were less able to demonstrate.[19] The fact that most cases (at least of those that survive) represent strife between elites seems to indicate that the courtroom was a forum primarily for elites, rather than nonelites:[20] the latter presumably had their own ways of working out disagreements.

Any citizen, rich or poor, could serve as a juror (*dikastēs*), provided that he was over thirty, not in debt to the state treasury, nor otherwise *atimos* ([Arist.] *Ath. Pol.* 63.3).[21] Jury pay of two obols was instituted by Pericles and was increased to three obols by Cleon ([Arist.] *Ath. Pol.* 62.2). Appar-

---

[15] On judicial procedure, see, e.g., Harrison 1971; MacDowell 1978, pt. 3; Hansen 1991, ch. 8; Todd 1995, 77–163. See also Allen 2000 on punishment.

[16] It is unclear whether the phrase *kan tini kata genos hierosunē genētai* ("and if a family priesthood came about for someone") refers to another type of case an ephebe could enter into, or to another valid reason (in addition to cases concerning estates and heiresses) for leaving the *ephebeia*; Rhodes 1981 *ad loc.* favors the latter interpretation.

[17] See, e.g., Christ 1998; Johnstone 1999.

[18] On court fees and statutory penalties, see Christ 1998, 28–30.

[19] See Ober 1989.

[20] See D. Cohen 1995.

[21] On jury service, see [Arist.] *Ath. Pol.* 63–65; MacDowell 1978, 33–40; Hansen 1991, 181–83; Liddel 2007, 259–60.

ently this sum, though paltry, was a real incentive for poorer citizens, especially the elderly (Aristoph. *Wasps*; Isoc. 7.54). In fact, some Athenians believed that the courts deteriorated as a result of Pericles's institution of jury pay, because now "ordinary" (*tuchontōn*) people could serve ([Arist.] *Ath. Pol.* 27.4).

After 451/0 BCE (with periodic exceptions), male citizens were restricted in their marital rights in that they had to marry citizen women if they wanted their offspring to be citizens. In the fourth century, marrying a noncitizen, and particularly having children with her, could lead to prosecution in a *graphē xenias* (see chapter 4).[22] Punishment for conviction in this type of suit was one thousand drachmas, a very large fine ([Dem.] 59.16).

Part of the *dokimasia* that took place in order to determine if one could hold office[23] involved being asked how one treated one's parents and where one's ancestral tombs were located ([Arist.] *Ath. Pol.* 55.3). The male citizen was obliged to care for his parents (and grandparents) and provide for their funerary rites; he could expect the same thing, in turn, from his own children.[24] If a son did not fulfill these obligations, he could be prosecuted on a charge of mistreating his parents (*graphē goneōn kakōseōs*) (Dem. 24.60, 102, 105; [Arist.] *Ath. Pol.* 56.6; Hyp. 4.6; Is. 8.32); if convicted, he was punished with total *atimia* (see chapter 7).[25] If, however, a father prostituted his son, the son, once grown, was relieved of the obligation to care for his father while the latter was still alive, but was still obligated to bury him and perform the customary funerary rites (Aesch. 1.13). If one did not have heirs, adoption was the primary way of guaranteeing that one would be supported in one's old age, and one's tomb cared for.[26]

Provided that there were direct heirs, inheritance was relatively straightforward. A male citizen automatically left his estate in equal shares to his sons, and in the absence of biological heirs, he generally adopted a son. If, however, there was no heir, the estate was claimed by the next-closest member of the circle of heirs (*ankhisteia*).[27] Oftentimes in these instances estates were contested, leading to a large number of inheritance cases among the speeches that have survived (see especially the orations of Isaeus).

---

[22] Cf. Kapparis 2005, 76–95.

[23] On the *dokimasia* for holding office, see Rhodes 1981, 614–21; Hansen 1991, 218–20; Lape 2010, ch. 5.

[24] On the obligations to one's parents, see Liddel 2007, 215–18.

[25] On punishment for mistreatment of one's parents, see Harrison 1968, 77–78; MacDowell 1978, 92; Todd 1995, 107–8.

[26] On adoption in Athens, see Rubinstein 1993; on reasons for adoption, see ch. 4.

[27] On the rules of succession and claiming an inheritance, see Harrison 1968, ch. 5; MacDowell 1978, 92–108; Todd 1995, 210–27.

In general, increase in status was difficult for male citizens. But whereas poor citizens had little chance of overcoming poverty and attaining a higher status, already-wealthy citizens could experience further gains in honor (that is, social status) in exchange for contributions to the city, whether mandatory (like liturgies) or supererogatory.[28] Downward mobility, on the other hand, was a real danger facing citizens. We have already seen how a citizen could be rendered *atimos* as punishment for a crime (see chapter 7) or even enslaved (see chapter 1), though the latter fate was relatively rare for Athenian citizens. There were, in addition, various other ways in which a citizen could lose his civic rights. During two periods in classical Athenian history, a number of citizens were temporarily stripped of their active political rights by short-lived oligarchical regimes: under the Four Hundred ([Arist.] *Ath. Pol.* 29–33) and under the Thirty Tyrants ([Arist.] *Ath. Pol.* 34–40). Moreover, if a deme register was ever lost (or thought to be lost), individual deme-members' civic status could potentially be contested (Dem 57.60–61).

Demes also periodically voted on the citizenship status of the individuals listed on their registers (a procedure called *diapsēphismos* or *diapsēphisis*). For our period, we know of one in 445/4 BCE and one in 346/5 BCE.[29] So, for example, Euxitheos (see chapter 9) was struck off the rolls of his deme in 346/5 BCE on the grounds that he was not born from two citizens; the basis for this allegation seems to have been that his father had a foreign accent and his mother was a ribbon-seller (Dem. 57). Anyone who was struck off the rolls in this way lost his citizenship (Is. 12 *hyp.*) and was reclassified as a metic (Dem. 57 *hyp.*). If he believed himself to be, or wanted to pass himself off as, a legitimate citizen, he could appeal the decision in court (see, e.g., Aesch. 1.114–15; Dem. 57; Is. 12), as Euxitheos does. But this was a risky endeavor, since if he lost the appeal, he would be sold into slavery (Dem. 57 *hyp.*; Is. 12 *hyp.*).[30] In one particularly interesting case, also after the scrutiny of 346/5, Timarchus (see chapter 7) claimed that a citizen named Philotades was actually his own freed slave and urged Philotades's deme-members to strike him from the rolls. The matter came to court, but once it was revealed that Timarchus had taken a bribe from Philotades's family (it is unclear whether they bribed him to bring the claim or to drop the case!), the case was thrown out and Philotades's civic status was safely restored (Aesch. 1.114–15).

Another measure putting citizens' status into jeopardy was the *graphē xenias*, a public suit alleging that someone was a foreigner masquerading

---

[28] On the mutually beneficial system of euergetism, see, e.g., Whitehead 1983; Liddel 2007 *passim*.

[29] On these scrutinies, see Lape 2010, 199–216, with bibliography.

[30] See Rhodes 1981, 501–2; but cf. Gomme 1934, 130–39, who argues that those who lost their appeals were sold only if they were already slaves.

as a citizen. A citizen was particularly susceptible to such a charge if he had enemies, since they might be inclined to use the legal system to attack him.[31] The only surviving speech from such a *graphē* is *Against Neaira* ([Dem.] 59),[32] but scattered evidence indicates that these suits were not uncommon (see, e.g., Aristoph. *Wasps* 718; Is. 3.17; Dem. 24.131). In a *graphē xenias*, each side would produce witnesses attesting to the defendant's status. If the defendant was convicted, he could appeal by bringing a *dikē pseudomarturiōn* (private lawsuit concerning false witness) against the witnesses who had testified against him.[33] While awaiting this trial for false testimony, he would be locked up in jail (Dem. 24.131). Through a series of legal suits, then, a citizen wrongly accused of being a foreigner might manage to regain his citizen status—but it was also possible that he might lose his case, and, as with the appeal trials following scrutinies of the deme rolls, ultimately be sold as a slave.

Notionally, a male citizen had nearly complete rights, as well as a number of obligations, in the sacral sphere.[34] All citizens, rich and poor alike, were expected to participate in the cult activities of their phratry, deme, and polis.[35] In fact, participation in these rites was a primary way for citizens to solidify and manifest their communal civic identity.[36] There were, however, some restrictions on full participation in the sacral sphere. Only some citizens participated in the cult activities of private religious associations[37] and of *genē* (noble kin groups),[38] and only members of *genē* could hold *genos*-specific hereditary priesthoods. Moreover, richer citizens could afford to make more lavish dedications and sacrificial offerings to the gods than could their poorer counterparts. Finally, all male citizens were forbidden from participating in festivals and rites restricted to women (see chapter 9).

In the political realm, the adult male citizen (that is, the male citizen over the age of eighteen) was at the pinnacle of the status spectrum. By the classical period, any citizen, including *thētes*, could in theory participate in the Ekklesia, which met three or four times a month and was

---

[31] On the lawcourts as a venue for pursuing feuds, see, e.g., D. Cohen 1995, esp. ch. 4 and 5.

[32] On this speech, see Lape 2010, 220–29, with bibliography. Cf. Kapparis 2005, 76–95, who argues that [Dem.] 59 is not a *graphē xenias*.

[33] On the use of the *dikē pseudomarturiōn* following a *graphē xenias*, see Scafuro 1994, 170–181; Kapparis 2005, 95–98.

[34] On participation in civic cults and festivals as an obligation, see Sinclair 1988, 53–54; Liddel 2007, 300–8. Liddel 2007, 300, lists four major religious obligations of the Athenian citizen: "the maintenance and dedication of cult objects, participation in religious activity, the duties of religious personnel, and the avoidance of impious behaviour."

[35] On phratry religion, see Lambert 1993, ch. 6; on deme religion, see Whitehead 1986c, ch. 7. See also Fisher 2011, who argues that after the reforms of Cleisthenes, rich and poor citizens participated together on (tribal) teams for choral and athletic events at civic festivals.

[36] See, e.g., Goldhill 1990 (focusing specifically on the Great Dionysia).

[37] On private religious associations, see Parker 1996, 333–42; N. F. Jones 1999, 249–67.

[38] On *genos* religion, see Parker 1996, ch. 5; N. F. Jones 1999, 242–49.

attended by at least 6,000 individuals.[39] Any citizen over thirty could also participate in the Boule ([Arist.] *Ath. Pol.* 43.2–49), the council that prepared the Ekklesia's business, for which 500 members (fifty from each tribe) were selected by lot each year.[40] The councilors from each tribe were in charge for one-tenth of a year, during which time they were said to hold the prytany (presidency). In order to serve on the Boule, one had to undergo a scrutiny (*dokimasia*) by the other Boule members ([Arist.] *Ath. Pol.* 45.3). In the fourth century, participation in both bodies was remunerated: participation in the Boule brought the modest sum of five obols a day ([Arist.] *Ath. Pol.* 62.2), and attendance at the Ekklesia brought a drachma a day for ordinary meetings, a drachma and a half for the *ekklēsiai kuriai*, special meetings at which the most important business took place ([Arist.] *Ath. Pol.* 62.2). However, while payment must have been an incentive for some, it was not the case that everyone was equally likely to participate in these bodies. *Thētes*, for example, were probably less inclined to participate because of financial and temporal constraints. Those living in the rural demes, especially poorer citizens, were also less likely to attend meetings except when they absolutely needed to, especially since many of them could not leave their farms. What this meant, in effect, was that poorer, rural citizens had less of a political "voice" than did richer, urban ones.[41] Moreover, it was probably the case that even among those who did attend, "ordinary" citizens had less of a voice in these bodies than the dominant public speakers (*rhētores*).[42]

Citizens over the age of thirty who came from the three highest Solonian property classes—and apparently by the fourth century from the *thētes* as well—could serve as magistrates. Most of the city's approximately 700 magistrates ([Arist.] *Ath. Pol.* 24.3) were selected by lot from among the citizen body ([Arist.] *Ath. Pol.* 43–62).[43] Military officers, however, were elected by a show of hands, presumably because their positions required specialized skills ([Arist.] *Ath. Pol.* 43.1; 61).[44] To serve as a magistrate one had to undergo a *dokimasia* by the Boule ([Arist.] *Ath. Pol.*

[39] Participating in the Assembly: A. H. M. Jones 1957, 108–33; Hansen 1987 and 1991, ch. 6.

[40] Serving on the Boule: A. H. M. Jones 1957, 105–8; Rhodes 1981, 510–71; Hansen 1991, ch. 10.

[41] See, however, Taylor 2007a, who argues that in the fourth century, as compared with the fifth, more nonwealthy citizens, and more citizens from outside the city area, became involved in politics (broadly defined).

[42] On the limits to full citizen participation in these bodies, see Sinclair 1988, 106–14 (Boule), 114–19 (Ekklesia); and Manville 1997 [1990], 17–18, with bibliography. On the elite status of *rhētores*, see Ober 1989, 112–18 and *passim*.

[43] On holding magistracies: Hansen 1980; Rhodes 1981, 510–697; and Hansen 1991, ch. 9.

[44] Elected officials in addition to military officers included the treasurer of military funds, the controller of theoric fund, and the superintendent of wells ([Arist.] *Ath. Pol.* 43.1). For evidence that election favored individuals from demes closer to the city, and therefore was less "democratic" than selection by lot, see Taylor 2007b.

55.2–5), and if one did not pass the scrutiny, one could appeal the decision in a courthouse (*dikastērion*) ([Arist.] *Ath. Pol.* 55.2).[45] Although magistracies were in general open to everyone, some offices were restricted by wealth, family, or age. For example, to be one of the ten Treasurers of Athena one technically had to belong to the class of *pentakosiomedimnoi*, "in accordance with the law of Solon." Ps.-Aristotle, however, tells us that even poor men could be selected by lot for this office ([Arist.] *Ath. Pol.* 47.1), presumably either because they might somehow be classified as *pentakosiomedimnoi* despite their poverty or because non-*pentakosiomedimnoi* could be selected despite Solon's law.[46] Moreover, some of the city's religious offices were reserved for members of particular *genē*: for example, although two of the four superintendents of the Mysteries were drawn from the entire citizen body, one was always drawn from the Eumolpidai *genos*, and one from the Kerkyes ([Arist.] *Ath. Pol.* 57.1).[47] Finally, some offices were age-specific: for instance, one had to serve as an arbitrator (*diaitētēs*) in one's sixtieth year, and not doing so, unless one was abroad or holding another office that year, was punishable with *atimia* ([Arist.] *Ath. Pol.* 53.4, 5).

A special class of magistrates was the archons, chosen by lot from those who were over thirty and presented themselves for selection ([Arist.] *Ath. Pol.* 55–59).[48] Their *dokimasia* took place first in the Boule, and a second time in a *dikastērion* ([Arist.] *Ath. Pol.* 55.2). The archons were nine in number: the eponymous archon, the chief magistrate and the nominal head of state who gave his name to the year in which he served ([Arist.] *Ath. Pol.* 56.2–6); the Basileus or "king" archon, who was responsible for religious ceremonies and presided over the Court of the Areopagos ([Arist.] *Ath. Pol.* 57); the polemarch, who initially was a war commander but who in the classical period took on legal duties concerning non-Athenians, as well as certain religious duties ([Arist.] *Ath. Pol.* 58); and finally six additional junior archons called Thesmothetai ("lawmakers") ([Arist.] *Ath. Pol.* 59.1–6). Because magistracies were not generously paid ([Arist.] *Ath. Pol.* 62.2), the self-selection process for archonships favored candidates who were, in general, among the wealthier citizens in the polis.[49] Membership in the Areopagos—a court solely for homicide cases from 462–403/2 BCE, at which point it began accumulating additional supervisory powers—was for life and was restricted to former archons.[50]

---

[45] But cf. Rhodes 1981, 615–17, who argues that by the time of the *Ath. Pol.*, a hearing by the *dikastērion* became a required step in the *dokimasia* process.

[46] See also Rhodes 1981 *ad loc.*

[47] On the evidence for the Eumolpidai, see Parker 1996, 293–97; on the Kerkyes, Parker 1996, 300–302.

[48] On the Athenian archonships, see Rhodes 1981, 612–68.

[49] Hansen 1991, 289.

[50] On the composition and powers of the Areopagos, see Hansen 1991, ch. 12.

Other duties of citizens in the political sphere were financial.[51] For instance, all citizens were subject to the *eisphora*, originally an exceptional wartime tax but by the mid-fourth century a regular annual tax. Citizens paid a certain amount based both on the value of their property and on the amount being levied in a particular year. A change to the levying of the *eisphora* was made in 378/7 BCE, at which point the wealthy citizens of Athens were divided into 100 tax groups called symmories, each of which was responsible for paying 1/100th of the total tax the city was levying. At this time, or perhaps shortly thereafter, the three wealthiest members of each symmory were required to make an advance payment (*proeisphora*) on behalf of their fellow members (Is. 6.60).[52] The richest citizens of the city were also responsible for annual liturgies or public services. As David Whitehead aptly puts it, liturgies represent a "paradoxical conjunction of burden and honour."[53] Services included festival liturgies, like financing the participation of choruses in festivals (*khorēgia*), and military liturgies, like financing the maintenance of warships (*triērarkhia*).[54] If a man was selected for a liturgy but thought he could find a richer man to take on the duty instead, he could challenge the latter, in a procedure called an *antidosis*, either to take on the liturgy himself or to exchange property with him. If the other party refused to do either, the matter would be referred to public trial.[55] Finally, citizens who were both very poor and physically disabled received welfare from the state. After being inspected by the Boule and having their qualifications confirmed, they were given a (publicly funded) food allowance of one to two obols a day (Lys. 24; [Arist.] *Ath. Pol.* 49.4).[56]

In the military sphere, male citizens had a number of privileges as well as duties.[57] The top three census classes could be conscripted to serve as heavy-armed infantry (hoplites), and the very wealthiest could elect to serve with the cavalry, which required more expensive equipment provided by the soldiers themselves (Hyp. 1.16–17). It is less clear whether *thētes* could serve as hoplites; all we can say with certainty is that they could volunteer to serve in the navy as rowers.[58] They may well have

---

[51] On financial obligations to the city, see Sinclair 1988, 61–65; Christ 2006, 146–55; Liddel 2007, 262–82, with bibliography.

[52] On the *eisphora*, see Thomsen 1964; Christ 2007.

[53] Whitehead 1977, 81.

[54] On the *khorēgia*, see Wilson 2000; on the *triērarkhia*, see Gabrielsen 1994.

[55] On the *antidosis*, see Gabrielsen 1987; Christ 1990. On tax evasion more broadly, see Christ 2006, ch. 4.

[56] By the time of [Arist.] *Ath. Pol.* (late fourth century BCE), the allowance was two obols; earlier in the fourth century (see Lys. 24.13, 26) it was one.

[57] On the obligations of military service, see Sinclair 1988, 54–61; Liddel 2007, 282–93. On *thētes*' apparent limitations in the military sphere, see Raaflaub 1996, 154–59.

[58] On the question whether *thētes* could serve as hoplites, see Hansen 1985, 48–49, 88–89 (yes, in the fourth century); Christ 2001, 415n65 (if so, it would have happened only after the Battle of Chaeronea); Rhodes 1981, 503 (no, they could not).

done this in an attempt to gain increased social status,[59] but they were under no obligation to do so. This fact leads Finley to point out a paradox: "the poorer Athenian citizen had the freedom to choose between serving and not serving and to be maintained by the state if he chose to serve, whereas the wealthier Athenian citizen had no freedom in this sphere."[60]

Even though all citizen-hoplites were ideologically equal, some factors contributed to the over-representation of certain groups of people in the ranks. In the fifth century, for instance, all hoplites had to provide their own equipment, which may have deterred those with fewer resources. Sometime in the fourth century, however, the state began providing a shield and spear to all new recruits ([Arist.] *Ath. Pol.* 42.4). A further change in the mid-fourth century involved the drafting of hoplites. Before that point, it was up to generals to handpick recruits from each of the city's ten tribes, drawing their names from draft lists called *katalogoi*. After the reform, the state would call up entire age groups at a given time,[61] leveling out the range of people called for service. Some citizens, however, were exempt from conscription, including, among others, those over fifty-nine ([Arist.] *Ath. Pol.* 53.4); those currently serving on the Boule (Lycurg. 1.37) or holding major magistracies; those currently serving as chorus members in dramatic festivals (Dem. 21.15), since doing so was an important component of civic identity; and those who were ill or disabled.[62] Military service, then, was a duty, at least for the top three classes. Anyone who avoided military service or deserted the battlefield could be charged with a public lawsuit: the *graphē astrateias* ([Dem.] 59.27; Lys. 15) or the *graphē lipotaxiou*, respectively (Lys. 14).[63] If convicted, they were punished with *atimia* (Andoc. 1.74; Aesch. 3.176).

In theory, all male citizens were equal. We have seen, however, that variation existed within the male citizen population, with some groups restricted (officially or unofficially) from holding office or compelled to pay extra taxes. Age was one determining factor, since one could be too young or too old to perform the full set of citizen rights. Wealth was another important factor, affecting in several ways the degree to which one could participate in the polis and also the level of *timē* one could attain. As we have seen, poor citizens, constrained by their limited resources and their obligation to perform labor, could not exercise

---

[59] Liddel 2007, 283. See also Strauss 1996 on the ways in which naval service gave *thētes* a sense of solidarity.

[60] Finley 1981 [1976], 89.

[61] On changes in the drafting of hoplites, see Christ 2001. The date for this reform is uncertain, but Christ posits the period 386–366 BCE.

[62] On exemptions from military service, see Hansen 1985, 16–21.

[63] On draft evasion, see Christ 2006, ch. 2; on desertion, see Christ 2006, ch. 3.

full-fledged citizenship and were socially degraded as compared to their richer fellow-citizens. Mostly likely, they also felt threatened by the existence of wealthy slaves (chapter 2) and rich metics (chapter 4), who despite their inferior legal status occupied a higher socioeconomic status than they did. Possessing the rights of citizenship—especially ones they could rarely exercise—may have been of small comfort to them.

CONCLUSION
Status in Ideology and Practice

THROUGH CLOSE ANALYSIS OF VARIOUS FORMS OF EVIDENCE—LITERARY, epigraphic, and legal—I have demonstrated that classical Athens had a spectrum of statuses, ranging from the base chattel slave to the male citizen with full civic rights. I have also shown that factors not previously taken into account alongside one another (e.g., property ownership, corporal inviolability, and religious rights) made for significant legal and social differences between groups of individuals in the city.

As we have seen, the status of the basest chattel slave (e.g., a mining slave; chapter 1) was characterized by a (nearly) complete lack of rights: he had no claims to property; no power over his own or others' labor and movement; no power to punish others, while being very susceptible to corporal punishment himself; no privileges in the judicial realm; virtually no privileges in the realm of family; limited opportunities for social mobility; little autonomy in the religious sphere; no involvement in politics; and a limited role in the military. The privileged chattel slave (e.g., a slave-banker; chapter 2) was distinguished from his baser counterpart by having (at least sometimes) de facto claims to property; greater control over his labor and movement; greater power over his subordinates (while at the same time remaining, like the baser slave, susceptible to corporal punishment); slightly greater judicial privileges, particularly in the fourth century; greater opportunities for social mobility, especially manumission; and slightly greater involvement in civic religion. The conditionally freed slave (chapter 3), in turn, possessed a status superior to the privileged slave, as manifested in his right to own property (if not land); his decreased susceptibility to bodily violence; his greater privileges in legal actions; and his greater privileges in the area of family, especially the right to marry. With these improvements in legal status from base chattel slave to conditionally freed slave came incremental increases in social status, though even the highest of these groups (the freedman bound to his former master) possessed relatively little honor.

Both freeborn and ex-slave metics (chapter 4) were higher in legal status than conditionally freed slaves—especially in the areas of freedom of movement, control over their own labor, and involvement in civic religion—and with this higher status came additional obligations to the polis, such as paying the *metoikion* tax and serving (albeit in segregated ranks) in the military. Although both categories of metic received less honor than citizens, ex-slaves bore a social stigma that their freeborn counterparts did not. Privileged metics (chapter 5), whose privileges came from the state, were superior both legally and socially to "regular" metics: some possessed the right to own land (*enktēsis*); others to pay taxes commensurate with those imposed upon citizens; still others to serve alongside citizens in the military; and any metic with privileges was more likely to gain additional rights (including naturalization) than was an unprivileged metic. In terms of legal status, bastards (chapter 6) were essentially identical to unprivileged metics. They differed from metics primarily in their *social* status (which sometimes had legal repercussions). Since they were born from at least one citizen parent, bastards had, at least in theory, access to a (citizen) support network, granting them protection in the event of physical or legal assault. In this way, they were superior to metics, even to privileged metics, who were fully foreign, but they were also inferior, in that they stood almost no chance of becoming citizens and occupied a marginal (and often uncomfortable) position within their households. Some disenfranchised citizens (*atimoi*; chapter 7) possessed greater rights than metics and bastards— e.g., they could own land, unless they were state debtors—but others, if banned entirely from the legal, political, and religious spheres, occupied a lower legal status. However, although *atimia* was more socially stigmatizing than *notheia*, it did not necessarily represent a permanent dishonor: periodic amnesties restored citizen status to *atimoi*; those with temporary *atimia* could eventually return to their status as full-fledged citizens; and at least some unconvicted *atimoi* might have been able to "pass" as enfranchised.

Naturalized citizens (chapter 8) were superior to *atimoi* in nearly all areas of civic life. As compared with natural-born citizens, they faced a handful of political and religious limitations, but their biggest liability was their foreign birth, which was a source of social stigmatization. Female citizens (chapter 9) in some respects had fewer rights than naturalized citizens, most if not all of whom were male, since they played little direct role in the courts and the political sphere (though their role in civic religion was substantial). Their pure Athenian blood, however, coupled with their capacity to produce citizen children, granted them a social status higher in many ways than that available to naturalized citizens. Finally, male citizens (chapter 10), although varying to some degree in social status, in theory possessed every available privilege and were susceptible to every obligation to the state, including the capacity to own all forms of property; to control their own labor and movement;

to punish subordinates (and to be free from corporal abuse themselves); to engage in judicial proceedings; to exercise marital and family rights; to be involved in the military; and, most representative of citizen status, to participate at all levels in the political system.

Mapping this spectrum of status has, furthermore, revealed a number of gaps between Athenian civic ideology, as found in much of our literary evidence, and the reality of citizenship in Athens. First, the existence of naturalized citizens (chapter 8)—foreign-born individuals who were granted citizenship for their services to the city—gives the lie to the myth that all Athenian citizens were autochthonous, the lineal descendants of ancestors who were "born from the earth."[1] This myth, which enshrines one of the most important strands of civic ideology, holds that the first two kings of Athens, Kekrops and Erekhtheus (or Erikhthonios), literally sprang from the soil of Attica. Bolstered by Pericles's citizenship law of 451/0 BCE, which mandated that citizens of Athens be of pure Attic stock on both sides, the myth of autochthony was the foundation for the Athenians' sense of a unique and shared identity, marking them as distinct from (and superior to) non-Athenians.

The practice of naturalization, then, had the potential to make citizens very uneasy, since it called into question one of the fundamental components of Athenian civic identity: namely, shared descent from an autochthonous ancestor. We see this discomfort expressed most explicitly when (in 330 BCE) the orator Lycurgus says, concerning Hyperides's proposal to naturalize foreigners (and well as manumit slaves and re-enfranchise *atimoi*) (see chapter 8):

> When many terrible things were happening against the city [i.e., the Battle of Chaeronea (338 BCE)], and all the citizens had suffered the greatest misfortunes, one would have especially grieved and shed tears at the misfortunes of the city upon seeing the demos decreeing that slaves become free, that foreigners become Athenians, and that the disenfranchised become enfranchised—a demos that previously boasted of being autochthonous [*autokhthōn*] and free. (Lycurg. 1.41–42)

Through his use of hyperbolic language, Lycurgus stresses how far Athens has fallen from its glory days, when the principle of autochthony was (at least notionally) respected. In this case, the fact that Hyperides's proposed measures were contested in court and never actually put in place may have dissipated some of the threat they posed to Athenian civic ideology. But not all decrees of naturalization were challenged, which

---

[1] On the discrepancy between the myth of autochthony and reality, see, e.g., Connor 1994, 35–38; Lape 2010.

meant that the Athenians did have to confront the reality—incongruous with their civic ideology—of non-autochthonous fellow citizens, and they did so with varying degrees of ease.[2]

Second, despite what is claimed by democratic ideology, not all citizens were in fact equal,[3] nor, as I have demonstrated, were members of any other status group: we may recall the wide variety of chattel slaves, ranging from the base laborer in the mines, to the semiprivileged domestic slave, to the wealthy and independent banker (chapters 1 and 2). The lack of equality within the citizen body has even led some scholars to classify Athenian citizens as either "active" or "passive," depending on their level of involvement in the political life of the city.[4] My discussion has built on this distinction by examining the participation (or lack thereof) of citizens not only in the political sphere, but also in other realms, perhaps most significantly in the sacral sphere.[5] In doing so, I have shown that some citizens exercised greater rights and possessed more social cachet than others, for a number of reasons, including age, money, and geography (chapters 9 and 10). Thus a rich male citizen living in the center of Athens had not only the leisure time to serve as an archon or on the Boule, but also the means, for example, to perform liturgies, thereby bringing more honor upon himself than a poor citizen living in the outskirts of Attica ever could. Likewise, a girl or woman from a prominent Athenian family would probably have a greater chance than her less-well-off counterparts of playing a distinguished role, even holding a position of leadership, in civic religion, and of marrying a high-status man, which would presumably bring her more honor, if only indirectly, via her husband and children.

Third, contrary to the tenet of Athenian civic ideology that (only) citizens "shared in" the city,[6] we have seen that a variety of noncitizens also received rights from and fulfilled obligations to the polis, including some privileged slaves, freedmen with conditional freedom, metics, privileged metics, bastards, and disenfranchised citizens (chapters 2–7).[7] These included, for example, the right to bring certain kinds of lawsuits and participate in various aspects of civic religion, as well as the obligation (itself also a symbolic privilege) to serve alongside citizens in the

---

[2] See also Lape 2010, ch. 6, who suggests that one of the ways the Athenians managed this reality, from an ideological perspective, was by framing naturalization as "adoption," akin to the commonplace practice of adopting sons.

[3] See, e.g., Finley 1981 [1976], 81; Raaflaub 1996.

[4] See Mossé 1979; Lotze 1981. Cf. Manville 1997 [1990], ch. 1, who argues that Athenian citizenship encompassed both (what we would call) "active" and "passive" citizenship.

[5] See, e.g., C. Patterson 2005 and Blok 2005 on citizenship entailing more than political involvement (pace Aristotle's Politics book 3).

[6] On citizenship in Athens as a "sharing in" the city, see, e.g., Ostwald 1996.

[7] On the idea of "sharing in" the city broadly, see, e.g., Hedrick 1994; E. E. Cohen 1994, 1997, 2003 [2000]; Ober 2005 [2000]; and more recently Wijma 2010, 311–23.

military and pay taxes commensurate with citizens'. This broadly distributed "sharing in" the city does not mean, however, that the Athenians referred to nearly all these individuals as "*astoi*" ("natives" or "locals") and enrolled them in their deme registers, as Edward Cohen has suggested.[8] Surveys of the term *astos* have shown, rather, that it consistently refers only to citizens,[9] differing from the more common term *politēs* only in that it stresses one's status as a native inhabitant more than one's role in the political realm.[10] Cohen is completely right, however, that we have to imagine a much larger sector of the population sharing in the city than citizens alone. Indeed, this book has attempted to flesh out some of the *range* of this participation.

In short, then, I hope to have shown that Athenian democracy was in practice both more inclusive and more exclusive than one might expect based on its civic ideology: more inclusive in that even slaves and noncitizens "shared in" the democratic polis (albeit to varying extents), more exclusive in that not all citizens were equal participants in the social, economic, and political life of the city.[11]

Another aim of this book has been to illuminate the flexibility of status boundaries, seemingly in opposition to the dominant ideology of two or three status groups divided neatly from one another: slave versus free, citizen versus noncitizen, or slave versus metic versus citizen.[12] This has been demonstrated by the elucidation of (at least) ten distinct status groups, as well as the possibility of both upward and downward mobility between statuses (chapters 1–10).

One explanation for this discrepancy between practice and ideology can be found in the fact that Greek thought, in general, was characterized by binaries.[13] A binary thought system also allows for the existence of clearly defined ternaries (e.g., when humans define themselves by their difference from the gods on the one hand, and nonhuman animals on the other). This way of thinking is one that stresses the sharpness of boundaries, and in the case of binary or ternary status groups, the

---

[8] See, e.g., E. E. Cohen 1997 and 2003 [2000].

[9] This was suggested as early as Chapelot 1929. For criticisms of E. E. Cohen's argument about the meaning of *astos*, see, e.g., Ober 2005 [2000], 117n40; C. Patterson 2005, 269n5; Fisher 2006, 340 and 2008, 137; Lape 2010, 20n73, 48n173; R. Osborne 2011, 92n44.

[10] For the different nuances of these terms, see C. Patterson 1986 and Blok 2005. Cf. R. Osborne 2011, 92–105, who argues that *astos* is the term used to stress one's role in the political realm (i.e., legal or political status), whereas *politēs* more broadly indicates membership in or belonging to a community.

[11] Cf. Taylor 2007a, who argues that the democracy became "more inclusive" in the fourth century, with the involvement of less wealthy citizens in politics.

[12] On the discrepancy between the ideology of fixed status groups and the reality of fluidity, see, e.g., Todd 1994 (with E. E. Cohen 1994); Connor 1994; Vlassopoulos 2007, 2009. See also Golden 1998 and 2008 on the ways in which Greek sport establishes distinctions between various statuses (e.g., Greek and non-Greek, slave and citizen, men and women, old and young), even when these boundaries are, in practice, fluid.

[13] On the significance of binaries in Greek thought, see Lloyd 1966. See also Cartledge 2002, with bibliography.

sharpness of status boundaries.[14] Since Athenian citizens defined themselves, collectively, in opposition to noncitizens and slaves,[15] they were invested in believing that the boundaries between status groups were well defined and impenetrable.[16] This was the case even though—or perhaps because—they were frequently confronted with the reality of status flux and the lack of clear-cut status markers (see, e.g., [Xen.] *Ath. Pol.* 1.10).[17] Therefore, except when necessary, they preferred not to acknowledge the spectrum of statuses and the possibility of movement between groups.[18] If, however, a particularly threatening form of status fluidity reared its head—perhaps most dramatically, when slaves and metics entered the citizen body—steps were taken to police the "naturally" rigid status boundaries.[19] As we have seen, this could take the form of judicial measures like the *dikē apostasiou* (chapters 3, 4), the *graphē paranomōn* (chapters 5, 8), and courtroom trials in which individuals had to prove their civic status (chapters 9, 10). Greek literature, especially through its ideologically motivated silences, also plays an important role in enforcing normative status boundaries. It does so, in part, by masking the participation of lower-status individuals in higher-status pursuits (e.g., slaves in the "citizen" army: chapters 1, 2), as well as that of citizens in lower-status occupations (e.g., those involving banausic labor: chapters 9, 10).

And yet, alongside these attempts to enforce the ideology of two or three fixed status groups stood the Athenians' recognition, in practice, of a range of statuses between which movement was in fact possible. I would argue there were both ideological and practical benefits to this recognition. First, as I mentioned in the Introduction, it has been suggested that the "intervening" status categories—those between slave and metic, and between metic and citizen—actually served an ideological purpose (as well as a practical one), since as "minor" statuses, they reified and reinforced the primacy of the "big three" status categories.[20] Second, and perhaps more important, institutionalized status change—whether the manumission of a slave (chapter 3), the granting of extra privileges to a metic (chapter 5), the disenfranchisement of a citizen (chapter 7), or the naturalization of a foreigner (chapter 8)—gave the population of Athens, citizens and noncitizens alike, incentives to behave in a manner beneficial to the polis. That is, encouraging the promotion of some individuals (those who helped the state) and the

[14] On dichotomic schemes and the sharpness of class divisions, see Ossowski 1963, 92–96.

[15] See Vidal-Naquet 1986 [1981], 164, followed by many scholars.

[16] On "penetrable" versus "permanent" status groups, see Ossowski 1963, 93.

[17] Cf. Osborne 2011, who argues that visual distinctions between statuses in classical Greece were often invisible in sculpture and painted pottery (and thus in reality).

[18] On anxieties about status-boundary crossing in Athens, see, e.g., Davies 1977/78; Jameson 2004 [1997].

[19] See Lape 2010, esp. ch. 5.

[20] Todd 1995, 173, 174.

demotion of others (those who harmed the state) affected not only the individuals in question but also the state itself, whether directly or indirectly. We might compare this system of incentives to other such systems in democratic Athens: for example, the recruitment of the elite citizens of Athens to deliver assistance, especially in the form of liturgies, to the demos (see chapter 10). As Josiah Ober has demonstrated, by drawing on this service in the courts, elites could display their commitment to the polis, thus appealing to the interests of the mass juries and potentially winning their cases.[21]

This does not mean, however, that there was not ambivalence about accommodating civic ideals to practical necessities. In the Parabasis of Aristophanes's *Frogs* (see chapter 7), the Chorus leader recognizes the practical advantages of offering citizenship to those who have aided the city (in this case, the slaves and foreigners fighting at Arginousai); in fact, he calls it the one smart thing the polis did (*Frogs* 695–96). Simultaneously, however, he finds it shameful that slaves and foreigners are being naturalized when genuine citizens are being disenfranchised (693–94), and laments the intrusion of base parvenus into the citizen body (730–32). In a similar way, we have seen that the polis was happy to reward privileged slaves like Pasion and Phormion with citizenship in exchange for their tremendous financial contributions, but at the same time, the opponents of such individuals in court could play on the jury's prejudices against status transgressors by calling them once-and-future slaves (chapters 2, 3, 8).

Athens, then, was faced with competing motivations, which were in tension but nonetheless coexisted. On the one hand, there was a desire to preserve an ideology of rigidly defined statuses; on the other, the city wanted to get the most out of its diverse lot of inhabitants, which necessitated setting up a ladder of incremental steps by which one could rise (or sink) in status. Rather than canceling each other out, however, these two apparently contradictory desires were both satisfied. That is, Athenian society was *both* a spectrum of statuses *and* a set of binaries or ternaries; it was *both* fluid *and* rigid.

[21] See Ober 1989.

BIBLIOGRAPHY

Allen, Danielle. 1997. "Imprisonment in Classical Athens." *CQ* ns 47: 121–35.
———. 2000. *The World of Prometheus: The Politics of Punishing in Democratic Athens.* Princeton: Princeton University Press.

Andreau, Jean. 1993. "The Freedman." In *The Romans*, edited by Andrea Giardina, 175–98. Translated by Lydia G. Cochrane. Chicago: Chicago University Press.

Antonaccio, Carla M. 2000. "Architecture and Behavior: Building Gender into Greek Houses." *CW* 93: 517–33.

Ault, Bradley A. and Lisa C. Nevett. 2005. "Summing Up: Whither the Archaeology of the Greek Household?" In *Ancient Greek Households: Chronological, Regional, and Social Diversity*, edited by Bradley A. Ault and Lisa C. Nevett, 160–75. Philadelphia: University of Pennsylvania Press.

Austin, M. M. and Pierre Vidal-Naquet. 1977 [1972]. *Economic and Social History of Ancient Greece: An Introduction.* Translated and revised by M. M. Austin. Berkeley: University of California Press.

Bäbler, Balbina. 1998. *Fleissige Thrakerinnen und wehrhafte Skythen: Nichtgriechen im klassischen Athen und ihre archäologische Hinterlassenschaft.* Stuttgart: Teubner.

Bakewell, Geoffrey. 2008/9. "Forbidding Marriage: *Neaira* 16 and Metic Spouses at Athens." *CJ* 104: 97–109.

Bearzot, Cinzia. 2005. "Né cittadini né stanieri: *apeleutheroi* e *nothoi* in Atene." In *Il cittadino, lo straniero, il barbaro, fra integrazione ed emarginazione nell'antichità*, edited by Maria G. Angeli Bertinelli and Angela Donati, 77–92. Rome: Giorgio Bretschneider.

Beauchet, Ludovic. 1976 [1897]. *Histoire du droit privé de la république athénienne,* vol. 2: *Le droit de famille.* New York: Arno Press.

Biscardi, Arnaldo. 1982. *Diritto greco antico.* Milan: Giuffrè.

Blok, Josine H. 2005. "Becoming Citizens: Some Notes on the Semantics of 'Citizen' in Archaic Greece and Classical Athens." *Klio* 87: 7–40.
———. 2009. "Perikles' Citizenship Law: A New Perspective." *Historia* 58: 141–70.

Boegehold, Alan L. 1994. "Perikles' Citizenship Law of 451/0 BC." In *Athenian Identity and Civic Ideology*, edited by Alan L. Boegehold and Adele C. Scafuro, 57–66. Baltimore: Johns Hopkins University Press.
——— and Adele C. Scafuro, eds. 1994. *Athenian Identity and Civic Ideology.* Baltimore: Johns Hopkins University Press.

Bömer, Franz. 1960. *Untersuchungen über die Religion der Sklaven in Griechenland und Rom,* vol. 2: *Die sogenannte sakrale Freilassung in Griechenland und die (δοῦλοι) ἱεροί.* Wiesbaden: Steiner.

Braund, David. 2011. "The Slave Supply in Classical Greece." In *The Cambridge World History of Slavery*, vol. 1: *The Ancient Mediterranean World*, edited by Keith Bradley and Paul Cartledge, 112–33. Cambridge: Cambridge University Press.

Brock, Roger. 1994. "The Labour of Women in Classical Athens." *CQ* 44: 336–46.

Calderini, Aristide. 1908. *La manomissione e la condizione dei liberti in Grecia.* Milan: Hoepli.

Camp, Stephanie H. 2004. *Closer to Freedom: Enslaved Women and Everyday Resistance in the Plantation South.* Chapel Hill: University of North Carolina Press.

Canevaro, Mirko. 2010. "The Decree Awarding Citizenship to the Plataeans ([Dem.] 59.104)." *GRBS* 50: 337–69.

Cantarella, Eva. 2005. "Gender, Sexuality, and Law." In *The Cambridge Companion to Ancient Greek Law,* edited by Michael Gagarin and David Cohen, 236–53. Cambridge and New York: Cambridge University Press.

———. 2009. "Women: Ancient Greek Law." In *The Oxford Encyclopedia of Legal History,* vol. 6, edited by Stanley N. Katz, 112–17. Oxford: Oxford University Press.

Carawan, Edwin. 2008. "Perikles the Younger and the Citizenship Law." *CJ* 103: 383–406.

Carey, C. 1991. "Apollodoros' Mother: The Wives of Enfranchised Aliens in Athens." *CQ* 41: 84–89.

Cartledge, Paul A. 1993. "Like a Worm i' the Bud?" *G&R* 40: 163–80.

———. 2002. *The Greeks: A Portrait of Self and Others.* Oxford: Oxford University Press.

Chapelot, V. 1929. "Astos." *REA* 31: 7–12.

Christ, Matthew R. 1990. "Liturgy Avoidance and *Antidosis* in Classical Athens." *TAPA* 120: 147–69.

———. 1998. *The Litigious Athenian.* Baltimore: Johns Hopkins University Press.

———. 2001. "Conscription of Hoplites in Classical Athens." *CQ* 51: 398–422.

———. 2006. *The Bad Citizen in Classical Athens.* Cambridge: Cambridge University Press.

———. 2007. "The Evolution of the *eisphora* in Classical Athens." *CQ* 57: 53–69.

Christensen, Kerry A. 1984. "The Theseion: A Slave Refuge at Athens." *AJAH* 9: 23–32.

Clerc, Michel. 1893. *Les métèques athéniens.* Paris: Thorin.

Cohen, David. 1989. "Seclusion, Separation, and the Status of Women in Classical Athens." *G&R* 36: 3–15.

———. 1991a. *Law, Sexuality, and Society: The Enforcement of Morals in Classical Athens.* Cambridge: Cambridge University Press.

———. 1991b. "Sexuality, Violence, and the Athenian Law of 'Hubris.'" *G&R* 38: 171–88.

———. 1995. *Law, Violence and Community in Classical Athens.* Cambridge.

———. 1998. "Women, Property and Status in Demosthenes 41 and 57." *Dike* 1: 53–61.

———. 2005. "Women in Public: Gender, Citizenship, and Social Status in Classical Athens." In *Symposion 2001: Vorträge zur griechischen und hellenistischen Rechtsgeschichte,* edited by Michael Gagarin and Robert W. Wallace, 33–46. Vienna: Verlag der Österreichischen Akademie der Wissenschaften.

Cohen, Edward E. 1973. *Ancient Athenian Maritime Courts.* Princeton: Princeton University Press.

———. 1991. "Banking as a 'Family Business': Legal Adaptations Affecting Wives and Slaves." In *Symposion 1990: Vorträge zur griechischen und hellenistischen Rechtsgeschichte,* edited by Michael Gagarin, 239–63. Cologne: Böhlau.

————. 1992. *Athenian Economy & Society: A Banking Perspective.* Princeton: Princeton University Press.

————. 1994. "Status and Contract in Fourth-Century Athens: A Reply." In *Symposion 1993: Vorträge zur griechischen und hellenistischen Rechtsgeschichte*, edited by Gerhard Thür, 141–52. Cologne: Böhlau.

————. 1997. "The Astoi of Attika: Nationality and Citizenship at Athens." In *Symposion 1995: Vorträge zur griechischen und hellenistischen Rechtsgeschichte*, edited by Gerhard Thür and Julie Vélissaropoulos-Karakostas, 57–87. Cologne: Böhlau.

————. 1998. "The Wealthy Slaves of Athens: Legal Rights, Economic Obligations." In *Le monde antique et les droits de l'homme*, edited by Huguette Jones, 105–29. Brussels: Université libre de Bruxelles.

————. 2003 [2000]. *The Athenian Nation.* Princeton: Princeton University Press.

————. 2003. "Athenian Prostitution as a Liberal Profession." In *Gestures: Essays in Ancient History, Literature, and Philosophy Presented to Alan L. Boegehold on the Occasion of His Retirement and Seventy-Fifth Birthday*, edited by Geoffrey W. Bakewell and James P. Sickinger, 214–36. Oxford: Oxbow.

————. 2006. "Free and Unfree Sexual Work: An Economic Analysis of Athenian Prostitution." In *Prostitutes and Courtesans in the Ancient World*, edited by Christopher A. Faraone and Laura K. McClure, 95–124. Madison: University of Wisconsin Press.

————. 2007. "Slave Power at Athens: Juridical Theory and Economic Reality." In *Individus, groupes et politique à Athènes de Solon à Mithridate*, edited by Jean-Christophe Couvenhes and Sílvia Milanezi, 155–70. Tours: Presses universitaires François-Rabelais.

Cole, Susan G. 2004. *Landscapes, Gender, and Ritual Space: The Ancient Greek Experience.* Berkeley: University of California Press.

Connelly, Joan B. 2007. *Portrait of a Priestess.* Princeton: Princeton University Press.

Connor, W. R. 1994. "The Problem of Athenian Civic Identity." In *Athenian Identity and Civic Ideology*, edited by Alan L. Boegehold and Adele C. Scafuro, 34–44. Baltimore: Johns Hopkins University Press.

Cox, Cheryl A. 1998. *Household Interests: Property, Marriage Strategies, and Family Dynamics in Ancient Athens.* Princeton: Princeton University Press.

Crowther, Nigel B. 1992. "Slaves and Greek Athletics." *QUCC* n.s. 40: 35–42.

Cudjoe, Richard V. 2010. *The Social and Legal Position of Widows and Orphans in Classical Athens.* Athens: Centre for Ancient Greek and Hellenistic Law, Panteion University of Social and Political Sciences.

Davidson, James N. 1997. *Courtesans and Fishcakes: The Consuming Passions of Classical Athens.* London: HarperCollins.

Davies, John K. 1971. *Athenian Propertied Families, 600–300 BC.* Oxford: Clarendon Press.

————. 1977/78. "Athenian Citizenship: The Descent Group and the Alternatives." *CJ* 73: 105–21.

————. 1981. *Wealth and the Power of Wealth in Classical Athens.* Salem, NH: Ayer.

de Ste. Croix, G. E. M. 1970. "Some Observations on the Property Rights of Athenian Women." *CR* 20: 273–78.

de Ste. Croix, G. E. M.. 1981. *The Class Struggle in the Ancient Greek World from the Archaic Age to the Arab Conquests*. Ithaca, NY: Cornell University Press.

Diller, Aubrey. 1935. "Scrutiny and Appeal in Athenian Citizenship." *CP* 30: 302–11.

———. 1937. *Race Mixture among the Greeks before Alexander*. Urbana.

Dillon, Matthew. 2002. *Girls and Women in Classical Greek Religion*. London: Routledge.

Dimopoulou-Piliouni, Athina. 2009. "*Apeleutheroi*: Metics or Foreigners?" *Dike* 11: 27–50.

Dow, Sterling. 1963. "The Athenian Anagrapheis." *HSCP* 67: 28–54.

duBois, Page. 1991. *Torture and Truth*. New York: Routledge.

———. 2003. *Slaves and Other Objects*. Chicago: University of Chicago Press.

Ducrey, Pierre. 1999 [1968]. *Le traitement des prisonniers de guerre dans la Grèce antique des origins à la conquête romaine*. Paris: E. de Boccard.

Ebbott, Mary. 2003. *Imagining Illegitimacy in Classical Greek Literature*. Lanham, MD: Lexington Books.

Ehrenberg, Victor. 1943. *The People of Aristophanes: A Sociology of Old Attic Comedy*. Oxford: Blackwell.

Eidinow, E. "'What Will Happen to Me if I Leave?' Ancient Greek Oracles, Slaves and Slave Owners." In *Slaves and Religions in Graeco-Roman Antiquity and Modern Brazil*, edited by Dick Geary and Stephen Hodkinson, 244–78. Newcastle upon Tyne: Cambridge Scholars Publishing.

Farenga, Vincent. 2006. *Citizen and Self in Ancient Greece: Individuals Performing Justice and the Law*. Cambridge: Cambridge University Press.

Finley, Moses I. 1968. "Slavery." In *International Encyclopedia of the Social Sciences*, vol. 14, edited by David L. Sills, 307–13. New York: Macmillan.

———. 1973. *The Ancient Economy*. Berkeley: University of California Press.

———. 1981 [1959]. "Was Greek Civilisation Based on Slave Labour?" In *Economy and Society in Ancient Greece*, edited by Brent D. Shaw and Richard P. Saller, 97–115. London: Chatto & Windus.

———. 1981 [1960]. "The Servile Statuses of Ancient Greece." In *Economy and Society in Ancient Greece*, edited by Brent D. Shaw and Richard P. Saller, 133–49. London: Chatto & Windus.

———. 1981 [1962]. "The Slave Trade in Antiquity." In *Economy and Society in Ancient Greece*, edited by Brent D. Shaw and Richard P. Saller, 167–75. London: Chatto & Windus.

———. 1981 [1964]. "Between Slavery and Freedom." In *Economy and Society in Ancient Greece*, edited by Brent D. Shaw and Richard P. Saller, 116–32. London: Chatto & Windus.

———. 1981 [1976]. "The Freedom of the Citizen in the Greek World." In *Economy and Society in Ancient Greece*, edited by Brent D. Shaw and Richard P. Saller, 77–94. London: Chatto & Windus.

———. 1981 [1977]. "The Ancient City: From Fustel de Coulanges to Max Weber and Beyond." In *Economy and Society in Ancient Greece*, edited by Brent D. Shaw and Richard P. Saller, 3–23. London: Chatto & Windus.

———. 1983. *Politics in the Ancient World*. Cambridge: Cambridge University Press.

———. 1985. *Ancient History: Evidence and Models*. New York: Viking.

———. 1998 [1980]. "The Emergence of a Slave Society." In *Ancient Slavery and Modern Ideology*, edited by Brent D. Shaw, 135–60. Princeton: Markus Wiener Publishers.

Fisher, N. R. E. 1992. *HYBRIS: A Study in the Values of Honour and Shame in Ancient Greece*. Warminster, U.K.: Aris & Phillips.

———. 1995. "*Hybris*, Status and Slavery." In *The Greek World*, edited by Anton Powell, 44–84. London: Routledge.

———. 2001 [1993]. *Slavery in Classical Greece*. London: Bristol Classical Press.

———. 2004. "The Perils of Pittalakos: Settings of Cock Fighting and Dicing in Classical Athens." In *Games and Festivals in Classical Antiquity: Proceedings of the Conference Held in Edinburgh 10–12 July 2000*, edited by Sinclair Bell and Glenys Davies, 65–78. Oxford: Archeopress.

———. 2006. "Citizens, Foreigners, Slaves." In *A Companion to the Classical Greek World*, edited by Konrad H. Kinzl, 327–49. Malden, MA: Blackwell.

———. 2008. "'Independent' Slaves in Classical Athens and the Ideology of Slavery." In *From Captivity to Freedom*, edited by Constantina Katsari and Enrico Dal Lago, 121–46. Leicester: University of Leicester, School of Archaeology & Ancient History.

———. 2011. "Competitive Delights: The Social Effects of the Expanded Programme of Contests in Post-Kleisthenic Athens." In *Competition in the Ancient World*, edited by N. R. E. Fisher and Hans van Wees, 175–219. Swansea: Classical Press of Wales.

Forsdyke, Sara. 2005. *Exile, Ostracism, and Democracy: The Politics of Expulsion in Ancient Greece*. Princeton: Princeton University Press.

Foucart, George. 1896. *De libertorum conditione apud Athenienses*. Paris: Klinksieck.

Foxhall, Lin. 1989. "Household, Gender and Property in Classical Athens." *CQ* 39: 22–44.

———. 1996. "The Law and the Lady: Women and Legal Proceedings in Classical Athens." In *Law in its Political Setting: Justifications not Justice*, edited by Lin Foxhall and A. D. E. Lewis, 133–52. Oxford: Clarendon Press.

———. 2005. "Response to D. Cohen, Women in Public: Gender, Citizenship, and Social Status in Classical Athens." In *Symposion 2001: Vorträge zur griechischen und hellenistischen Rechtsgeschichte*, edited by Michael Gagarin and Robert W. Wallace, 47–50. Vienna: Verlag der Österreichischen Akademie der Wissenschaften.

Gabrielsen, Vincent. 1987. "The Antidosis Procedure in Classical Athens." *C&M* 38: 7–38.

———. 1994. *Financing the Athenian Fleet: Public Taxation and Social Relations*. Baltimore: Johns Hopkins University Press.

Gagarin, Michael. 1996. "The Torture of Slaves in Athenian Law." *CP* 91: 1–18.

———. 1998. "Women in Athenian Courts." *Dike* 1: 39–52.

Garlan, Yvon. 1987. "War, Piracy and Slavery in the Greek World." Translated by Marie-Jo Roy. In *Classical Slavery*, edited by Moses I. Finley, 9–27. London: F. Cass.

———. 1988 [1982]. *Slavery in Ancient Greece*. Translated by Janet Lloyd. Ithaca, NY: Cornell University Press.

Garland, Robert. 1992. *Introducing New Gods: The Politics of Athenian Religion*. London: Duckworth.

Garnsey, Peter. 1998. *Cities, Peasants and Food in Classical Antiquity: Essays in Social and Economic History*, edited with addenda by Walter Scheidel. Cambridge: Cambridge University Press.

———. 1999 [1996]. *Ideas of Slavery from Aristotle to Augustine*. Cambridge: Cambridge University Press.

Gärtner, Martine. 2008. "L'affranchissement dans le corpus lysiaque: une pratique contestée: Le regard d'un métèque sur l'affranchissement." In *La fin du statut servile? Affranchissement, liberation, abolition*, vol. 2, edited by Antonio Gonzales, 453–66. Besançon: Presses universitaires de Franche-Comté.

Gastaldi, Enrica C. 2004. *Le prossenie ateniesi del IV secolo a.C.: gli onorati asiatici*. Alessandria, Italy: Ed. dell'Orso.

Gauthier, Philippe. 1972. *Symbola: Les étrangers et la justice dans les cites grecques*. Nancy: Université de Nancy.

———. 1974. "'Generosité' romaine et 'avarice' grecque: sur l'octroi du droit de cité." In *Mélanges d'histoire ancienne offerts à William Seston*, 207–15. Paris: E. de Boccard.

———. 1985. *Les cités grecques et leurs bienfaiteurs*. *Bulletin de correspondance hellénique*. Supplement XII. Paris: Diffusion de Boccard.

———. 1986. "L'octroi du droit de cité à Athènes." *REG* 99: 119–33.

———. 1988. "Métèques, périèques, paroikoi." In *L'étranger dans le monde grec: actes du deuxième Colloque sur l'étranger, Nancy, 19–21 septembre 1991*, edited by Raoul Lonis, 23–46. Nancy: Presses universitaires de Nancy.

Geary, Dick and Stephen Hodkinson, eds. 2012. *Slaves and Religions in Graeco-Roman Antiquity and Modern Brazil*. Newcastle upon Tyne: Cambridge Scholars Publishing.

Geertz, Clifford. 1973. *The Interpretation of Cultures*. New York: Basic Books.

Gernet, Louis. 1954. *Démosthène: Plaidoyers civils*, vol. 1. Paris: Les Belles Lettres.

———. 1955. *Droit et société dans la Grèce ancienne*. New York: Recueil Sirey.

Gilhuly, Kate. 2009. *The Feminine Matrix of Sex and Gender in Classical Athens*. Cambridge: Cambridge University Press.

Glazebrook, Allison. 2005. "Prostituting Female Kin (Plut. *Sol.* 23.1–2)." *Dike* 8: 33–52.

———. 2011. "*Porneion*: Prostitution in Athenian Civic Space." In *Greek Prostitutes in the Ancient Mediterranean, 800 BCE–200 CE*, edited by Allison Glazebrook and Madeleine M. Henry, 34–59. Madison: University of Wisconsin Press.

——— and Madeleine M. Henry, eds. 2011. *Greek Prostitutes in the Ancient Mediterranean, 800 BCE–200 CE*. Madison: University of Wisconsin Press.

Goff, Barbara E. 2004. *Citizen Bacchae*. Berkeley: University of California Press.

Golden, Mark. 1985. "*Pais*, 'Child' and 'Slave.'" *AntCl* 54: 91–104.

———. 1998. *Sport and Society*. Cambridge: Cambridge University Press.

———. 2008. *Greek Sport and Social Status*. Austin: University of Texas Press.

———. 2011. "Slavery and the Greek Family." In *The Cambridge World History of Slavery*, vol. 1: *The Ancient Mediterranean World*, edited by Keith Bradley and Paul Cartledge, 134–52. Cambridge: Cambridge University Press.

Goldhill, Simon. 1990. "The Great Dionysia and Civic Ideology." In *Nothing to Do with Dionysos? Athenian Drama in its Social Context*, edited by John J. Winkler and Froma I. Zeitlin, 7–129. Princeton: Princeton University Press.

———. 1994. "Representing Democracy: Women at the Great Dionysia." In *Ritual, Finance, Politics: Athenian Democratic Accounts Presented to David Lewis*, edited by Robin Osborne and Simon Hornblower, 347–69. Oxford: Clarendon Press.

Gomme, A. W. 1925. "The Position of Women in Athens in the Fifth and Fourth Centuries." *CP* 20: 1–25.

———. 1934. "Two Problems of Athenian Citizenship Law." *CP* 29: 123–40.

Gould, J. 1980. "Law, Custom and Myth: Aspects of the Social Position of Women in Classical Athens." *JHS* 100: 38–59.

Grace, Emily. 1975. "A Note on Dem. XLVII 72: τούτων τὰς ἐπισκήψεις εἶναι." *Eirene* 13: 5–18.

Halperin, David M. 1990. *One Hundred Years of Homosexuality: and Other Essays on Greek Love*. London: Routledge.

Hansen, M. H. 1974. *The Sovereignty of the People's Court in Athens in the Fourth Century BC and the Public Action Against Unconstitutional Proposals*. Odense, Denmark: Odense University Press.

———. 1976. *Apagoge, Endeixis and Ephegesis against Kakourgoi, Atimoi and Pheugontes*. Odense, Denmark: Odense University Press.

———. 1980. "Seven Hundred *Archai* in Classical Athens." *GRBS* 21: 151–73.

———. 1985. *Demography and Democracy: The Number of Athenian Citizens in the Fourth Century BC*. Herning, Denmark: Systime.

———. 1987. *The Athenian Assembly*. Oxford: Blackwell.

———. 1991. *The Athenian Democracy in the Age of Demosthenes: Structure, Principles and Ideology*. Translated by J. A. Crook. Norman, OK: University of Oklahoma Press.

Hanson, Victor D. 1999 [1995]. *The Other Greeks: The Family Farm and the Agrarian Roots of Western Civilization*. Berkeley: University of California Press.

Harris, Edward M. 1992. "Women and Lending in Athenian Society: A Horos Re-examined." *Phoenix* 46: 309–21.

———. 2004. "Notes on a Lead Letter from the Athenian Agora." *HSCP* 102: 157–70.

Harrison, A. R. W. 1968. *The Law of Athens*. Vol. 1. Oxford: Clarendon Press.

———. 1971. *The Law of Athens*. Vol. 2. Oxford: Clarendon Press.

Headlam, J. W. 1893. "On the πρόκλησις εἰς βάσανον in Attic Law." *CR* 7: 1–5.

Hedrick, Charles W., Jr. 1994. "The Zero Degree of Society: Aristotle and Athenian Citizen." In *Athenian Political Thought and the Reconstruction of American Democracy*, edited by J. P. Euben, John R. Wallach, and Josiah Ober, 289–318. Ithaca, NY: Cornell University Press.

Henry, Alan S. 1983. *Honours and Privileges in Athenian Decrees: The Principal Formulae of Athenian Honorary Decrees*. Hildesheim, Germany: G. Olms.

Hereward, Daphne. 1952. "New Fragments of IG II2 10." *ABSA* 47: 102–17.

Herman, Gabriel. 1987. *Ritualised Friendship and the Greek City*. Cambridge: Cambridge University Press.

———. 2006. *Morality and Behaviour in Democratic Athens: A Social History*. Cambridge: Cambridge University Press.

Hermann-Otto, Elisabeth. 2009. *Sklaverei und Freilassung in der griechisch-römischen Welt.* Hildesheim, Germany: G. Olms.

Hohfeld, Wesley N. 1919. *Fundamental Legal Conceptions as Applied in Judicial Reasoning.* Edited by Walter W. Cook. Westport, CT: Greenwood Publishing.

Hopkins, Keith. 1978. *Conquerors and Slaves.* Cambridge: Cambridge University Press.

Humphreys, S. C. 1974. "The Nothoi of Kynosarges." *JHS* 94: 88–95.

Hunt, Peter. 1998. *Slaves, Warfare and Ideology in the Greek Historians.* Cambridge: Cambridge University Press.

———. 2001. "The Slaves and Generals of Arginusae." *AJP* 122: 359–80.

Hunter, Virginia. 1989a. "Women's Authority in Classical Athens: The Example of Kleoboule and Her Son (Dem. 27–29)." *ECM/CV* n.s. 8: 39–48.

———. 1989b. "The Athenian Widow and Her Kin." *JFH* 14: 291–311.

———. 1992. "Constructing the Body of the Citizen: Corporal Punishment in Classical Athens." *EMC/CV* n.s. 11: 271–91.

———. 1994. *Policing Athens: Social Control in the Attic Lawsuits.* Princeton: Princeton University Press.

———. 2000a. "Introduction: Status Distinctions in Athenian Law." In *Law and Social Status in Classical Athens,* edited by Virginia J. Hunter and J. C. Edmondson, 1–29. Oxford: Oxford University Press.

———. 2000b. "Policing Public Debtors in Classical Athens." *Phoenix* 54: 21–38.

———. 2006. "Pittalacus and Eucles: Slaves in the Public Service of Athens." *Mouseion* 3rd ser. 6: 1–14.

Jacob, Oscar. 1928. *Les esclaves publics à Athènes.* Bibliothèque de la faculté de philosophie et lettres de l'université de Liège. Vol. 35. Liège: H. Vaillant-Carmanne.

Jameson, Michael H. 1977/78. "Agriculture and Slavery in Classical Athens." *CJ* 73: 122–45.

———. 1990a. "Domestic Space and the Greek City-State." In *Domestic Architecture and the Use of Space: An Interdisciplinary Cross-Cultural Study,* edited by Susan Kent, 92–113. Cambridge: Cambridge University Press.

———. 1990b. "Private Space and the Greek City." In *The Greek City: From Homer to Alexander,* edited by Oswyn Murray and S. R. F. Price, 171–95. Oxford: Oxford University Press.

———. 2004 [1997]. "Women and Democracy in Fourth-Century Athens." In *Ancient Greek Democracy: Readings and Sources,* edited by Eric W. Robinson, 281–92. Oxford: Blackwell.

Johnstone, Steven. 1994. "Virtuous Toil, Vicious Work: Xenophon on Aristocratic Style." *CP* 89: 219–40.

———. 1999. *Disputes and Democracy: The Consequences of Litigation in Ancient Athens.* Austin: University of Texas Press.

———. 2003. "Women, Property, and Surveillance in Classical Athens." *CA* 22: 247–74.

Jones, A. H. M. 1957. *Athenian Democracy.* Oxford: Blackwell.

Jones, Nicholas F. 1999. *The Associations of Classical Athens: The Response to Democracy.* New York: Oxford University Press.

Jordan, D. R. 2000. "A Personal Letter Found in the Athenian Agora." *Hesperia* 69: 91–103.

Joshel, Sandra R. and Lauren H. Petersen. Forthcoming. *The Material Life of Roman Slaves*. Cambridge: Cambridge University Press.

Just, Roger. 1989. *Women in Athenian Law and Life*. London: Routledge.

Kagan, Donald. 1963. "The Enfranchisement of Aliens by Cleisthenes." *Historia* 12: 41–46.

Kamen, Deborah. 2009. "Servile Invective in Classical Athens." *SCI* 28: 43–56.

———. 2010. "A Corpus of Inscriptions: Representing Slave Marks in Antiquity." *MAAR* 55: 95–110.

———. 2012. "Manumission, Social Rebirth, and Healing Gods in Ancient Greece." In *Slaves and Religions in Graeco-Roman Antiquity and Modern Brazil*, edited by Dick Geary and Stephen Hodkinson, 174–94. Newcastle upon Tyne: Cambridge Scholars Publishing.

———. Forthcoming. "Reconsidering the Status of *khōris oikountes*." *Dike*.

Kantzara, V. 2007. "Status." In *The Blackwell Encyclopedia of Sociology*, vol. 9, edited by George Ritzer, 4749–53. Malden, MA: Blackwell.

Kapparis, K. 1995. "The Athenian Decree for the Naturalisation of the Plataeans." *GRBS* 36: 359–78.

———. 1999. *Apollodoros "Against Neaira" [D. 59]*. Berlin and New York: W. de Gruyter.

———. 2005. "Immigration and Citizenship Procedures in Athenian Law." *RIDA* 52: 71–113.

Kazakévich, Emily G. 2008 [1960]. "Were the χωρὶς οἰκοῦντες Slaves?" Edited by Deborah Kamen. *GRBS* 48: 343–80.

Klees, Hans. 1998. *Sklavenleben im Klassischen Griechenland*. Forschungen zur antiken Sklaverei 30. Stuttgart: F. Steiner.

———. 2000. "Die rechtliche und gesellschaftliche Stellung der Freigelassenen im klassischen Griechenland." *Laverna* 11: 1–43.

Kopytoff, Igor. 1986. "The Cultural Biography of Things: Commoditization as Process." In *The Social Life of Things*, edited by Arjun Appadurai, 64–91. Cambridge: Cambridge University Press.

Koschaker, Paul. 1931. *Über einige griechische Rechtsurkunden aus den östlichen Randgebieten des Hellenismus: mit Beiträgen zum Eigentums- und Pfandbegriff nach griechischen und orientalischen Rechten*. Abhandlungen der Philologischen-historischen Klasse der Sächsischen Akademie der Wissenschaften 42. Leipzig: Hirzel.

Krentz, Peter. 1980. "Foreigners against the Thirty: IG II2 Again." *Phoenix* 34: 298–306.

Kurke, Leslie. 1997. "Inventing the *Hetaira*: Sex, Politics, and Discursive Conflict in Archaic Greece." *CA* 16: 106–50.

Labarre, Guy. 1998. "Les métiers du textile en Grèce ancienne." *Topoi* 8: 791–814.

Lacey, Walter K. 1968. *The Family in Classical Greece*. London: Thames and Hudson.

Lambert, S. D. 1993. *The Phratries of Attica*. Ann Arbor: University of Michigan Press.

———. 2006. "Athenian State Laws and Decrees, 352/1–322/1: III. Decrees Honouring Foreigners; A. Citizenship, Proxeny and Euergesy." *ZPE* 158: 115–58.

Lanni, Adriaan. 2006. *Law and Justice in the Courts of Classical Athens*. Cambridge: Cambridge University Press.

Lape, Susan. 2010. *Race and Citizen Identity in the Classical Athenian Democracy*. Cambridge: Cambridge University Press.

Lauffer, Siegfried. 1979. *Die Bergwerkssklaven von Laureion.* Weisbaden: F. Steiner.

Lewis, David M. 1959. "Attic Manumissions." *Hesperia* 28: 208–38.

———. 1968. "Dedications of Phialai at Athens." *Hesperia* 37: 368–80.

Liddel, Peter P. 2007. *Civic Obligation and Individual Liberty in Classical Athens.* Oxford: Oxford University Press.

Lipsius, Justus H. 1966 [1905–1915]. *Das attische Recht und Rechtsverfahren.* Hildesheim: G. Olms.

Llewellyn-Jones, L. 2003. *Aphrodite's Tortoise: The Veiled Woman of Ancient Greece.* Swansea: The Classical Press of Wales.

Lloyd, G. E. R. 1966. *Polarity and Analogy: Two Types of Argumentation in Early Greek Thought.* Cambridge: Cambridge University Press.

Loraux, Nicole. 1993. *The Children of Athena: Athenian Ideas about Citizenship and the Division of the Sexes.* Princeton: Princeton University Press.

Lotze, Detlef. 1981. "Zwischen Politen und Metöken: Passivbürger im klassischen Athen?" *Klio* 63: 159–78.

MacDowell, Douglas M. 1962. *Andokides, "On the Mysteries."* Oxford: Clarendon.

———. 1963. *Athenian Homicide Law in the Age of the Orators.* Manchester: Manchester University Press.

———. 1976. "Bastards as Athenian Citizens." *CQ* 26: 88–91.

———. 1978. *The Law in Classical Athens.* Ithaca, NY: Cornell University Press.

Mactoux, Marie M. 1988. "Lois de Solon sur les esclaves et formation d'une société esclavagiste." In *Forms of Control and Subordination in Antiquity*, edited by Tōru Yuge and Masaoki Doi, 331–54. Tokyo: Society for Studies on Resistance Movements in Antiquity.

———. 2008. "Regards sur la proclamation de l'affranchissement au théâtre à Athènes." In *La fin du statut servile? Affranchissement, liberation, abolition*, vol. 2, edited by Antonio Gonzales, 437–51. Besançon: Presses universitaires de Franche-Comté.

Maffi, A. 1997. "Processo di libertà e rivendicazione in proprietà dello schiavo a Gortina e ad Atene." In *Symposion 1995: Vorträge zur griechischen und hellenistischen Rechtsgeschichte*, edited by Gerhard Thür and Julie Vélissaropoulos-Karakostas, 17–25. Cologne: Böhlau.

Manville, Philip B. 1997 [1990]. *The Origins of Citizenship in Ancient Athens.* Princeton: Princeton University Press.

Marek, Christian. 1984. *Die Proxenie.* Frankfurt am Main: P. Lang.

Meillassoux, Claude. 1975. "Introduction." In *L'esclavage en Afrique précoloniale*, edited by Claude Meillassoux, 11–26. Paris: Maspero.

———. 1986. *Anthropologie de l'esclavage: Le ventre de fer et d'argent.* Paris: Presses universitaires de France.

Mennen, Inge. 2011. *Power and Status in the Roman Empire, AD 193–284.* Leiden: Brill.

Meyer, Elizabeth A. 2010. *Metics and the Athenian Phialai-inscriptions: A Study in Athenian Epigraphy and Law. Historia Einzelschriften* vol. 208. Stuttgart: Steiner.

Middleton, Marci M. 2008. "Social Status." In *International Encyclopedia of the Social Sciences*, vol. 7, edited by William A. Darity, Jr., 621–22. 2nd ed. Detroit: Macmillan.

Mikalson, Jon D. 2010. *Ancient Greek Religion.* 2nd ed. Malden, MA: Blackwell.

Millett, Paul. 1991. *Lending and Borrowing in Ancient Athens*. Cambridge: Cambridge University Press.

Mirhady, David. 1996. "Torture and Rhetoric in Athens." *JHS* 116: 119–31.

———. 2000. "The Athenian Rationale for Torture." In *Law and Social Status in Classical Athens*, edited by Virginia J. Hunter and J. C. Edmondson, 53–74. Oxford: Oxford University Press.

———. 2010. "Marriage and Divorce: Greek Marriage." In *The Oxford Encyclopedia of Ancient Greece and Rome,* vol. 4, edited by Michael Gagarin, 350–53. Oxford: Oxford University Press.

Morgan, Janett. 2010. *The Classical Greek House*. Exeter: Bristol University Press.

Morris, Ian. 2011. "Archaeology and Greek Slavery." In *The Cambridge World History of Slavery*, vol. 1: *The Ancient Mediterranean World*, edited by Keith Bradley and Paul Cartledge, 176–93. Cambridge: Cambridge University Press.

Morrow, Glenn R. 1937. "The Murder of Slaves in Attic Law." *CP* 32: 210–27.

———. 1939. *Plato's Law of Slavery in Its Relation to Greek Law*. Urbana: University of Illinois.

———. 1960. *Plato's Cretan City: A Historical Interpretation of the* Laws. Princeton: Princeton University Press.

Mossé, Claude. 1979. "Citoyens 'actifs' et citoyens 'passifs' dans les cités grecques." *REA* 81: 241–49.

Nafissi, Mohammad. 2004. "Class, Embeddedness, and the Modernity of Ancient Athens." *CSSH* 46: 378–410.

Németh, György. 2001. "Metics in Athens." *AAntHung* 41: 331–48.

Nevett, Lisa C. 1994. "Separation or Seclusion? Towards an Archaeological Approach to Investigating Women in the Greek Household in the Fifth to the Third Centuries BC." In *Architecture and Order: Approaches to Social Space*, edited by Michael P. Pearson and Colin Richards, 98–112. London: Routledge.

———. 1995. "Gender Relations in the Classical Greek Household: The Archaeological Evidence." *ABSA* 90: 363–81.

———. 1999. *House and Society in the Ancient Greek World*. Cambridge: Cambridge University Press.

Niku, Maria. 2007. *The Official Status of the Foreign Residents in Athens 322–120 BC*. Helsinki: Suomen Ateenan-instituutin säätiö.

Ober, Josiah. 1989. *Mass and Elite in Democratic Athens*. Princeton: Princeton University Press.

———. 1991. "Aristotle's Political Sociology: Class, Status, and Order in the *Politics*." In *Essays on the Foundations of Aristotelian Political Science*, edited by Carnes Lord and David K. O'Connor, 112–35. Berkeley: University of California Press.

———. 2005 [2000]. "Quasi Rights: Participatory Citizenship and Negative Liberties." In *Athenian Legacies: Essays on the Politics of Going On Together*, 92–127. Princeton: Princeton University Press.

Ogden, D. 1995. "Women and Bastardy in Ancient Greece and the Hellenistic World." In *The Greek World*, edited by Anton Powell, 219–44. London: Routledge.

———. 1996. *Greek Bastardy in the Classical and Hellenistic Periods*. Oxford: Oxford University Press.

Oliver, Graham. 2007. "Citizenship: Inscribed Honours for Individuals in Classical and Hellenistic Athens." In *Individus, groupes et politique à Athènes de Solon à Mithridate*, edited by Jean-Christophe Couvenhes and Silvia Milanezi, 273–92. Tours: Presses universitaires François Rabelais.

Omitowoju, Rosanna. 2002. *Rape and the Politics of Consent in Classical Athens*. Cambridge: Cambridge University Press.

Osborne, Michael J. 1981. *Naturalization in Athens*, vol. 1. Brussels: Paleis der Academiën.

——. 1982. *Naturalization in Athens*, vol. 2. Brussels: Paleis der Academiën.

——. 1983. *Naturalization in Athens*, vols. 3–4: *Testimonia; The Law and Practice*. Brussels: Paleis der Academiën.

Osborne, Robin. 1995. "The Economics and Politics of Slavery at Athens." In *The Greek World*, edited by Anton Powell, 27–43. London: Routledge.

——. 1997. "Law, the Democratic Citizen and the Representation of Women in Classical Athens." *P&P* 155: 3–33.

——. 2000. "Religion, Imperial Politics, and the Offering of Freedom to Slaves." In *Law and Social Status in Classical Athens*, edited by Virginia J. Hunter and J. C. Edmondson, 75–92. Oxford: Oxford University Press.

——. 2011. *The History Written on the Classical Body*. Cambridge: Cambridge University Press.

Ossowski, Stanisław. 1963. *Class Structure in the Social Consciousness*. Translated by Sheila Patterson. New York: Free Press.

Ostwald, Martin. 1986. *From Popular Sovereignty to the Sovereignty of Law*. Berkeley: University of California Press.

——. 1990. "The Solonian Law of *Hubris*." In *NOMOS: Essays in Athenian Law, Politics, and Society*, edited by Paul Cartledge, Paul Millett, and Stephen Todd, 139–45. Cambridge: Cambridge University Press.

——. 1996. "Shares and Rights: 'Citizenship' Greek Style and American Style." In *Dēmokratia: A Conversation on Democracies, Ancient and Modern*, edited by Josiah Ober and Charles W. Hedrick, Jr., 49–61. Princeton: Princeton University Press.

Paoli, Ugo E. 1974 [1930]. *Studi di diritto attico*. Milan: Bemporad.

Parker, Robert. 1983. *Miasma: Pollution and Purification in Early Greek Religion*. Oxford: Clarendon Press.

——. 1996. *Athenian Religion: A History*. Oxford: Clarendon Press.

——. 2005. *Polytheism and Society at Athens*. Oxford: Oxford University Press.

——. 2011. *On Greek Religion*. Ithaca, NY: Cornell University Press.

Patterson, Cynthia. 1981. *Pericles' Citizenship Law of 451–50*. New York: Arno Press.

——. 1986. "*Hai Attikai*: The Other Athenians." In *Rescuing Creusa: New Methodological Approaches to Women in Antiquity*, edited by Marilyn Skinner. A Special Issue of *Helios* 13: 49–67.

——. 1990. "Those Athenian Bastards." *CA* 9: 40–73.

——. 1998. *The Family in Greek History*. Cambridge, MA: Harvard University Press.

——. 2000. "The Hospitality of Athenian Justice: The Metic in Court." In *Law and Social Status in Classical Athens*, edited by Virginia J. Hunter and J. C. Edmondson, 93–112. Oxford: Oxford University Press.

———. 2005. "Athenian Citizenship Law." In *The Cambridge Companion to Ancient Greek Law*, edited by Michael Gagarin and David Cohen, 267–89. Cambridge and New York: Cambridge University Press.

———. 2009. "Status: Ancient Greek Law." In *The Oxford International Encyclopedia of Legal History*, vol. 5, edited by Stanley N. Katz, 354–58. Oxford: Oxford University Press.

Patterson, Orlando. 1982. *Slavery and Social Death: A Comparative Study.* Cambridge, MA: Harvard University Press.

Pearson, Lionel. 1972. *Demosthenes: Six Private Speeches.* Norman, OK: University of Oklahoma Press.

Pečírka, Jan. 1966. *The Formula for the Grant of Enktesis in Attic Inscriptions.* Prague: Universita Karlova.

Perotti, Elena. 1974. "Esclaves χωρὶς οἰκοῦντες." Translated from the Italian by Michèle Pesce. In *Actes du Colloque 1972 sur l'esclavage*, 47–56. Paris: Les Belles Lettres.

———. 1976. "Contribution à l'étude d'un autre categorie d'esclaves attiques: les ἀνδράποδα μισθοφοροῦντα." In *Actes du Colloque 1973 sur l'esclavage*, 181–94. Paris: Les Belles Lettres.

Pomeroy, Sarah B. 1975. *Goddesses, Whores, Wives, and Slaves: Women in Classical Antiquity.* New York: Schocken Books.

———. 1997. *Families in Classical and Hellenistic Greece: Representations and Realities.* Oxford: Clarendon Press.

Pritchett, W. K. 1953. "The Attic Stelai: Part I." *Hesperia* 22: 225–99.

———. 1956. "The Attic Stelai: Part II." *Hesperia* 25: 178–328.

———. 1991. *The Greek State at War.* Part 5. Berkeley: University of California Press.

Raaflaub, Kurt. 1996. "Equalities and Inequalities in Athenian Democracy." In *Dēmokratia: A Conversation on Democracies, Ancient and Modern*, edited by Josiah Ober and Charles W. Hedrick, Jr., 139–74. Princeton: Princeton University Press.

———. 2004. *The Discovery of Freedom in Ancient Greece.* Translated by Renate Franciscono. Chicago: University of Chicago Press.

Rädle, Herbert. 1969. *Untersuchungen zum griechischen Freilassungswesen.* Dissertation. University of Munich.

———. 1971. "Freilassung von Sklaven im Theater (Inschriftliche Zeugnisse)." *RIDA* 18: 361–64.

———. 1972. "Platons Freigelassenengesetze als Ausdruck attischer Standespolitik de 4. Jahrhunderts." *Gymnasium* 79: 305–13.

Randall, R. H., Jr. 1953. "The Erechtheum Workman." *AJA* 57: 199–210.

Reitzammer, L. 2008. "Aristophanes' *Adōniazousai*." *CA* 27: 282–333.

Rhodes, P. J. 1978. "Bastards as Athenian Citizens." *CQ* 28: 89–92.

———. 1981. *Commentary on the Aristotelian* Athenaion Politeia. Oxford: Clarendon Press.

———. 1991. "The Athenian Code of Laws, 410–399 BC." *JHS* 111: 87–100.

——— and Robin Osborne. 2003. *Greek Historical Inscriptions, 404–323 BC.* Oxford: Oxford University Press.

Rihll, Tracey. 2010. "Skilled Slaves and the Economy: The Silver Mines of Laurion." In *Antike Sklaverei: Rückblick und Ausblick. Neue Beiträge zur Forschungsgeschichte und zur Erschließung der archäologischen Zeugnisse*, edited by Heinz Heinen, 203–20. Stuttgart: Steiner.

Robertson, Bruce. 2000. "The Scrutiny of New Citizens at Court." In *Law and Social Status in Classical Athens*, edited by Virginia J. Hunter and J. C. Edmondson, 149–74. Oxford: Oxford University Press.

Robertson, Noel. 1990. "The Laws of Athens, 410–399: The Evidence for Review and Publication." *JHS* 110: 43–75.

Robinson, Rachel S. 1924. *The Size of the Slave Population at Athens during the Fifth and Fourth Centuries before Christ*. Urbana: University of Illinois.

Rosivach, Vincent J. 1989. "*Talasiourgoi* and *Paidia* in *IG* 2² 1553–78: A Note on Athenian Social History." *Historia* 38: 365–70.

———. 1999. "Enslaving *Barbaroi* and the Athenian Ideology of Slavery," *Historia* 48: 129–57.

Rubinstein, Lene. 1993. *Adoption in IV. Century Athens*. Copenhagen: Museum Tusculanum Press.

Samuel, Alan E. 1965. "The Role of Paramone Clauses in Ancient Documents." *JJP* 15: 221–311.

Scafuro, Adele. 1994. "Witnessing and False Witnessing: Proving Citizenship and Kin Identity in Fourth-Century Athens." In *Athenian Identity and Civic Ideology*, edited by Alan L. Boegehold and Adele C. Scafuro, 156–98. Baltimore: Johns Hopkins University Press.

Schaps, David M. 1975. "Women in Greek Inheritance Law." *CQ* 25: 53–57.

———. 1979. *Economic Rights of Women in Ancient Greece*. Edinburgh: Edinburgh University Press.

———. 1998. "What Was Free about a Free Athenian Woman?" *TAPA* 128: 161–88.

Sealey, Raphael. 1983. "How Citizenship and the City Began in Athens." *AJAH*: 97–129.

———. 1984. "On Lawful Concubinage in Athens." *CA* 3: 111–33.

———. 1990. *Women and Law in Classical Greece*. Chapel Hill: University of North Carolina Press.

Shaw, Brent D. and Richard P. Saller. 1981. "Editors' Introduction." In *Economy and Society in Ancient Greece*, edited by Brent D. Shaw and Richard P. Saller, ix–xxvi. New York: Viking Press.

Shipton, Kirsty M. W. 1997. "The Private Banks in Fourth-Century BC Athens: A Reappraisal." *CQ* 47: 396–422.

Sickinger, James P. 1999. *Public Records and Archives in Classical Athens*. Chapel Hill: University of North Carolina Press.

Simms, Ronda R. 1988. "The Cult of the Thracian Goddess Bendis in Athens and Attica." *AncW* 18: 59–76.

Sinclair, Robert K. 1988. *Democracy and Participation in Athens*. Cambridge: Cambridge University Press.

Sokolowski, F. 1954. "The Real Meaning of Sacral Manumission." *HThR* 47: 173–81.

Sourvinou-Inwood, Christiane. 1988. *Studies in Girls' Transitions: Aspects of the Arkteia and Age Representation in Attic Iconography*. Athens: Kardamista.

Strauss, Barry S. 1996. "The Athenian Trireme, School of Democracy." In *Dēmokratia: A Conversation on Democracies, Ancient and Modern*, edited by Josiah Ober and Charles W. Hedrick, Jr., 313–25. Princeton: Princeton University Press.

Stroud, Ronald S. 1968. *Drakon's Law on Homicide*. Berkeley: University of California Press.

———. 1974. "An Athenian Law on Silver Coinage." *Hesperia* 43: 157–88.

Tamiolaki, Hélène-Melina. 2008. "La liberation et la citoyenneté des esclaves aux Arginuses Platéens ou Athéniens? Un vers controversé d'Aristophane (Gren. 694) et l'idéologie de la société athénienne." In *La fin du statut servile? Affranchissement, liberation, abolition*, vol. 2, edited by Antonio Gonzales, 53–63. Besançon: Presses universitaires de Franche-Comté.

Taylor, Claire. 2007a. "A New Political World." In *Debating the Athenian Cultural Revolution: Art, Literature, Philosophy, and Politics, 430–380 BC*, edited by Robin Osborne, 72–90. Cambridge: Cambridge University Press.

———. 2007b. "From the Whole Citizen Body? The Sociology of Election and Lot in the Athenian Democracy." *Hesperia* 76: 323–45.

Thompson, Wesley E. 1981. "Athenian Attitudes toward Wills." *Prudentia* 13: 13–23.

Thomsen, Rudi. 1964. *Eisphora: A Study of Direct Taxation in Ancient Athens*. Copenhagen: Gyldendal.

Thür, Gerhard. 1977. *Beweisführung vor den Schwurgerichtshöfen Athens: die Proklesis zur Besanos*. Vienna: Österreichische Akademie der Wissenschaften.

Tod, Marcus N. 1950. "Epigraphical Notes on Freedmen's Professions." *Epigraphica* 12: 3–26.

Todd, Stephen. 1990. "The Purpose of Evidence in Athenian Courts." In *NOMOS: Essays in Athenian Law, Politics, and Society*, edited by Paul Cartledge, Paul Millett, and Stephen Todd, 19–39. Cambridge: Cambridge University Press.

———. 1994. "Status and Contract in Fourth-Century Athens." In *Symposion 1993: Vorträge zur griechischen und hellenistischen Rechtsgeschichte*, edited by Gerhard Thür, 125–40. Cologne: Böhlau.

———. 1995. *The Shape of Athenian Law*. Oxford: Clarendon Press.

———. 1996. "Lysias Against Nikomachos: The Fate of the Expert in Athenian Law." In *Greek Law in its Political Setting: Justifications not Justice*, edited by Lin Foxhall and A. D. E. Lewis, 101–31. Oxford: Clarendon Press.

———. 1997. "Status and Gender in Athenian Public Records." In *Symposion 1995: Vorträge zur griechischen und hellenistischen Rechtsgeschichte*, edited by Gerhard Thür and Julie Vélissaropoulos-Karakostas, 113–24. Cologne: Böhlau.

Tompkins, Daniel P. 2006. "The World of Moses Finkelstein: The Year 1939 in M. I. Finley's Development as a Historian." In *Classical Antiquity and the Politics of America: From George Washington to George W. Bush*, edited by Michael Meckler, 95–125. Waco, TX: Baylor University Press.

Trevett, Jeremy. 1992. *Apollodoros, the Son of Pasion*. Oxford: Clarendon Press.

Tucker, C. W. 1982. "Women in Manumission Inscriptions at Delphi." *TAPA* 112: 225–36.

van Wees, Hans. 2006. "Mass and Elite in Solon's Athens: The Property Classes Revisited." In *Solon of Athens: New Historical and Philological Approaches*, edited by Josine Blok and A. P. M. H. Lardinois, 351–89. Leiden: Brill.

Vidal-Naquet, Pierre. 1986 [1981]. *The Black Hunter: Forms of Thought and Forms of Society in the Greek World*. Translated by Andrew Szegedy-Maszak. Baltimore: Johns Hopkins University Press.

Vlassopoulos, Kostas. 2007. "Free Spaces: Identity, Experience and Democracy in Classical Athens." *CQ* 57: 33–52.

———. 2009. "Slavery, Freedom and Citizenship in Classical Athens: Beyond a Legalistic Approach." *ERH/REH* 16: 347–63.

———. 2011. "Greek Slavery: From Domination to Property and Back Again." *JHS* 131: 115–30.

von Reden, S. 2003 [1995]. *Exchange in Ancient Greece*. London: Duckworth.

Walbank, Michael B. 1978. *Athenian Proxenies of the Fifth Century BC*. Toronto: S. Stevens.

———. 1994. "Greek Inscriptions from the Athenian Agora: Lists of Names." *Hesperia* 63: 169–209.

Wallace, M. B. 1970. "Early Greek *Proxenoi*." *Phoenix* 24: 189–208.

Wallace, R. W. 1998. "Unconvicted or Potential 'átimoi' in Ancient Athens." *Dike* 1: 63–78.

Walters, K. R. 1983. "Perikles' Citizenship Law." *CA* 2: 314–36.

Weiler, Ingomar. 2001. "Eine Sklavin wird frei: Zur Rolle des Geschlechts bei der Freilassung." In *Fünfzig Jahre Forschungen zur antiken Sklaverei an der Mainzer Akademie, 1950-2000: Miscellanea zum Jubiläum,* edited by Heinz Bellen and Heinz Heiner, 113–32. Stuttgart: Franz Steiner.

Westermann, William L. 1945a. "Between Slavery and Freedom." *AHR* 50: 213–27.

———. 1945b. "Slave Maintenance and Slave Revolts." *CP* 40: 1–10.

———. 1946. "Two Studies in Athenian Manumission." *JNES* 5: 92–104.

Whitehead, David. 1977. *The Ideology of the Athenian Metic*. Cambridge: Cambridge University Press.

———. 1983. "Competitive Outlay and Community Profit: *Philotimia* in Democratic Athens." *C&M* 34: 55–74.

———. 1986a. "Women and Naturalization in Fourth-Century Athens: The Case of Archippe." *CQ* 36: 109–14.

———. 1986b. "The Ideology of the Athenian Metic: Some Pendants and a Reappraisal." *PCPS* 212: 145–58.

———. 1986c. *The Demes of Attica: 508/7-ca. 250 BC: A Political and Social Study*. Princeton: Princeton University Press.

Wijma, Sara M. 2010. *Joining the Athenian Community: The Participation of Metics in Athenian Polis Religion in the Fifth and Fourth Centuries BC*. Dissertation. University of Utrecht.

Wilamowitz-Möllendorff, Ulrich von. 1887. "Demotika der Metoeken." *Hermes* 22: 107–28, 211–59.

Wilson, P. 2000. *The Athenian Institution of the* Khoregia: *The Chorus, the City and the Stage*. Cambridge: Cambridge University Press.

Wood, E. M. 1988. *Peasant-Citizen and Slave: The Foundations of Athenian Democracy*. London: Verso.

Wrenhaven, Kelly L. 2009. "The Identity of the 'Wool-Workers' in the Attic Manumissions." *Hesperia* 78: 367–86.

————. 2012. *Reconstructing the Slave: The Image of the Slave in Ancient Greece*. London: Bristol Classical Press.

Wright, Erik O. 2005. "Social Class." In *Encyclopedia of Social Theory*, vol. 2, edited by George Ritzer, 717–24. Thousand Oaks, CA: Sage Publications.

Wyse, W. 1904. *The Speeches of Isaeus*. Cambridge: Cambridge University Press.

Yunis, Harvey. 1988. "Law, Politics, and the *graphe paranomon* in Fourth-Century Athens." *GRBS* 29: 361–82.

Zelnick-Abramovitz, Rachel. 2005. *Not Wholly Free: The Concept of Manumission and the Status of Manumitted Slaves in the Ancient Greek World*. Leiden: Brill.

————. 2009. "Freed Slaves, Their Status and State Control in Ancient Greece." *ERH/REH* 16: 303–18.

————. 2012. "Slaves and Role Reversal in Ancient Greek Cults." In *Slaves and Religions in Graeco-Roman Antiquity and Modern Brazil*, edited by Dick Geary and Stephen Hodkinson, 96–132. Newcastle upon Tyne: Cambridge Scholars Publishing.

INDEX LOCORUM

GENERAL INDEX

CPSIA information can be obtained
at www.ICGtesting.com
Printed in the USA
JSRC021048040322
23611JS00001B/2